THE
NORTHERN
WORLD

EDITED BY DAVID M. WILSON

THE NORTHERN WORLD

THE HISTORY AND HERITAGE OF NORTHERN EUROPE · AD 400–1100

TEXTS BY
CHRISTINE E. FELL · H. AMENT · CATHERINE HILLS
JAMES GRAHAM-CAMPBELL · ELSE ROESDAHL
DAVID M. WILSON · JOACHIM HERRMANN
JÖRAN MJÖBERG

Harry N. Abrams, Inc., Publishers,
New York

Endpapers: carved wooden doorway from the stave
church at Urnes, Norway.

Half-title page: circular motif on a seventh-century
gold buckle from the Sutton Hoo ship burial.

Frontispiece: picture stone from Tjängvide, Gotland,
Sweden. The lower field shows a sailing vessel full of
armed warriors. Above them a rider on an eight-
legged horse is greeted by a woman apparently
holding a drinking horn and standing in front of a
building which may represent the entrance to
Valhalla.

Maps: Shalom Schotten
Translators: Kathleen Cheesmond (Chapter 2), Eva
Wilson (Chapters 5, 8), Gillian Wilson (Chapter 7)

Library of Congress Cataloging in Publication Data
Main entry under title:

The Northern world.

Bibliography: p.
Includes index.
1. Art—Europe, Northern. 2. Art, Medieval—Europe,
Northern. 3. Europe, Northern—Civilization. 4. Eu-
rope, Northern—Antiquities. I. Wilson, David McKenzie.
N6750.N67   948   79–21745
ISBN 0–8109–1365–8

Library of Congress Catalog Card Number: 79–21745

Filmset in Great Britain by Keyspools Ltd, Golborne Lancs
Text and illustrations printed in the Netherlands by Smeets B.V. Weert

CONTENTS

INTRODUCTION

DAVID M. WILSON

IN A TIME when European unity is under constant consideration we may look back to our roots and examine the validity of the concept, particularly in so far as it concerns northern Europe. To those who speak English, Dutch, German, Flemish and the Scandinavian languages these roots are clearly grounded in language; but to Slav-speakers and those in the west who speak the ancient British languages, our common heritage is less clear. Political manoeuvring and cultural contact have over the years brought all these people closer together. In many ways we speak the same cultural language, but the differences are marked and are occasionally used to heighten distance or tension. The purpose of this book is to examine the origins of both the common and the different elements of the peoples of northern Europe, of the peoples whose centres lie around the North Sea and the Baltic rather than around the Mediterranean. That there are valid cultural similarities between the various modern countries which make up this region is beyond doubt. But these similarities are often exaggerated, as the differences are forced. It is simply not true to say that the speech of the people of western Jutland can be understood by the people of eastern Yorkshire (to whom they are related by more than a thousand years of distinct polarity) any more than it is true that German and Dutch are the same language. In moments of national peril or national euphoria, the nothern nations will rally under the banner of a common heritage, based on language or religion. But just as often they will fight or quarrel with a surprising lack of understanding.

The sentiments expressed by Alfred, Lord Tennyson on the marriage of Princess Alexandra of Denmark to Edward, Prince of Wales, in 1863:

> Sea-Kings' daughter from over the sea . . .
> Saxon or Norman or Dane are we,
> Teuton or Celt . . .

sounded grand, idealistic and bore more than an element of truth; but soon Dane and Teuton were at war over Schleswig-Holstein, while England looked on and said nothing. As a result of this war the Danes lost control of the great monument that had formed their southern boundary with Germany – the Danevirke – for the first time for a thousand years and the brotherly attitude of the northern peoples was once again seen to be fragile in the face of political convenience.

We are the hostages of history in this century as we have been for so long. The political perversions engendered by Alfred Rosenberg and Adolf Hitler encompassed a pan-Germanism, based on a myth of Aryan or Nordic racial supremacy, more rabid than the worst pan-Slavism or the most extreme excesses of Celtic nationalism. The correlation of Germanic race with Aryanism was not only false but stupid and the idea of race associated with it was at best unscientific, at worst inflammatory. Yet in the Nazi period archaeological objects achieved a symbolism out of all proportion to their significance. The common bow-brooch of the fifth and sixth centuries, for example, was regarded by some as symbolic of pan-Germanism – those who did not have it (or were alleged not to have had it, as the Slavs) were considered *Untermensch*.

On a more academic (but still political) level the consideration of the problems inherent in the rise of the Russian state has been the subject of pamphleteering since the eighteenth century. To the scholar it cannot matter who founded the Russian state: the point is that a vital Slav culture – fuelled by mercantile influences from northern Europe as well as from Byzantium and the Arab world – flowered in the region centred on Kiev. That Scandinavians were instrumental in some of the activities of the Kiev state is incontrovertible, but it is as unimportant as the contribution they made to Irish culture before the Norman conquest of 1169. It is arguable that the present troubles in Ulster have their roots in the Viking economic domination of Dublin and the western seaways of Europe, in that this must have been a major factor in the conquest of Ireland by the English who wanted to develop this trade themselves.

Writing is the bridge between history and prehistory and all the peoples covered by this book – the Germanic tribes, the Celts, the Norsemen, the Slavs – learned to write between the third and twelfth centuries. Runic, a Germanic script, is first found in the third century. The ancient Celtic script probably appeared at the same time.

Ogham is found exclusively on stones, the corner often forming the central element and the letters made up of sloping or straight lines on each side. It is read from bottom to top. Shown here is an example of Pictish ogham. (1,2)

The origin of the Germanic runic script is disputed, but it is perhaps ultimately derived from the Greek alphabet. Its angular letters were originally developed for writing on wood, but are also well suited for stone. Several examples are shown elsewhere (including its use on whalebone on the Franks Casket, pp. 30–31). This stone from Ed, near Stockholm, was erected by 'Ragnvild who . . . was in Greece, the leader of the host'. (3,4)

ᚠᚢᚦᚨᚱᚲᚷᚹ ᚺ ᚾᛁᛃᛈ ᛇᚱᛊ ᛏᛒᛖᛗᛚᛜᛞᛟ
f u þ a r k g w h n i j p e R s t b e m l ng d o

Such historical politicking is of doubtful value and limited use. What is important is that for fifteen hundred years the nations of northern Europe have been in continuous contact. These nations emerged during the period covered by this book, between say 400 and 1100. It is, therefore, of interest to examine the process by which they emerged and the inter-relationships which grew up between them. The common elements and the different features of our heritage – and not only of our heritage as Europeans, but also of much of the heritage of the North American nations – can in some cases be explained.

In this period northern Europe emerged from practical illiteracy and anonymity into a closely knit and inter-related series of established states, mostly Christian by religion, bearing in their breasts the seeds of great literature and enormous practical achievement. The power of Rome collapsed, barbarian attacks out of Asia and Africa were countered, America was discovered (although its potential was not realized), many of the cities of northern Europe were founded, ruling dynasties emerged and with them national identities.

It is fair to ask if literacy and Christianity were the two elements which made the new nations, for so they are often seen to be by historians grounded in the strong coherent traditions and well-documented justification of the classical countries of the Mediterranean world. Rome even today is one of the most potent intellectual elements in the thought of western man. Seventeenth-century artistic achievement in Italy is competent but well known, while contemporaneously northern Europe was producing great and original art and architecture, which is less appreciated than it should be. For every hundred men who know the name of Galileo, there is probably only one who knows the achievements of Tycho Brahe who built in Denmark what was probably the world's first observatory and paved the way for the ideas of Kepler and Galileo. Mediterranean centricity in history is more noticeable the further we move backwards in time. The finger of accusation – if not of scorn – is levelled at the *barbares du nord*. The brutality of barbarians is an easy target; but it is well to remember the brutalities of the allegedly civilized. It is clear that the sophistication of the Mediterranean is missing from northern Europe, but it is valid to question whether the presence of good timber in the north – with little need to use stone – might not cloud our judgment of the comparative strengths of the classical and northern cultures. It is true that the Anglo-Saxons regarded the ruined masonry of Roman towns as 'the wondrous work of giants'; it is also true that the economic and political base of Germanic power was narrow. On the other hand, the technical achievement of the Germanic smith, the sophistication of the Scandinavian boat-builder, the engineering skills of the Slavs, the inventiveness of the Anglo-Saxon and Celtic historian and the brilliance and depth of the Germanic poet induce a consideration of these comparisons. As Rome destroyed itself and as Byzantine power faded the lacunae they left were filled quickly and imaginatively in the North. The process was sometimes messy, often sordid, but ultimately it was northern Europe that had – at least temporarily – the vision.

The early seventh-century 'Cathach [literally; 'battler'] of St Columba' is perhaps the earliest surviving Irish manuscript. Here for the first time are seen two features of Insular manuscripts — the distorted and decorated initial and the diminution of letters in the first line of text. (5)

Part of a Latin Bible (a page from the Second Book of Kings) written in Northumbria at the beginning of the eighth century, under the patronage of Ceolfrid, abbot of Jarrow and Wearmouth: one of the most accomplished and sophisticated Anglo-Saxon manuscripts. (6)

This book tells the story of Germanic Europe from 400 to 1100 and of the lands, Celtic and Slav, which bordered it. The survey is not quite complete, for one major Germanic people – the Franks – had so quickly adopted a Mediterranean, Romance role and language that by about 800 they had become in effect an extension of the Mediterranean world. It has also proved impossible to follow to their ultimate destination such people as the Visigoths and Burgundians who turned culturally in the same direction as the Franks. The Germanic tribes of southern Germany are not treated after the year 800, as to a large extent they (like the Franks) came under the sway of the revived 'Roman' empire of Charlemagne.

The Slavs and Celts are discussed because they were the two people who mingled with and struggled against their German contemporaries. In small things they affected each other. Harald Bluetooth, the tenth-century king who built a strong Danish state, married a Slav princess. Fine spiral ornament of Celtic origin was for a short time enthusiastically adopted by Anglo-Saxon artists. But these people also had important long-lasting and deep relations with each other. The Anglo-Saxon Church, as well as the Church of certain other Germanic countries, received some of its major inspiration from the older, well-established Church of Ireland and Scotland. The Slavs were one of the most potent martial influences in northern Europe. Their state of almost constant warfare internally and externally may well have had considerable influence, for example in the field of military engineering, on the Danish state.

The story revealed in these pages depends on a vast amount of evidence of mixed character. Primary historical records do exist, but are often one-sided and in need of careful elaboration. Primary sources are most scarce in the Viking and Slav homelands, although the Primary Russian Chronicle and the Scandinavian runic inscriptions do provide the historian with some contemporary material. On the other hand there is a vast literature concerning the Vikings and the Slavs written from outside Scandinavia. A Byzantine emperor, Constantine Porphyrogenitus, writes of Vikings and Slavs, as does an Anglo-Saxon king, Alfred. Their information came at second hand; closer perhaps to life are the writings of Arab travellers in the Slav lands who met Scandinavians and Slavs and recorded their impressions, sometimes in rather lurid detail. Historians also treat of these same people; a German cleric, Adam of Bremen, is a mine of information – and misinformation – about the immediate neighbours of the great north German diocese of Hamburg-Bremen. The Royal Frankish Annals illuminate for a short time at the turn of the eighth and ninth centuries a small fragment of Danish history; but such mentions are tenuous.

Anglo-Saxon England (and to some extent Ireland) is well served by historians, particularly after the end of the sixth century. The Venerable Bede, writing at Jarrow in the early eighth century, was an innovator as an historian and took considerable trouble to check his sources. The Irish annals are less reliable, while Pictish histories have almost completely disappeared. The period of the break-up of the Roman Empire is also

When the Saxons in Germany were converted to Christianity about 820, the oath imposed upon them was recorded in a mixture of Latin and Saxon, the latter written in a script based on the Latin alphabet but with additional letters for purely Germanic sounds. (7)

Part of the Anglo-Saxon Chronicle, recording events of 871 (Alfred's defeat of the Danes at Ashdown) but written in the late eleventh century. Here again most of the forms are based on Latin (including the date at the beginning). (8)

documented, with varying degrees of accuracy and obfuscation, in many of the Germanic areas; but generally the further one moves from Rome, the less reliable and useful the historical sources.

Much traditional material survives in later literary productions. Classic in this context are the Scandinavian sagas written down in the later Middle Ages. These have been used and misused with great abandon, particularly in the service of Scandinavian nationalism, and this aspect is treated here by Dr Mjöberg. The poetry of the Edda particularly has been used to elucidate the religion of the north. Like the sagas, the Eddic poems may be used, with the aid of extremely careful analysis, to illuminate darker areas of man's thought during the period covered by this book. They give us access to at least part of the more imaginative corners of man's mind at this time.

The second great source of knowledge is archaeology. Excavation reveals more and more of the material facts concerning the life of Europe in the post-Roman period. In some areas it is practically the only surviving evidence: the Isle of Man, for example, which is rarely mentioned in literature before the eleventh century, had a flourishing Celtic and Viking economy and social structure. Even where literature provides rich material, archaeology can clothe it with new facts and visual immediacy. Thus, for example, the excavations at York in the last few years have illuminated in an exciting fashion the daily and official life of this well-documented town, described or mentioned in dozens of sources from the time of Bede to the Norman Conquest. Anglo-Scandinavian sculpture, coins, metal-working

tools, weapons and ornaments testify to the deeply Scandinavian character of York in the ninth and tenth century. The countryside has been revealed in a new light by the archaeologist's spade. The great north German villages – Warendorf, Tofting, Ezinge – tell of the life of the ordinary peasant in the early Migration Period. Houses have been found in plenty, which we may imagine as the dwellings of farmers and their families; animal bones, seeds and pollen tell of the basic food and economy of life, of the standard of husbandry and of the peasant's dependence – or lack of it – on hunting and fishing.

For much of the first three centuries after the collapse of the Roman Empire cemeteries were furnished throughout most of northern Europe outside the Christian areas with objects of everyday use – women's brooches, men's weapons, smiths' tools, pots, food, boats and animals. The practice of accompanied burial in the more pagan parts of Europe (particularly in north Germany and Scandinavia) continued for many centuries – often until the tenth century. The objects found in such graves have been easily recognizable to the casual finder and have flooded into museums to provide the basis for much study and analysis by scholars. For many years, until the development of sophisticated, scientifically based dating techniques, these grave-goods provided much of the chronological framework for the non-literate parts of Europe. They are still used in this fashion, but they may also be used to provide all manner of information about the people who buried their dead in this way. They tell of cultural contact, illuminate our ideas of dress, demonstrate technical achievements and industrial processes and throw light on the artistic abilities and inspiration which form so important a part of the northern European inheritance. The graves are beginning to tell other stories: the bones themselves tell of disease and diet, even possibly of the area of origin of the dead; they tell of life expectancy and infant mortality; and by their position and by the elaborate nature of their ritual may hint at social structure and religious belief.

Archaeology also depends to some extent on casual finds. Of primary importance are hoards of precious metal, laid down in times of trouble or in the hope of security and never reclaimed by the owner. Hoards of gold are comparatively rare, but (particularly in the Migration Period in Scandinavia) can be very large. In the Viking period silver was the currency throughout the north and vast quantities have been found, particularly in Scandinavia where some of it at least reflects the Danegeld (the political ransom paid by the countries attacked by the Vikings). The hoards also include, or consist entirely of, objects of precious metal, ornamented to express the taste of the conspicuously wealthy or of the deeply religious; objects like the Ardagh chalice from Ireland, which dates from about 700 and is one of the finest pieces of metalwork of all time, or the great fifth-century hoard of the Goths from Szilagy Somlyo between Hungary and Romania.

But not all casual finds are hoards. Some are objects lost by their owners and found centuries later by a ploughman or construction worker, a particularly remarkable example being the great golden horns of Gallehus. Important also are finds which have been abandoned to the elements, like a ninth-century boat from Graveney in Kent or wooden cult figures from Schleswig-Holstein, and the remarkable ritual deposits (laid down to celebrate a god or a victory) in the bogs of south Scandinavia. Such deposits encompass objects of daily life: tools, belts, boats, as well as weapons and other objects of war which may have been sacrificed as thanksgiving for victory.

To history and archaeology can be added a wide range of disciplines which help the scholar to build up a picture of the total life of northern Europe in the period between 400 and 1100. The place-names of farms, villages and towns each tell a story, sometimes obscure but often full of significance. The town of Derby in England was originally called Northworthy (to use a modern spelling); it achieved its present name in the ninth century, when it became one of the major towns of Viking-settled England. The name in its present form is completely Scandinavian and means 'settlement with a deer park'. There are many names which enshrine other ideas. Kaupang in Norway, for example, means 'market place', and here excavation has revealed imported objects and goods made for foreign traders. The place-name Novgorod (literally, 'the new fortification') indicates how the early Slav settlers conceived this important settlement. Not only place-names but also the surviving languages demonstrate cultural contact and foreign influence – thus the English word *law* has a Scandinavian root and the dialect word *kirk* of north Britain is common to the Scandinavian countries, from which it is derived.

History, archaeology and philology are but three of the many disciplines used by the student of this period. Hence the wide-ranging content of this book. Among the many disciplines which could be added to this list are those of the literary historian, the soil scientist, the legal historian and the ethnologist. Here they can merely be drawn together without great acknowledgement or elaboration. The contributions to this volume are drawn from a variety of disciplines, from a variety of countries. They present a picture at once incomplete and synthetic: the picture is, however, a true, if impressionistic, portrait (with all its faults) of the foundation of northern Europe.

The Norse sagas were written down in the thirteenth and fourteenth centuries. Shown here is a detail from the Flateyjarbók of 1387–94: part of the Greenlanders' Saga, probably composed some two centuries earlier. (9)

*It would seem fitting for a Northern folk, deriving
the greater and better part of their speech, laws and customs
from a Northern root, that the North should
be to them, if not a holy land, yet at least a place more
to be regarded than any part of the world
beside, that howsoever their knowledge widened of
other men, the faith and deeds of
their forefathers would never lack interest for them,
but would always be kept in remembrance.*

William Morris

1
GODS
AND HEROES
OF THE
NORTHERN
WORLD

CHRISTINE E. FELL

'What dream is that? quoth Odin –
I thought to rise ere daybreak
To make Valhalla ready
For troops of slain.
I roused the champions,

Bade them rise swiftly
Benches to strew,
To wash the beer-flagons;
The Valkyries to pour wine,
As a prince were coming.'

Poetic Edda

Before the thirteenth century

The gods of the North have suffered two eclipses – first by the advent of Christianity, which destroyed their shrines and condemned the old stories as pagan and even diabolical; and then by the classical Renaissance, which (as early as the twelfth century) gave Europe a repertoire of Greek and Roman myths that almost completely obliterated the Germanic. Odin, Thor, Freyja and Sigurd are therefore shadowy figures compared to Jupiter, Mars, Venus and Hercules; the literature that embodies them is relatively meagre, and they scarcely live in the few works of art that have come down to us. Yet the memory of them never entirely disappeared, and in the nineteenth century their very mystery was a source of emotive power.

Odin – or Woden – was the chief of the gods, and was regarded by the Anglo-Saxons as the ancestor of their kings, a belief still current in the Middle Ages. In a thirteenth-century manuscript now at Cambridge, the genealogy of the English kings is traced from Adam, through Woden, to Henry II. A full-page illustration (*opposite*) shows him dressed in contemporary costume and holding a gold flower. The crowned heads in the margins are his seven sons.

Our main source of information about Odin, as about most other Germanic myths, is the Prose Edda of Snorri Sturluson, written in Iceland in the thirteenth century. How far the stories that he recorded really reflect the religion of a thousand years earlier it is difficult to say. There is reason to believe that Odin was not originally the chief of the gods. Some early writers equate him with Mercury; others allude to forgotten legends whose significance is lost. But certainly by the early Middle Ages his position in the Germanic pantheon was secure, and to later poets and artists he was 'the High One', 'Lord of the Spear', 'the All-father'. (1)

On previous page: Thor fishing for the serpent of Midgard, a detail from the Gosforth Cross (see p. 161). Thor is on the left holding his hammer in one hand and the line, baited with an ox's head, in the other. The figure on the right is Hymir, ready to cut the line with an axe. (1)

Two of the stories told by Snorri are confirmed by archaeology. *Above*: Odin's eight-legged horse Sleipnir, the offspring of Loki when he had turned himself into a mare, on a ninth-century picture stone. Another offspring of Loki was Fenrir, the wolf. At the time of the destruction of the gods, Fenrir's great jaws stretched from the earth to the sky. *Above right*: Fenrir devouring Odin (note the raven by his shoulder) on a stone relief from the Isle of Man. (2,3)

In 1812 the Swedish artist Pehr Hörberg drew Odin building his town of Sigtuna. All the details are vaguely classical or Asiatic except one – the carved stone near the centre, clearly copied from a real Viking rune-stone. (4)

A modern Odin (*right*) is depicted on the door of Oslo Town Hall, riding the eight-legged Sleipnir. Above him fly the two ravens Hugin ('thought') and Munin ('memory') who roam the world gathering information for their lord. (6)

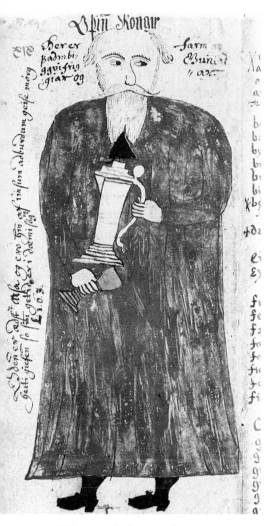

'The mead of poetry' was a miraculous beverage which made anyone who drank it a poet and a sage. Odin possessed it, dispensing it to those he favoured, who became the bards. This naïve illustration (*above*) is from a seventeenth-century manuscript miscellany including Eddic material, now in Copenhagen. (5)

The bronze doors of the Historical Museum of Stockholm (*right*) combine several myths associated with the primeval figure of Odin, shown with one eye, since he sacrificed the other to gain Mimir's draught of wisdom. On the left is his voluntary self-sacrifice, hanging from the branches of Yggdrasil, the world ash. (7)

19

The hammer of Thor

Thor was the warrior god who with his mighty hammer Mjöllnir could smash the skulls of giants, serpents and monsters. The serpent of Midgard lay coiled in the great ocean round the earth ('midgard' = 'middle earth'). The first time Thor fought the serpent was from the fishing boat of the giant Hymir, when he baited his hook with an ox's head, but Hymir cut the line and the serpent escaped. This fight is illustrated in a mid-eighteenth-century Icelandic manuscript (*below*) and – far more dramatically – by Henry Fuseli (*left*), 1790. *Opposite*: Thor's fight with the giants, by the Swedish artist, M. E. Winge, of 1872. Thor rides in a chariot drawn by goats. (8,9,11).

Miniature hammers may have been worn as amulets, in the same way as crosses were worn by Christians. During the period of conversion (tenth-to-eleventh century) the same person might well have owned both and moulds (*right*) have actually been found with which both hammers and crosses could be made. With it are two enriched hammers discovered in graves. (10)

Odin, Thor and Frey from a twelfth-century embroidery, once in Skog church, Sweden. The small figure in the background is Freyja. (13)

The enigmatic Balder, young, beautiful, universally beloved, was killed through the agency of Loki. His brother Hermod penetrated the underworld and was promised that if the whole earth wept for Balder he would be allowed to return. Everything on earth did weep, except one old giantess – Loki in disguise! To the Romantics Balder had something Christ-like, a parallel made explicit in Bengt Fogelberg's statue (*right*) of about 1840, through its resemblance to Thorwaldsen's *Risen Christ*. (14)

22

Freyja, Balder and Loki

Her chariot drawn by cats and surrounded by cupids that seem to have strayed into Norse mythology from a sunnier clime, Freyja, goddess of youth and love, rides across the sky seeking her husband Od. The Swedish artist Nils Blommér painted the picture (*left*) in Rome in 1852 and signed it *in runic* on the baton in Freyja's right hand. Later writers (followed by Wagner) conflated Freyja and Idun, who guarded the golden apples that kept the gods young. *Right*: an illustration by Arthur Rackham to Wagner's *The Ring of the Nibelung*, showing the slender goddess with the apple tree and, again, two attendant cats. (12,16)

Loki the trickster, the betrayer, the father of monsters, is the Satan of Germanic mythology. *Right*: a carving by H. E. Freund, 1822, stresses his cynicism and mockery. On one occasion the gods seized him and tied him to a rock below a poisonous snake. His wife Sigyn (*above*) caught the poison in a bowl, but whenever she went away to empty it, poison fell on Loki's face and he shook the earth with his struggles. The painting is by M. E. Winge. (15,17)

The birth and death of the world

In the beginning, according to the Elder, or Poetic, Edda, living things emerged from the primeval ice – first the giant Ymir (whose body was to be the earth and his blood the sea), then Buri, then Bor, the father of Odin. Ymir was nourished by the cow Audumla. This strange subject was chosen by the Danish artist N. A. Abilgaard when in the late eighteenth century the Norse myths were becoming associated with Scandinavian nationalism. While Ymir sucks the milk of Audumla, she licks the ice to release Buri and Bor. (18)

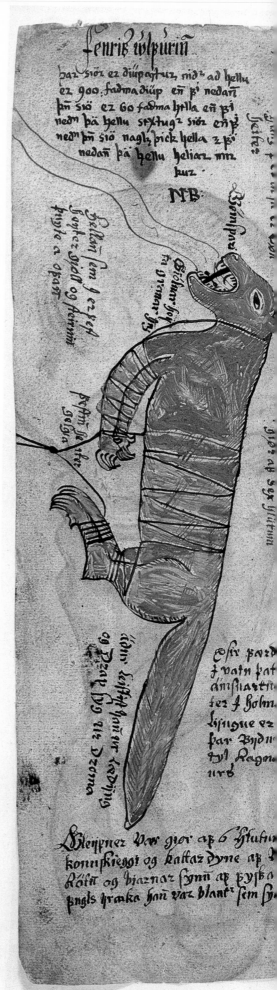

The end will come when the wolf Fenrir breaks his bonds and with his brood roams the world spreading death and destruction. Then the world ash, Yggdrasil, upon which all things rest, will be shaken. Odin and the gods will perish and a new race inherit the earth. *Centre*: a page from the same seventeenth-century manuscript illustrated on p. 32. It is provided with copious annotations, mostly quoted or paraphrased from Snorri. On the left is Fenrir, still bound; 'the saliva runs from his mouth, that is the river which is called Vøn. The Æsir brought the wolf to the lake which is called Amsvartner on to the island which is called Lyngve. He will remain there till *Ragnarok* [the End of the world].' On the right is Yggdrasil. 'Harts run about the branches of the ash and bite the shoots. An eagle sits in the branches of the ash' ('he is wise about many matters, and between his eyes sits that hawk which is called Vedrfolnir' – Snorri). The serpent, Nidhogg, gnaws the roots of the tree, and the squirrel, Ratatosk, 'carries words of ill-will between the eagle and Nidhogg'. (19)

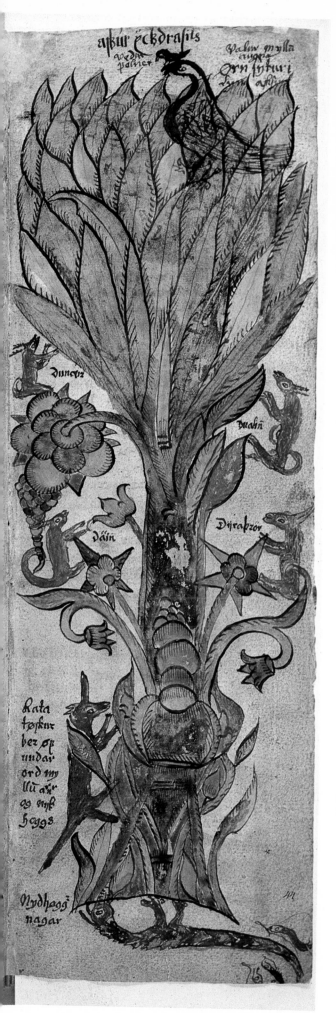

A twentieth-century version of Yggdrasil, painted by
Axel Revold in 1933, is to be seen in the vestibule of the
University Library in Oslo. *Below*: an even more recent
representation of Fenrir, on the island of Asköy, near
Bergen, by Arne Vinje Gunnerud. (20,21)

25

Sigurd the Volsung

Of the Norse heroes, Sigurd, or Siegfried, was by far the most popular. Not only does he appear in the Eddas, the *Nibelungenlied* and the Norse *Volsunga saga*, but his story is one of the few that can be identified in contemporary art. A thirteenth-century chair at Heddal church, Norway (*left*), shows Brynhild in the centre, wooed by Sigurd and Gunnar. On the doorway of Hylestad church, Norway (*below*), a whole series of scenes is contained within interlaced foliage. Three are shown here: in the first, Regin forges a sword for Sigurd, with Sigurd working the bellows; in the second, Sigurd tests the weapon by cleaving the anvil; in the third, he slays the dragon, Fafnir. (22–25)

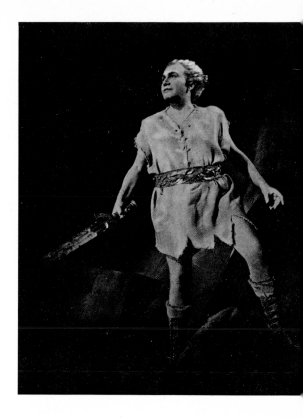

For Wagner, the figure of Siegfried carried a political and moral meaning. While Wotan (Odin) symbolizes the old order, compromised by the struggle for power, Siegfried represents fearless youth, innocent of the sins of his predecessors and therefore able to redeem the world through sacrifice and love. The *Ring* was first produced at Bayreuth in 1876. Bernd Aldenhoff (*above*) sang the part in Wieland Wagner's production of 1951. (27)

Kriemhild finds the body of Siegfried: an intensely Romantic rendering of the scene by the German artist Peter Cornelius, *c.*1820. Following the *Nibelungenlied*, Cornelius gives the story a medieval setting (note the Gothic architecture) and makes Kriemhild a more sympathetic figure than her rival Brynhild. 'From that moment her dole began; for, with his death, she took leave of all joy. She sank on the floor speechless; they saw the miserable woman lying there. Kriemhild's woe was great beyond measure, and after her swoon she cried out that all the chamber rang.' (26)

Fritz Lang's film of the *Nibelungenlied*, made in 1924 (*right*), returned the legend to the Dark Ages, creating a strange, magical, hauntingly poetic world. (28)

The epic of the Nibelungs

The Middle Ages in Germany, drawing on the same mythological sources as the sagas, wove them into a new pattern, introducing real historical figures. *Left*: the meeting of Siegfried and Kriemhild, from a fifteenth-century manuscript of the *Nibelungenlied*: 'And lo! the fair one appeared, like the dawn from out the dark clouds. The beloved one, his sweet lady, stood before him in her beauty.' (29)

Rediscovered in the late eighteenth century, the *Nibelungenlied* was hailed as one of the glories of the German people. Between 1827 and 1834 Schnorr von Carolsfeld painted a series of large frescoes from it in the Munich Residenz. *Below*: 'Hagen sprang back and gripped his spear; and while Siegfried drank from the stream, Hagen stabbed him, that his heart's blood spurted out on the traitor's clothes.' *Opposite*: Siegfried is buried in Worms Cathedral, and Hagen, who has denied the killing, is accused by the grief-stricken Kriemhild: 'Hagen's guilt was plain to all. The wounds burst open and bled as they had done afore, and they that had wept already now wept much more.' (30,31)

The Franks Casket

Weland the smith was a household name to the Norsemen and Anglo-Saxons, but his story has come down to us only in a fragmentary and ambiguous form. A metalworker of marvellous powers, he was persecuted by Nidhad, against whom he took revenge by killing his sons and raping his daughter Beadohild. In this scene on the Franks Casket (*below*) the figure on the left seems to be Weland, holding the head of a murdered prince in one hand and offering a cup to Beadohild with the other. On the right, Weland may be catching birds to help him make his escape.

The Casket, made from whalebone in the eighth century, displays a bewildering assortment of themes, pagan and Christian, inscribed in a mixture of Latin script and runes. *Opposite*, from top to bottom: Egil the archer defending his home from attack (from *Egils saga*); the sack of Jerusalem by the Crusaders; the story of Romulus and Remus; and a scene that seems to represent the death of Sigurd. Next to the Weland scene (*left*) comes the Adoration of the Magi. (32–37)

fym hundrud Dyra Op Biørn
stugu sva hygg ek Valhøll vera
átta hundrud einherria ganga u
einóm Dyru I Ben þa er þeir þara
at vitne at vega

Heidm heiter geit er stendur hællu a
skapt ker hun fylla skal Jnz skikza
mradar kna at Su veig vanas

eikþyrner

Heijmdøllur

miðgards Ormurin

Gunnar, thrown bound into a snake pit by his brother-in-law Atli (Attila the Hun), plays the harp with his toes in order to charm the snakes: a carving from the Norwegian church of Hylestad. (2)

GODS AND HEROES OF THE NORTHERN WORLD

IN ATTEMPTING to define and discover what the pagan Germanic tribes believed or what religious ceremonies they practised, a first essential is to assess the nature of our problems. We are dealing with a subject that extends over a vast area both geographically and chronologically. Our earliest identifiable written evidence for beliefs or ceremonies among Germanic tribes is the record by the Roman historian Tacitus in the first century AD. At the other end of the scale an Icelandic historian, Snorri Sturluson, in the first part of the thirteenth century gives details of what purport to be pagan beliefs. Neither of these historians is writing with first-hand knowledge. Tacitus is a foreigner, probably reporting what he has heard from travellers. Snorri is a Christian writing about the religion of his ancestors. Yet because our information from elsewhere is scattered and scanty, both the foreigner Tacitus and the Christian Snorri have been widely accepted as authorities on Germanic paganism, and what they say about it is repeatedly quoted as evidence of value.

Snorri is by no means the only medieval Christian historian to write of pagan beliefs and practice, but the trouble is that among the Germanic tribes Christianity and literacy tended to arrive hand-in-hand. Pre-

◁ **Valhalla and the serpent of Midgard**, as depicted in the Copenhagen manuscript, *c*.1680. Valhalla, identified with charming directness by a flag bearing the letters VH, was the palace of Odin. Here he held court in his great hall, feasting the heroes who had died in battle. High up, on the left, is the hart, Eikthyrner, 'who stands in Valhalla and bites the branches of [the tree] Laered; from her horns flows a stream into [the well] Hvergelmir'; and on the right, the goat Heidrun. 'From her teats', says Snorri, 'runs the mead with which she fills a cauldron every day, so that all the Einherjar [Odin's champions] can get full drink from it.' The figure in the doorway is Heimdall. The serpent of Midgard has been encountered earlier (p. 20). In this drawing, it is about to take the ox's head suspended on the line which conceals the hook of Thor. (38)

Christian Anglo-Saxons and Scandinavians did have an alphabet, which they used for carving fairly short texts on stone, wood, bone or metal, but long literary records in manuscript form are the product of a Christian and Latin education. It follows, therefore, that before we can have any full native record of a pagan practice or concept, a prerequisite is that the man who writes of it shall have been educated out of it. Missionary zeal in Anglo-Saxon England did not allow much scope for records of this kind, and we are obliged to interpret a rather limited range of references as competently as we can. The Scandinavian material is more extensive.

The foreigners' insight into Germanic religion may have been hampered by lack of full understanding of such rituals as they observed or heard described. What the Christians said about it may have been distorted by their wish to present it in the worst possible light as superstition, idolatry or devil-worship. But even when a text has been interpreted with the maximum amount of care, the resulting discovery may apply to only a small section of the Germanic community as a whole. Anglo-Saxon, Swede, Frisian or Icelander came originally from a common ethnic stock, presumably with common religious beliefs and practices. But it would be absurd to assume that with geographical distribution and the passing of centuries all these beliefs and practices remained static. What we read in an Anglo-Saxon text, even if we believe it to be true, of the religious outlook of a pagan monarch in Kent in the sixth century, is not necessarily true of a Norwegian farmer's in the eighth century or a Swedish mercenary's in the tenth. Yet all these characters would be, in some sense of the words, both Germanic and pagan.

Before we start using native written sources it is necessary to take note of the very great disparity in the volume of surviving literary material from Scandinavia and from the other Germanic countries. It is necessary, too, to take notice of the disparity in date. Anglo-Saxon England became Christian or was becoming Christian from the sixth century onwards, but Anglo-Saxon England was abruptly terminated by the Norman Conquest in 1066. In looking at the records between these dates, we are therefore looking at some of our earliest sources, especially our earliest vernacular texts. The Anglo-Saxons were, if one may generalize, interested in their past but not in their paganism. The store of legend they preserve is considerable, but the references to their pre-Christian religion are meagre, and scattered in homily, charter, medical miscellany and other improbable documents. Thus what we have is of great value because of its early date, but there is not much of it. Missionaries came later to Germany and Scandinavia, and in Germany there was no immediate and obvious side-effect by way of a literary corpus. Scandinavia, on the other hand, was uniquely served by one of its colonies. In the ninth century, Iceland was discovered by a Scandinavian and subsequently settled largely from Norway. Over the later medieval period, Iceland produced a body of literature that in extent and quality is unlike anything else from the medieval world.

Of this literature we are particularly concerned with three branches. In the first place, there is a corpus of poetry containing stories of gods and heroes. At least some of these heroes were those whose stories were being told by other Germanic firesides. Some of the gods are those common to the Germanic world. The collection of these poems, preserved mainly in one thirteenth-century manuscript, is now known as the Elder Edda or the Poetic Edda.

In the second place, Snorri Sturluson (1172–1241), Icelandic historian, scholar and politician, wrote in prose many tales and anecdotes about gods and heroes, mainly, he says, because it is difficult to understand Scandinavian poets if you cannot catch their allusions to these stories. His work is therefore in intention an aid to critical appreciation and understanding of Viking Age poetry. In this it succeeds. But it also tells us legends about the gods that we know from no other sources. This work is the Prose Edda.

In the third place, Icelanders in the late Middle Ages were writing the story of their past. In a vast number of prose vernacular works, known collectively as the Icelandic family sagas, they told the story of their pagan Viking ancestors who had settled Iceland. They told in other sagas histories of the kings of Norway. In yet more sagas they wrote down stories of the far legendary past, a past so remote that it includes names of such formidable heroes as Attila the Hun and Ermanaric the Goth. All these sagas are a curious mixture of history, fiction, folk-tale and anecdote. They include poems said to have been composed by the men who people the sagas, and some may indeed be authentic compositions from the Viking Age. They have a great deal to tell us about early Scandinavian society, and they are splendid reading in their own right. But for our present purposes the interest is in the odd aside, the occasional reference to pagan belief, practice, behaviour or superstition, whether by the writer of the saga, or, more importantly, in the poems he preserves. The range of material in Edda, prose and poetic, and in saga is vast, rich, varied and unreliable. The material has to be sifted with the utmost care before we can use it as evidence. Iceland's literary age, like Anglo-Saxon England's, is remote from its pagan past. The difference is mainly that the Icelanders were interested, and they preserved and recorded far more.

What we read does not, of course, provide the full sum of our evidence. Archaeologists who excavate temples and graves and market-towns from the pagan world can, for example, demonstrate with exactitude pagan burial practices in identifiable contexts. To some extent such evidence is open to further interpretation and deductions may be made from the nature of the burial about the current beliefs concerning the afterlife. Artifacts such as amulets or carved stones may also add details to our records. The distribution patterns of the names of Germanic gods as surviving place-name elements also can help us a good deal in locating specific cults. Yet even when all the disciplines have contributed their peculiar skills and kinds of knowledge, the final picture we have of Germanic mythology can never be as comprehensive or as sharply focused as we should like. Though we find out more every year we still do not know enough.

The realm of Thor

For the pagan Anglo-Saxon, important deities included Thunor, Woden, Tiw and Frig. Thunor, whose name was also the common noun 'thunder', is the same god as Scandinavian Thor. The various dialects of German record his name in forms closer to the English variant, *Thuner* in Old Low German, *Donar* in Old High German. This god has given his name to Thursday in most of the appropriate languages, German *Donnerstag*, Dutch *Donderdag*, Swedish and Danish *Torsdag*. The Scandinavian name Thor seems to have become the most popular usage in recent centuries and it may be a variant of Thor rather than Thunor which is preserved in the first element of 'Thursday'. The earliest Anglo-Saxon records have the form *Thunresdæg*, 'Thunor's day'. The paganism of the Viking invaders of England did not have a violent impact on a country by then fully Christianized, but this is one possible linguistic trace.

If we wish to probe further into the nature and powers of Thunor, the records of the Anglo-Saxons cannot take us very far. It is clear that Thunor is the name of a god, for when the Anglo-Saxons read Latin they sometimes wrote the gloss *Thunor* over their Latin reference to Jove or Jupiter. The Anglo-Saxon monk Ælfric, writing a homily against false gods *De falsis deis* in the days when Viking pagans were settling the north of England, used the Viking name Thor rather than the English Thunor, and wrote: 'Jove is the foremost of all the gods that the heathen worship in error. He is called Thor among some nations and the Danish people love him most.'

Scholars writing of Scandinavian paganism sometimes suggest that whereas Odin (Anglo-Saxon Woden) is the god of the king, warrior and poet, Thor is the god of the farmer and peasant. Whether or not a similar statement could be made of Anglo-Saxon England is doubtful, yet it is suggestive that whereas most Anglo-Saxon kings trace their ancestry back to Woden, none do so to Thunor. His name is rarely found as an element in English personal names, though Scandinavian sources are full of people whose names begin with the element *Thor*: Thorhall, Thorolf, Thormod, etc. The list could be continued almost indefinitely. But in both England and Scandinavia his name is found frequently enough in place-names. English Thunderfield, Thurstable, Thunderley, etc. may well have been original centres of Thunor worship. On the mainland of Scandinavia there are Thor place-names in abundance, and he is the god whose name is most frequently taken to Scandinavia's Atlantic colonies. Caithness, Scotland, has Thurso, 'Thor's estuary', the Faroe Islands Tórshavn, 'Thor's harbour', Iceland a minimum of eighteen names compounded with the element Thor.

Scandinavia and England can both offer place-name evidence, but for further record we have to turn from the scanty references in English documents to the rich if unreliable Scandinavian material. I do not think Anglo-Saxon England tells us of Thunor as a hammer-bearing deity, though his name means 'thunder' and the hammer may be thought to symbolize a thunderbolt. But Scandinavia is full of evidence in both literature and artifact associating the hammer with Thor. The stories which the Icelanders relate of Thor deal largely with his ability to rout the enemies of the gods, such as hill-giants and frost-giants, by swinging his hammer Mjollnir, and smashing the skulls of his opponents to gravel. A casual reference in the sagas tells us of a Christian king making the sign of the cross over his drink and being accused of doing so by his pagan subjects. His friends, quicker on the uptake than he is, claim that he is making the sign of Thor's hammer. Amulets in the shape of hammers, which could perhaps be worn as pendants, are found in a range of pagan graves of the tenth and eleventh centuries throughout Scandinavia. Writers and painters have delighted in depicting Thor with hammer and girdle of strength embarking on one of his many fights, whether with the giants or with the monstrous world-serpent, the Midgardsorm, 'who lies about all lands and whose length scarcely suffices for his tail and head to meet round the earth'. It is difficult to be sure with early

Thor, Woden and Friga (Thor, Odin and Frey) from Aylett Sammes's 'Britannia Antiqua' of 1676. The seventeenth century saw an increasing interest in England's pre-Christian past. (3)

carvings whether a depiction of a serpent and serpent-killer is a pagan god Thor and world-serpent, a hero dragon-slayer, or even a Christian St Michael fighting the devil. But there are a couple of carved stones, one at Altuna in Sweden, another at Gosforth, Cumberland, which may show Thor fishing on the famous occasion when, according to Snorri, he took an ox-head as bait and caught the world-serpent on his hook 'and it can be said that no one has seen a terrifying sight who did not see how Thor glared at the serpent, and how the serpent glared back and blew poison'.

The stress from Scandinavia appears to be on Thor as a god of immense physical strength, in many ways the defender of the gods from their violent enemies. The corollary to this is the emphasis in the Icelandic comic tales on Thor as slow-witted. A story in the Prose Edda tells us how the giants deceived the gods by optical illusions so that when Thor, having boasted of his capacity for drink, was invited to drain a horn of ale he failed to finish it, not having perceived that the far end of the horn was in the sea. Invited to pick up a cat from the ground – 'a grey one and quite big' – he did not see that it was the world-serpent in disguise. Invited to wrestle with an old woman he could not work out that he was fighting against Old Age herself. Snorri tells us these tales, but there is evidence for their being in circulation before Snorri, some evidence therefore that he is recording a tradition rather than inventing a delightful fiction. In a poem, probably authentic, ascribed to a Norwegian chieftain of the ninth century, Old Age is spoken of as 'Thor's wrestling-partner'.

The mood of the later writers towards Thor seems one more of tolerant affection than of veneration, which

*Stories of fights between heroes and dragons
passed from pagan to Christian mythology.
A Saxon carving now incorporated into
Southwell Minster shows St Michael
fighting Satan but the Scandinavian style of
the dragon betrays its pre-Christian origins.
On the left Samson wrestles with the lion.
(4).*

is appropriate enough since these records date from a
time when active worship of Thor had ceased. We
cannot tell how far this tone of friendliness rather than
awe is a continuation of an earlier attitude. One saga
writer describes an eleventh-century pagan Norseman
in Greenland who, in casual friendly fashion, called his
patron Thor 'the Redbeard'. The record of the
settlement of Iceland names an early settler, Helgi, as 'of
mixed faith. He believed in Christ, but still invoked
Thor before voyages or difficult enterprises.' Such
tolerant acceptance seems a long way from the firm
Anglo-Saxon rejection of paganism, or from the ninth-
century Old Saxon renunciation formula spoken at
Christian baptism: 'I forsake Thunaer and Uuoden . . .
and all those devils who are their companions.' An
attempt to serve both pagan and Christian gods in the
early days of Anglo-Saxon Christianity is recorded by
Bede. He says that the East Anglian king Redwald had
one altar dedicated to Christ and another, a little one, on
which victims were offered to devils. But where the late
Icelandic writer records 'mixed faith' without comment, Bede's condemnation in the early eighth century
is severe.

Odin, the All-father

The god whom the English called Woden and is found
in the early forms of German as Wodan or Wuotan is
also the Scandinavian Odin. The loss of the initial
consonant in the Old Norse form is usual (cf. Old
English *wulf*, 'wolf', as against Old Norse *ulfr*). That
Woden occurs alongside Thunor in the Old Saxon
renunciation formula quoted above suggests that for
this tribe these two were major gods as they clearly
were also for Anglo-Saxon and Viking. Woden has
given his name to Wednesday in most of the Germanic
dialects. The Old English spelling is *Wodnesdæg*, Old
Norse *Odinsdagr*, in modern Danish and Swedish
contracted to *Onsdag*. In Scandinavian literature Odin is
described as the All-father, the highest of the gods, but,
as we have already seen, for the educated Anglo-Saxon
Thunor rather than Woden was the god equivalent to

Jove, ruler of the Olympic pantheon. The same learned
Anglo-Saxon saw Woden as the equivalent to the
Roman god Mercury, for Woden translates Mercurium
in a Latin/Anglo-Saxon dictionary from the eighth
century. Ælfric in *De falsis deis* has a little to tell us about
the worship of Mercurius, whom the Danes, he says,
call Odin. He says that high mountains are the places
where Odin receives sacrifice, but his source says much
the same of Mercury, and we cannot be sure that his
statement reflects any precise knowledge of Odin
worship among Ælfric's Viking contemporaries. It is
appropriate to remember that the literate Anglo-Saxon
would probably have read as much on classical
paganism as he would have heard related about the
Germanic variety. Ælfric, writing in the eleventh
century, may also have known quite clearly that the
gods the Danish invaders worshipped had had Anglo-
Saxon counterparts back in the mists of time, but at no
stage does he say so unequivocally. He is writing
explicitly, not about the gods of his English ancestors,
but about the gods of heathen foreigners. Another
writer of homilies, Wulfstan, slightly adapts Ælfric's
material on false gods to produce a homily of his own
on the same subject. The surviving manuscript of this
has marginal additions which make it clear that one
scribe at any rate could identify Odin and Woden. The
marginalia include the phrase *Othon unde Wodones dæg*,
'Odin, whence Wednesday'.

Earlier writers than Ælfric and Wulfstan mention
Woden rarely, and the references can be hard to
understand. An Anglo-Saxon charm tells us how
Woden dealt with a serpent: 'Woden took nine twigs of
glory and struck the adder.' This approach was
evidently successful since the creature flew into nine
parts, but the significance is obscure. It is, however,
interesting to note that Woden figures also in a ninth-
century German charm of healing, linking 'bone to
bone, blood to blood' to cure a damaged foot. One
Anglo-Saxon poem draws a clear antithesis between the
achievements of the pagan and the Christian gods:
'Woden created idols, the Almighty created glory, the

broad heavens.' This is a variant version of the statement in Psalm 96, 'all the gods of the nations are idols: But the Lord made the heavens', but is still of interest in that Woden is the god chosen for the antithesis. Otherwise the main place of Woden in Anglo-Saxon documents is in the genealogical lists of the royal families. We find these in the Latin Chronicle of the Anglo-Saxon writer Æthelweard who quite clearly links Woden as ancestor of the Anglo-Saxon royalty with Odin, god of the heathen. Æthelweard's statement is that the leaders of the first Anglo-Saxon invasion of England were Hengist and Horsa, 'descendants of Woden, a king of the barbarians. And after his death the pagans, honouring him as a god with respect not fit to be mentioned, offered him sacrifice in order to have victory or be courageous.' Later Æthelweard says also: 'The heathen northern peoples . . . worship him as a god to the present day.' In the manuscripts of the Anglo-Saxon Chronicle Woden appears as the ancestor of the royal houses of Wessex, Mercia and Northumbria, sometimes as the first progenitor named, sometimes as one in a list linked with biblical names to provide a complete genealogy back to Adam. The interest taken by the Anglo-Saxons in these lists is demonstrated by the fact that they also occur independently of the Chronicle.

It is tempting, and people have been tempted, to use what we know of Odin from Scandinavian sources to interpret artifacts and texts of Anglo-Saxon England. It is true that Viking poets call Odin 'lord of the spear'. But it is very difficult to say with certainty that, for example, a seventh-century buckle from Finglesham, Kent, with the motif of a male figure, nude except for horned helmet and belt, carrying a spear, must depict Woden or even one of his followers. Nor is it more p.73(1) demonstrable that the stag figure on the whetstone in the Anglo-Saxon royal burial at Sutton Hoo is firm evidence of a Woden cult. The bearded faces on the sides of that whetstone have, on the other hand, been said to be pictures of Thunor, but doubtless there were other beards, other stags and other spears than those of the gods, even in pagan Anglo-Saxon England.

The place-name evidence for Woden worship in England is re-examined fairly often. If a site contains the god name Woden, this is not in itself clear and unmistakeable evidence of a cult-site, but where the second element of the name is one normally associated with pagan worship as, for example, Woodnesborough (Old English *Wodnesbeorg*), 'Woden's hill', we can assume it to be so. Place-names containing the Scandinavian form Odin are found regularly in mainland Scandinavia, the best known being Odense in Denmark, but less regularly elsewhere. Roseberry Topping in the north of Yorkshire, however, occurs in twelfth-century records with the spelling *Othenesberg*, 'Odin's hill', which contains the same two elements as

Danish *Onsbjærg*. This would be a perfectly appropriate Viking equivalent to *Wodnesbeorg*.

The Scandinavian sources, especially the two Eddas, have a good deal to say about Odin, all of it interesting, some of it incomprehensible, some of it perhaps contaminated by Christianity. The wearing of a Thor hammer amulet may be not so much an independent pagan habit as a pagan answer to the wearing of the crucifix, and in the same way some of the characteristics of pagan gods, especially of Odin, as described in the later centuries, may well have been acquired after their worshippers had been exposed, however casually, to Christian belief. The tenth-century Icelander Egil Skallagrimsson, who describes himself as a devotee of Odin in his poetry, received some sort of Christian initiation, according to the writer of his saga. We are told that King Æthelstan of England 'asked Thorolf and Egil to let themselves be provisionally baptized. It was a common custom to do so both among merchants and among those mercenaries who joined with Christians, since men who received provisional baptism had full contact with Christians and heathens, but kept whatever faith they were inclined to.'

Thus when the Eddic poem *Havamal*, 'sayings of the High One', tells us of Odin, 'I know that I hung on the windy tree for nine full nights, wounded with a spear, given to Odin, myself to myself', it is not immediately clear whether this god-sacrifice or some details of it have been drawn from the Crucifixion. On the other hand there is no suggestion in the Icelandic source that Odin's motive was redemption of mankind. Through suffering he acquires knowledge. After this sacrifice, according to the poem, he 'took up the runes, shrieking grasped them'. The term 'runes', in general meaning no more than the letters of an alphabet, could also have meant knowledge, especially secret knowledge. It is not clear exactly what Odin acquires in acquiring runes, but it is undoubtedly knowledge of some kind and of some value. The Prose Edda tells us of another occasion when Odin gave an eye in exchange for a drink from the spring of Mimir 'in which is wisdom and understanding'. He too is the god who, by a complicated process told at length in the Prose Edda, acquired the 'mead' or gift of poetry, and poets in the Viking Age, therefore, looked to Odin as their patron.

Thor, the god of physical strength, is seen in Icelandic sources as the protagonist in one comedy after another. There is little that is comic about Odin. If strength and stupidity are seen to go hand in hand, so are wisdom and cunning. One can see such a development in the downward path of the adjectives 'crafty' and 'cunning' themselves, for both now have pejorative overtones, but both in the first place described a man of talent or knowledge. Odin seems often enough to be a sinister figure, using his formidable powers to harm rather than help, to betray those who trust him, to promote strife and oath-breaking. But the Viking poet Egil Skallagrimsson claimed, in his superb poem lamenting the death of his sons, that though Odin has taken his children from him Odin has given him two great gifts. One of these is the art of poetry. The other is 'the temper which made known enemies out of tricksters'. Thus one worshipper of Odin at any rate saw him not as using guile but as helping to expose it.

The link that the Anglo-Saxons made between Woden and Mercury is also found in the Old Icelandic version of the Bible. Where our version of Acts of the Apostles reads, 'The gods are come down to us in the likeness of men. And they called Barnabas Jupiter; and Paul, Mercurius, because he was the chief speaker', the Icelandic text says 'they called Paul, Odin, but Barnabas they called Thor'. It is possible that the Scandinavians made this parallel independently, seeing their god of poetry as the most appropriate 'chief speaker', but it is more likely, I think, that the Anglo-Saxon missionaries who were instrumental in the conversion of Iceland taught their converts this equation of the classical pagan gods with their own.

Many facets of Odin are described in the late sources, but it is difficult to check the stories against other forms of evidence. Poets of the Viking Age describe him as god of the hanged, god of the spear and god of the raven, and all these indicate a relationship with death, either in sacrifice or war. The raven of course is the bird of prey that feeds on corpses. Odin is linked in many tales with the fortunes of heroes and kings, with battle and hostilities. Snorri tells us that Norwegians drank a toast to Odin for victory but the medieval chronicler Adam of Bremen claims more dramatically that the Swedes sacrificed to Odin for victory. Late and confused sagas preserve the traditions of a spear being hurled over an enemy host, accompanied by the words 'you belong to Odin', or of a victorious leader giving the dead to Odin. It is difficult to identify behaviour of this type in the pictorial evidence, but there is a carved stone that rather charmingly corroborates one trivial piece of information about Odin from the Prose Edda. Snorri's tale is that the god Loki, being obliged to distract a giant's horse from its work, turned himself into a mare for the occasion. The distraction worked admirably and, later, Loki gave birth to a foal. 'It was grey and it had eight legs and that horse is the best among gods and men.' Elsewhere, Snorri records further: 'The horses of the gods are called thus: Sleipnir is best; Odin owns him; he has eight legs.' Sleipnir is named if not described in two Eddic poems. It follows therefore that when we find a picture showing a rider on an eight-legged horse there is some reason for assuming that it shows Odin on Sleipnir, and that the tradition of the god's eight-legged horse was not uncommon.

2, 6

Tyr, Frey and Freyja

After Thunor/Thor and Woden/Odin, the international evidence for the veneration of the gods grows less. Anglo-Saxon Tiw, Scandinavian Tyr, is in Old Norse sources the name of a god of combat, and his presence in the hierarchy from early days is suggested by the fact that he gives his name to Tuesday, Old English *Tiwesdæg*, Old Norse *Tysdagr*. In England the place-name evidence is inconclusive. Until lately a fairly large number of names were thought to contain the name of the god, but recent scholarship has reduced them, and leaves us with only Tysoe, 'Tiw's hill-spur', in Warwickshire as a fairly definite example. Ælfric in his homily on false gods does not even give the vernacular name, though he identifies the god of Tuesday as a god of war. He says 'on the third day they honoured Mars, their battle-god'. Ælfric, as we have seen, normally suggests parallels between Roman and northern gods. This is the only time he gives the Roman name by itself avoiding explicit reference to the clear Germanic equivalent.

In Scandinavia, Tyr worship is suggested by place-names in Denmark but there are not many in the other northern countries. Tiw/Tyr is, in both Old English and Old Norse, the name of a letter in the runic alphabet. Most of these letter names are simply common nouns, such as 'thorn' or 'ash' or 'water', but at least one Scandinavian source makes it clear that this rune-name was also thought of as the god-name. The twelfth-century Norse runic poem that names each letter of the runic alphabet says of the letter Tyr that 'Tyr is the one-handed among the gods'. One curious indication of Tyr's popularity is the extent to which his name is used in periphrastic reference to other gods, particularly Odin. It is a common feature of Viking Age poetry to link the name of one god with the attribute of another. Thus if the poet says 'Tyr' he means Tyr, whereas if he says 'Tyr of the hanged' he means Odin. Such usage incorporating Tyr's name is extremely common, but the only narrative information we receive about Tyr is, as usual, from Snorri, who tells a pretty story of how Tyr came to lose his hand: 'When the gods enticed the wolf Fenrir to let the fetter Gleipnir be placed on him, he did not believe that they would loose him until they put Tyr's hand in his mouth as a pledge. Then when the gods did not wish to loose Fenrir he bit off the hand, at the place now called the wolf-joint' (wrist).

Anglo-Saxon England seems to know little or nothing of the brother and sister, Frey and Freyja, who occupy so large a part of the tales and chronicles from Scandinavia. The names themselves are of interest, for the cognate words in other Germanic languages are not names of deities but the common nouns for 'lord' and 'lady'. One possible interpretation of this is that the names Frey and Freyja are late, having taken over from other earlier appellations, though they are early enough for a wide range of Scandinavian place-names to be based on them. Freyja is in Scandinavian material the equivalent of Greek Aphrodite or Roman Venus, the goddess of love and beauty. Such a goddess in England and Germany gave her name to Friday, but her name must have been Frig (in some form), the equivalent not of Norse Freyja but of Frigg, Odin's wife, a different character altogether. It is the name Fricg which Ælfric uses in *De falsis deis*, where he describes the lady as a shameless goddess. His statement that she is the Danish answer to Venus suggests either that in his Scandinavian sources Frigg was the goddess of love (in which case the cult of Freyja may be a later, more literary development), or on the other hand that Ælfric's knowledge of far-off Anglo-Saxon paganism confused his record of current Scandinavian nomenclature. 'Shameless', however, seems a description that would suit Freyja better than Frigg if we are to go by what the late Norse texts say. In one Eddic poem, Freyja is taunted with her promiscuity: 'Of the gods and elves here . . . Each one has been your lover.'

There is much in recent works on mythology about Frey, Freyja and their father Njord, partly because in Scandinavian literature there are two races of gods named, and a battle and truce between them described. One group, in Old Norse the Æsir, includes Thor, Odin and Tyr. The other group, the Vanir, includes Frey, Freyja and Njord, all of them apparently connected with fertility and wealth. Those scholars who concern themselves with parallels in world mythology see the battle between the Æsir and the Vanir as being fought out in other heavens and hierarchies than the Norse one. There is not space to examine the evidence for these claims, but one certain point is the antiquity of Scandinavian Njord, who is undoubtedly descended from the early Germanic pantheon. The Roman historian Tacitus, writing his *Germania* in the first century AD, refers to a German goddess Nerthus and the rituals of her cult, thereby demonstrating the antiquity of Njord's name, if not of his sex. It may be that originally the cult was of brother and sister divinities like the subsequent one of Frey and Freyja.

The Scandinavian list of gods extends indefinitely, but it becomes increasingly difficult to make comparisons with English and German traditions. Some of the Norse gods are well known to us, Balder, for 14, example, because the story of his death inspired so 18 many poets, but there are others such as Bragi, god of poetry, of whom we know next to nothing. Snorri also enumerates various improbable goddesses: 'the second is Saga; she lives at Sokkvabekk which is a big place. The third is Eir; she is an excellent doctor. The fourth is Gefjon; she is a virgin and those serve her who die unmarried.' And so on. What we would really like to know is Snorri's evidence. The names occur in extant Eddic poems, but the context is usually obscure.

The gods in folklore: Valkyries, giants and elves

It is largely from Snorri that the delightful wealth of detail and anecdote comes which make the characters of gods and goddesses so vivid. So long as his stories are read for fun and not pressed for evidence beyond what they can yield we can get great pleasure from the thought of Freyja 'in her chariot drawn by two cats', 12 Freyja weeping 'tears of red gold', Freyja 'snorting with rage' because Thor lightly suggested she be married off to a giant in order that he might recover his stolen hammer. Snorri's stories of Frey's love for the giantess Gerd or Njord's marriage with the giantess Skathi have both been interpreted as the marriage of fertility gods with the frost-giant clan, i.e. with a goddess of winter and death. But what we remember is the picture of Frey, disconsolate lover, after his first sight of Gerd: 'And when he came home he did not speak; he did not sleep; he did not drink. No one dared to try and get a word out of him.' The incompatible couple Njord and Skathi complain bitterly about the early morning noises in each other's terrain. Njord, god of the sea, finds the howling of the wolves unpleasant when he sleeps in the hills. Skathi, hill-giantess, resents the screaming of the sea-birds and cannot sleep on the bed of the sea. It is not surprising that they part.

One of the areas in which we can perhaps trust Snorri is where he describes superstitions, though we do not know if his explanation is right. There will be few people who can forget, once having read it, his description of how the ship to be let loose at the last day, Naglfar, is built out of the nails of dead men. 'If a man dies with uncut nails that man adds greatly to the building material for the ship Naglfar which gods and men hope will be built slowly.' Nails are one thing, leather quite another, and bits of leather may be wasted, for these help the gods not their enemies. Vidar who fights the wolf Fenrir 'has on his foot a shoe which has been in preparation throughout all time. It is made of the scraps which men cut from their shoes round the toes and heels. Therefore he who wants to come to the help of the gods will throw away such bits.' These are interesting comments on what may have been surviving superstitions even in Snorri's day. A man does not have to believe firmly and fully in Naglfar or Fenrir to think that it is 'lucky' or 'unlucky' to perform certain actions.

Superstition, folk-tale and place-names have also kept alive the lingering traces of some lesser beings of the Germanic supernatural world, which appears to have been peopled by a healthy assortment of giants, elves, dwarfs, witches and water-monsters. In the Norse literature many of these are shown as creatures of power, stature and terror. The women who ride to choose the slain, the Valkyries (Old Norse *valkyrja*; plural *valkyriur*), have inspired many a modern painter, sculptor and writer, though they seem to have spent at least some of their time in a more domestic capacity. In the tenth-century poem *Eiriksmal*, describing the welcome for a dead king in Valhalla, Odin, the host in charge of the reception, instructs the Valkyries to 'strew the benches [with cushions], wash the goblets, and serve wine'. In Old English texts the cognate word *wælcyrige* survives. The meaning of the compound in both the lost English word and the recently revived Norse one is the same. The first element is 'the dead' or 'the slain', the second element 'chooser'. It seems quite likely that in the early stages of Anglo-Saxon paganism these beings had the same function as their Scandinavian sisters. The word occurs in English, translating the name of Roman goddesses of war such as Bellona, in one early dictionary translating, perhaps with more exactitude, the name of the avenging furies, the Erinyes. In one manuscript of a Latin work by Aldhelm, the Anglo-Saxon scribe has written in above the name Venus the Old English words for 'goddess' and, surprisingly, 'valkyrie'. The alliterative phrase *wyccan and wælcyrian*, 'witches and valkyries', occurs in several late Old English texts, and even in one Middle English poem. It is likely that the concept had lost power, and that the enfeebled caricature of a witch on her broomstick was already replacing the terrible Valkyrie; but it is fairly surprising that the word survived at all.

The giants of Scandinavian mythology are formidable enemies, who are destined to overcome gods and men in the final battle. The chief of them is sometimes called lord of the *thursar*, and the word occurs in such compounds as *hrimthurs*, 'frost-giant'. Anglo-Saxon texts also know of a *thyrs* who, unhappy creature, lives in the marsh alone in the land. This description occurs alongside such straightforward statements as 'a fish lives in water'. Clearly to be alone in a marsh is regarded as the natural habitat of a *thyrs*. There are other occasional references in the early literature, and the word survives in dialectal *thurse* meaning 'goblin', which seems something of a descent in the social scale. Scholars suggest that the creature can still be found lurking in such place-names as Thursden.

The Anglo-Saxon epic poem *Beowulf* is firm in its statement that all such beings as giants and elves are the progeny of Cain and the enemies of God, but elves at any rate get a kindlier press elsewhere. A list of creatures from classical mythology translated into Old English offers us the following equations:

Oreades   *muntælfen*   'mountain-elves'
Dryades   *wuduelfen*   'wood-elves'
Moides   *feldelfen*   'field elves'
Hamadryades   *wylde elfen*   'wild elves'
Naiades   *sæelfen*   'sea-elves'

Catalides   *dunelfen*   'hill-elves'

The adjective *Ælfsciene*, 'beautiful as an elf', is used to describe favourite heroines of Anglo-Saxon literature. In Norse sources, notably Eddic poetry, elves are often linked with the gods as a group of beings with similar status. Snorri divides them into light elves and dark elves. It is, perhaps, the Anglo-Saxon equivalent of the dark elves who are responsible for the illnesses against which they had so many remedies, 'elf-disease', 'water-elf disease', 'elf-shot cattle', 'elf-shot horses'. One remedy clearly faults the whole tribe, for the remedy is against *ælfcynn*, 'the race of elves'. The plant, enchanter's nightshade, is known as *ælfthone*, and is apparently efficacious against elf-disease.

Worlds of the living and the dead

There is not space to enumerate all the beings who have pretensions to inhabit the world of Germanic belief, whether as figures within the formal mythological framework or as creatures of superstition. It is, however, appropriate to look at the kind of universe they inhabit. Here we know very little from Anglo-Saxon sources. The fact that Anglo-Saxon pagan graves are furnished, sometimes richly, with grave-goods suggests some kind of belief in a continuation of life after death; the use of the ship for pagan burial, whether actually as at Sutton Hoo or in literary description as in *Beowulf*, suggests the concept of death as a journey. Bede, in his description of the conversion of Northumbria, gives a speech purporting to be that of one of King Edwin's counsellors:

Your Majesty, when we compare the present life of man with that time of which we have no knowledge, it seems to me like the swift flight of a lone sparrow through the banqueting-hall where you sit in the winter months to dine with your thanes and counsellors. Inside there is a comforting fire to warm the room; outside, the wintry storms of snow and rain are raging. This sparrow flies swiftly in through one door of the hall and out through another. While he is inside, he is safe from the winter storms; but after a few moments of comfort, he vanishes from sight into the darkness whence he came. Similarly man appears on earth for a little while, but we know nothing of what went before this life, and what follows. Therefore if this new teaching can reveal any more certain knowledge, it seems only right that we should follow it.

This is a profound statement and a fine poetic passage, and it is very difficult indeed to know how much reliance we can place on it. On the one hand Bede is inevitably presenting the pagan view from his own Christian ideological standpoint, on the other hand the anecdote sounds remarkably like a bit of genuinely preserved oral tradition. The idea of the unknown nature of the after-life is also presented to us by the poet of *Beowulf*, a Christian poet describing a pagan's funeral. The body of the dead king is placed in a ship: 'They let the sea carry him, they gave him to the ocean. Men, dwellers in the hall, heroes of the earth, do not know how to say truly who received that cargo.'

Viking and Anglo-Saxon had the same word for the human world. Earth is in Old English *middangeard*, in Old Norse *midgard*, 'the middle earth'. 'Middle' suggests some kind of central cosmic position, but Norse sources offer such a bewildering number of worlds that the structure is not always clearly comprehensible. With worlds of gods, giants, elves, men and the dead to be fitted in, the picture becomes a complex one. Snorri's version describes the world tree, 19,20 Yggdrasil, the branches of which 'spread out over all the world and reach up beyond heaven'. Various worlds were positioned among its roots. Snorri tells us in graphic detail of the beasts that inhabit or devour Yggdrasil, the eagle in the branches, the hawk perched between the eagle's eyes, the harts that 'run about the branches of the ash-tree and bite the shoots', the serpents among the roots. 'A squirrel called Ratatosk runs up and down the ash and carries words of ill-will between the eagle and the serpent Nidhogg.'

It cannot be said, I think, that the average Norseman could have 'believed' in anything as complex as these sources describe. There are clearly several concepts of the world of the dead. One involves Odin and his choice of heroes to help the gods in their last battle, one is linked with Hel, goddess of the underworld and the shadowy dead, another suggests that the dead continued some form of life in the burial mound. The range of belief suggested by sagas is considerable and must have shifted a good deal from one district to another and one century to another. The Viking poet Egil Skallagrimsson combines two ideas in one poem lamenting his sons' deaths when on the one hand he speaks of his dead son 'coming to Odin's home', and on the other hand describes his own wait and welcome for 'Hel, standing on the headland'.

The idea of Odin collecting together the dead champions of the human race in Valhalla is intimately linked with the concept of the last battle, the end of the world and the doom of the gods. In both Eddic prose and Eddic poetry there is a great deal of detailed description of this terrifying future, but again it is hard to say how closely such description is linked to genuine pagan belief. It may well have been influenced by Christian ideas of doom. It is here that we meet for the last time those superb monsters the Midgard serpent and the wolf Fenrir as they and the gods die together. 3 Odin is summarily disposed of: 'The wolf swallows Odin; that will be his death.' Thor, having killed the Midgard serpent, 'steps away nine feet' but then drops dead from the poison of the serpent's breath. More significant than these excellent stories are the details of how morality and integrity among humanity will come to an end. This is so close to certain Christian Anglo-

Saxon sermons that it is hard to see how one literature and mythology can have been uninfluenced by the other. The Eddic poem *Voluspa* prophesies: 'Brothers will fight and kill each other, kin commit incest, men will know misery, adulteries be multiplied.' The tone of all this is very close to Archbishop Wulfstan's famous 'Sermon of the Wolf to the English'. The sermon goes on rather longer than *Voluspa* but even short quotations are indicative: 'Also we fully know . . . that a father has sold his son for money, and a son his mother, and one brother has sold another into the power of strangers.' And again: 'This nation has become sinfully corrupted . . . through attacks on kin and through killings . . . through adultery, incest and various fornications.' It is worth remembering that the Anglo-Saxon world was educated in the Christian belief that the world was due to end in the year 1000. When it failed to do so the urgency was merely postponed a little, for they assumed they should have been calculating from the year of Christ's death not his birth, and the end of the world would therefore be AD 1033. Thus not only did the Christian Anglo-Saxon literature deal rather fully with the decline and impending doom of the world and the imminent day of judgment, but also those Vikings mentioned earlier who came into contact with Christianity, while adhering to what belief they pleased, may well have heard a good deal of thinking along these lines. It would hardly be reasonable to read this magnificent range of prophecy in Icelandic prose and poetry as if it were an integral part of the Germanic and pagan view of life and death. It is impressive as literature, but there is no overwhelming reason for accepting it as a formal, clear-cut and accurate guide to Germanic mythology.

When we are reading any piece of literature from these early times it is always necessary to bear in mind the possibility of two longish intervals in the transmission process. In the first place the work was very probably composed orally, and when first written down may already have passed through the memories of several generations and been altered in the process. The man who writes down a poem in England, a saga in Iceland, may be doing some final and personal reshaping and structuring, but we are in no position now to identify and differentiate the separate layers from the first oral composition to the first written text. In the second place we are dealing with the centuries before the invention of printing when the only way of obtaining multiple copies of anything was to produce further manuscripts of them. Every scribe copying anything makes mistakes, even the most conscientious and scholarly, and there are plenty of unscholarly, even of incompetent and careless scribes. It is often possible to see quite clearly in a manuscript a passage where the scribe has become tired, or perhaps hurriedly tried to finish off something while there was light enough, and his mistakes suddenly multiply. Second and third, or even twenty-second and thirty-third scribes copying from bad copies are in no position to restore an original reading, though they may sometimes try to make sense out of nonsense. Thus in reading the literature of the period it is self-evidently absurd to make literary critical judgments about the author's intention or even the author's accuracy. It may not even be entirely sensible to use the word 'author', though it is difficult to see what can be used instead. But it is always necessary to bear in mind these two intervals, perhaps of several centuries, the one between composing and writing, the second between the first manuscript (almost certainly lost) and the accidental survivor which we are obliged to use.

Weland the smith

There may have been in England, Scandinavia and Germany dozens of poems and stories about the smith Weland, the dragon-killer Beowulf, the yet more famed dragon-killer Sigmund (or Sigurd or Siegfried), the divided loyalties of Ingeld. We do not know dozens, but we do find similar stories about these characters turning up in different parts of the northern world. As with the mythological material we sometimes find evidence that a story was known because a detail from it was carved on wood or ivory or stone, or because a casual allusion to it is contained in a text dealing primarily with quite other material.

In England there is a good deal of evidence that the Anglo-Saxons were so familiar with the talents of a smith called Weland that his name had only to be mentioned for an audience to respond appropriately. Two heroic poems use, independently, the phrase *Welandes weorc*, 'the work of Weland', when they want to stress the magnificence of a sword or piece of armour. There could be no point in the phrase unless the poet was able to anticipate an informed audience. There may have been an implicit suggestion that the work of Weland was the work of a man with more than ordinary mortal talents. One of the Norse sources calls him *alfa liodi* and *visi alfa* 'prince' or 'lord of the elves'.

King Alfred, translating the *Consolation of Philosophy* in the ninth century from the Latin original of Boethius, came across the phrase, 'Where are the bones of Fabricius?' Evidently assuming with his customary good sense that since Fabricius was of no particular interest to the Anglo-Saxons it would be better to substitute a name with strong emotive associations, he asks instead: 'Where now are the bones of the wise and well-known goldsmith Weland?' Alfred adds a rider which may have been intended, from a Christian standpoint, to forestall any suggestion that he was referring to a man of supernatural skills. 'I call him wise for the craftsman may never lose his craft . . . .' A little later he reiterates the elegiac note: 'Where now are the

bones of Weland, or who knows now where they were?' The question is rhetorical, but the people of Berkshire might have offered an answer. Present-day maps of Berkshire show a feature named 'Wayland Smith's Cave'. The first known variant of this name in an Anglo-Saxon charter for the year AD 955 calls the same phenomenon 'Weland's smithy'.

The fullest reference to Weland in our Anglo-Saxon sources is in the poem *Deor*. The poem is found in one manuscript only, the *Exeter Book*, a poetic miscellany written towards the end of the tenth century. The date of the poem itself is uncertain. It has been ascribed by scholars to a variety of centuries from the fifth onwards. The first stanza of the poem opens with the name Weland, the second with the name Beadohild, mother of Weland's son. The other stanzas do not have any narrative connection with the first two for the pattern of the poem is not one of sequence but of parallel example. Weland and Beadohild are the first two examples of misfortune:

> *Weland knew persecution by the sword,*
> *steadfast hero, he endured misery;*
> *he had for comrades sorrow and longing,*
> *wintercold misery; he often knew distress*
> *after Nidhad placed fetters on him,*
> *supple sinew-bonds on the better man.*
> *That passed: this can too.*
>
> *Beadohild was not for her brothers' deaths*
> *so bitter at heart as for her own trouble,*
> *after she had clearly recognized*
> *that she was pregnant. She could not ever*
> *fully grasp how this had come about.*
> *That passed: this can too.*

This shows clearly that details of the Weland legend, quite apart from the smith's reputation, were known to the Anglo-Saxons, but it is only because Norse sources tell us the details that we are able to follow it. The link between Weland and Beadohild, for instance, which is implied though not stated in the poem, is clarified for us if we turn to the superb Eddic poem *Volundarkvida* (Old Norse *Völundr* = Old English Weland). From this poem we learn that the man named in the first stanza of *Deor*, Nidhad who captured Weland, is the father of Beadohild, and that Weland's revenge is the killing of this man's sons and the rape of his daughter. But where we have to be guided to an understanding of the poem by extraneous material, it is clear that the poet expected his audience to grasp understated allusions immediately. There are difficulties in the English poem which the fuller Norse version may help to clarify. 'Supple sinew-bonds' could refer to ropes of captivity, and perhaps does; but the Eddic poem refers to the cutting of Weland's sinews, crippling him to prevent escape, and it is possible that the English poet, relying on his audience's knowledge, could use the irony of the cut sinews serving as bonds in one graphic phrase.

Similarly, where *Deor* does not explain how Beadohild achieved pregnancy without knowing how, *Volundarkvida* suggests that she was drugged: 'he carried strong drink to her; he knew more than she did'.

37 The beautiful carved ivory box known as the Franks Casket, eighth century or possibly earlier, shows in one panel a series of scenes that can hardly be anything other than the Weland story. Scholars have interpreted some of the details differently, but there seems to be general agreement that the panel shows Weland's revenge: first the figure of Weland himself, a pair of tongs in one hand holding the head of the murdered prince, a cup of drink in the other, being offered to Beadohild. The second female figure may be a second depiction of Beadohild, though other ideas have been put forward; and the third scene, the figure catching birds, cannot be explained by anything in English sources. Once again we need the help of the Scandinavian material. *Volundarkvida* makes it clear that Weland finally escaped by flying; another Scandinavian source describes how Weland's brother shot birds so that the feathers might be used in making wings for Weland's escape.

Where and when the Weland story originated is not a problem that can be analyzed here. Nor can we make a comprehensive survey of what journeys it took and through what stages it passed to appear as and how it does, in a carving, a poem or a place-name. That it was firmly entrenched as part of the general Germanic corpus of story and legend is clearly shown by the fact that we use an Icelandic poem from a thirteenth-century manuscript to help us understand *Deor* and the Franks Casket in Anglo-Saxon England, and that even the writer of the Latin epic *Waltharius*, in tenth-century Germany, says of a particularly fine piece of armour that it is *Wielandia fabrica*, 'the work of Weland'.

The story of Sigurd

The problem with the story of the dragon-killer Sigurd or Siegfried and his troubled love life is that we, in the twentieth century, are all half-aware of the details as transmitted through Wagner's Ring Cycle. The story clearly took a hold on the imagination of the Germanic world, and we find indications that it was known in Anglo-Saxon England, vast quantities of material, as usual, from Scandinavia, but this time literature from Germany as well. The hero who is German Siegfried is Norse Sigurd and Old English Sigmund. For general reference I shall use the Norse nomenclature and orthography for all the characters in the story.

In the Anglo-Saxon epic poem *Beowulf* a story is told, occupying a mere twenty-five lines or so, of a hero whose deeds and fame may be considered analogous to Beowulf's. This is the dragon-killer Sigmund. The names given are Sigmund's own (he is also called

Wælsing or 'son of Wæls'), and that of his nephew, Fitela. These correspond to Sigmund, Volsung and (Sin)fjotli in the Norse sources, where it is not Sigmund but his son Sigurd who kills the dragon, there named Fafnir. In German the hero is Siegfried, son of Sigmund. *Beowulf*'s unequivocal statements are that Sigmund killed a dragon which died violently, melting in its own heat, and he obtained thereby vast quantities of treasure. He was known as the greatest of adventurers. More tantalizing are phrases such as the one describing the relationship of Sigmund and Fitela. In Norse texts Sinfjotli is the son of an incestuous union between Sigmund and his sister Signy. In the Old English epic, Sigmund is described as Fitela's maternal uncle, and we remain ignorant of whether the poet deliberately understated what his audience would have known, or whether the tradition behind the English version did not include the incest motif.

The link between the English version and the Norse is unmistakable, but it stops at the dragon-killing. *Beowulf* does not mention Brynhild, nor battle between Nibelungs and Huns. It is, however, worth noticing that at least one early Norse poem, a panegyric on the dead Eirik Bloodaxe, the tenth-century *Eiriksmal*, names the heroes of Valhalla who welcome Eirik as Sigmund and Sinfjotli. The hero Sigurd, who subsequently eclipsed his father's fame in Norse legend, is not mentioned.

Scandinavia is full of pictures of the dragon-killing, 5 but names are not named and we cannot tell at what stage in Norse tradition Sigurd not Sigmund took the centre of the stage. On the whole the pictures on the stones and the details we are told in Eddic poems, nearly half of which deal with the Sigurd cycle, tend to reinforce each other. Pictures and poems show us a hero 25 killing a dragon, gaining knowledge of bird-speech, winning gold. Viking Age poets named the dragon Fafnir and Sigurd's horse Grani, using metaphors for gold, such as 'Fafnir's bane' and 'Grani's burden'.

It is not entirely clear how one should visualize a dragon with precision, but to both Norse and Anglo-Saxon poets as to Norse artists it was obviously kin to a great serpent. The pictures show serpent-shaped beasts with varying degrees of sophistication. The Anglo-Saxon poet uses the words *draca*, 'dragon', and *wyrm*, 'serpent', as synonyms. (This use of the word for outlandish monsters survives in the 'loathly worms' of ballad and folk-song.) For Scandinavian poet and saga-writer the word is *ormr*, cognate to Old English *wyrm*, and the same word that is used for the world-serpent Midgardsorm: this of course is one reason why visual representations of Thor killing the one and Sigurd killing the other cannot always be distinguished.

The briefest possible outline of the subsequent Sigurd story should perhaps be given. I base the following on the full-length prose version of the story

22–28 in Norse, the *Volsunga saga*, but most of it is common to all versions. Sigurd saw and became betrothed to Brynhild. He was later induced by drugged or magical potion to forget this and betroth himself instead to 29–31 Gudrun. For Gudrun's brother Gunnar, and by supernatural trickery, he obtained Brynhild as bride. After the marriages have taken place Gudrun reveals the trickery to Brynhild, who induces her husband Gunnar and his brothers to kill Sigurd in revenge. She then kills herself. Gudrun marries again. This time her husband is Atli (the Norse form of the name Attila).

There is a significant difference between the *Volsunga saga* story, which is basically also that of the Eddic poems, and the German version as told in the early thirteenth-century poem the *Nibelungenlied*. In both versions Gunnar and his brother Hogni, who in German are Gunther and Hagen, visit their sister and brother-in-law. In both they are betrayed and killed. The difference is in the role played by their sister. In the Eddic poem *Atlakvida*, as in the *Volsunga saga*, Gudrun, suspecting the treachery of her husband Atli, tries to warn her brothers, and when they are dead takes terrible vengeance on Atli, killing her children by him and serving their hearts and blood to him for food and drink. In the *Nibelungenlied*, Kriemhild (Gudrun) plans the death of her brothers in revenge for the killing of her first husband Siegfried (Sigurd). Neither version makes an obvious issue of divided loyalties, but it is plain that in the Norse texts quoted the kinship tie is paramount, the woman still seeing herself (still being seen) as more closely part of the family she was born into than the one she marries into. In the German version the pre-eminence either of sexual passion or of marital loyalty has taken over.

It is interesting and curious to compare the *Volsunga saga* with the *Nibelungenlied*. The characters of the German poet move in a feudal, aristocratic, ritualized world. When Kriemhild (Gudrun) and Brunhild (Brynhild) quarrel it is initially over precedence and takes place on the steps of the cathedral. In the *Volsunga saga* the quarrel is still over precedence, but takes place as the two women are bathing in the river. The river is called the Rhine, but we feel ourselves to be more in the world of quarrels within Icelandic farmsteads than in the courts of kings. Yet the Norse text is far more sophisticated in its handling of the supernatural, where the German version relies on clumsy magical devices. When Sigurd wins Brynhild for Gunnar he has to overcome formidable barriers (different ones according to different versions). In the *Volsunga saga* this is done by the simple device of shape-changing. Sigurd performs the actions but he is wearing the likeness of Gunnar, and Brynhild is deceived. In the German, however, the poet invents a 'cloak of invisibility' so that an invisible Sigurd is constantly at Gunnar's side. The whole thing becomes ridiculous and burlesque. The

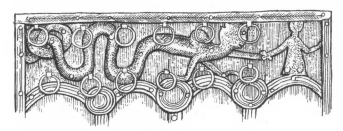

A church door from Västergötland, Sweden, displays this naïve outline in wrought iron of a swordsman facing a dragon. St Michael and Satan? Sigurd and Fafnir? (5)

character of Brynhild too has suffered in the *Nibelungenlied* recension. In Norse texts she is a wronged and tragic figure, a woman of power and dignity as well as beauty. Phrases such as 'she gave thoughtful answer from where she sat like a swan on the wave' come easily to the saga writer. The German poet's approach is unsympathetic. Any hint of a previous betrothal between herself and Sigurd is blurred, and she emerges unpleasantly as a cross between a virago and an Amazon, while the poet's praise is reserved for his Kriemhild (Gudrun), beautiful, dutiful, a submissive, almost doll-like creature before the loss of her husband transforms her into an avenging fury.

The carvings of Scandinavia show, of course, the most visually exciting parts of the story. There is one very delightful representation of Gunnar and Sigurd both attempting the flame-barrier that surrounds Brynhild, Gunnar's horse failing, but Sigurd's advancing. Gunnar's imprisonment by Atli in a snake-pit, 2 where, his arms tied, he played the harp with his toes, is a favourite subject for the artist. Other recurrent scenes are the forging of Sigurd's sword, his own death and Brynhild's funeral pyre. The Eddic poems on the other hand tend to be cast in the form of individual laments, in which we see a section only of the long and complex tale. Poems with the names of Gudrun, Sigurd or Atli in their title focus sharply on one role or aspect, but, like the Old English poems, take a good deal of background knowledge in the audience entirely for granted.

The heroic ethos
The Sigurd legend was so much part of general knowledge that the poet of the quite unrelated *Volundarkvida* can use casually a phrase about Weland's riches – 'that gold was not on Grani's path' – assuming that we will all catch the allusion to Sigurd's gold and Sigurd's horse. Names, not only of horses, but of men, women, places and peoples linger through centuries of stories in the Germanic world, and it seems likely that the ethos of much early Germanic literature, with its stress on courage, loyalty, memorable and honourable

behaviour, also has its roots in this period. An obscure battle involving Frisians and Danes in the fifth century or earlier is the subject of two pieces of Old English literature, one a poem, *The Fight at Finnsburg*, of which only a manuscript fragment survives, the other a long digression in *Beowulf*. No other source tells us anything about the characters involved and it is with difficulty that we try and piece together a coherent story from the fragment on the one hand and the allusive style of the *Beowulf* poet on the other. Yet we do not need precision of knowledge to understand the involvement of both poet and audience in this tale of conflicting loyalties and heroic death. When Hnæf, the Dane, and his men are attacked in the Frisian guest-hall and the poet tells us 'no men ever better repaid the bright mead than Hnæf's retainers did to him', we have a clear and immediately comprehensible statement on the relationship between lord and follower in both practical and emotional terms. The *Beowulf* poet tells us of Hildeburh, wife of the Frisian Finn, sister of the Danish Hnæf, who, the morning after the fight between these two tribes sees on the one side her brother, dead, on the other her son, and orders her son's body to be placed on the funeral pyre beside his uncle's, as she grieves for them both. In this violent age a woman's role was often seen as 'peace-weaver' in the hope that a marriage alliance between tribes might prevent future hostility, yet the actuality must often have been Hildeburh's, and the poet's comment, 'she was an unhappy woman', is a typical understatement of tragedy. We are not told about Hildeburgh's ultimate fate, except for her return to Denmark, but other women caught up in a similar situation of divided loyalties sometimes take more dramatic action. Signy, sister of Sigmund, in *Volsunga saga*, knows that her husband is responsible for the death of her father and brothers, and she aids Sigmund, her one surviving brother, to take vengeance on her husband. Her famous last words are: 'Everything I have done has been to bring about King Siggeir's death. I have done so much to achieve revenge that life is no longer possible. I shall now die willingly with King Siggeir whom I married unwillingly.' A wife in a happy marriage where there are no kinship ties pulling in the opposite direction may still find herself faced with such a choice. In *Njals saga* the protagonists are not from ancient legend but from the late Viking Age. Njal and his sons are about to be burned in their home, but Njal's wife Bergthora is offered a safe exit. She refuses in a mood of determined heroism not unlike Signy's: 'I was given young in marriage to Njal. I have promised him that our fate will be the same.'

Saga writers apparently liked their women to die with solemn courage. Perhaps it would not have been seemly for a female to die wittily. Men on the other hand could do this with perfect propriety, and the character who looked at the spear which had mortally wounded him, saying 'these broad-bladed spears are all the fashion nowadays', is typical. To accept death lightly and jestingly was to merit approbation, for though life is transient reputation lasts. So we are assured by the philosophy of Anglo-Saxon and Norse poet alike. An Eddic poem claims: 'cattle die, kinsmen die, one dies oneself. I know one thing that never dies, each dead man's reputation.' In England the poet of *The Seafarer* wrote, 'age or sickness or violence press life from the bold man, doomed. The best of epitaphs for every hero is the praise of the living, of those speaking after.' It is difficult for us to appreciate the stark reality of this repeated stress on the transience of life until we remember that Anglo-Saxon cemeteries are full of the skeletons of those who died in their thirties. The ambition to achieve reputation, to speak or live or die memorably, when the life-span was so short, makes the courage, the boasting, the jokes at the point of death more comprehensible.

Perhaps the most useful approach to understanding northern culture and northern thought in these early centuries is to look closely at the Old English heroic poem, *Beowulf*. As with so much of the literature, the scene of *Beowulf* is the scene of a past both remote and foreign. The date of the poem itself is hotly debated, though some scholars agree in attributing it to the eighth century. The date of the only surviving manuscript is early eleventh century. The date of the action in the poem is the fifth and the sixth century, the location Scandinavia. The hero Beowulf himself is a Geat, a nationality that ceased to exist after his death, for one of the poem's themes is the impending destruction of the Geats as an independent people, and their absorption by their powerful Swedish neighbours. Beowulf hears that the Danes are suffering from the depredations of a monster, Grendel, and he travels to the court of Denmark to offer help in ridding the Danes of their persecutor. In this he succeeds, and subsequently succeeds also in killing Grendel's mother, an attacker no less dreadful than her son. Beowulf returns home and ultimately takes the Geat throne. At the end of his life he is killed fighting a dragon that has attacked his own people.

Such is the bald outline of the plot, on the surface apparently no more than a monster-killing folk-tale. But, for the poet, the two monsters, Grendel and his mother, are creatures of darkness, outcasts from humanity and from God, representative therefore of evil which has to be fought in both human and Christian terms. They are seen as human in appearance, but human only in the sense that the trolls and giants of Scandinavian legend are human: they resemble man in shape alone, in all else they are alien to him. They are linked, too, with descendants of Cain and with devils out of hell. Like the fallen angels, they are maddened by human joy. Grendel's first attack on the great hall,

Heorot, is because he, 'living in darkness, heard each day the joy loud in the hall, where rang the sound of the harp, sweet song of the poet'.

In the early part of the poem the mood is on the whole one of joy and triumph. Disasters have been met and overcome. The Danish people suffered for a long while lordless, but the great Scyld came to rule over them, giving them security and victories. Scyld's descendant Hrothgar built the splendid gold-adorned hall of Heorot, symbol of peace, festivity and again security. 'Its light shone over many lands.' The monster Grendel is a threat to the Danes, but the young Geat heroes arrive, bright in their armour, rightly confident of success. There is much in the poem describing the delights of comrades in the hall, the mead-drinking and gold-giving symbolic of the friendships and loyalties. Yet even in the first part of the poem we are never allowed to forget the threats to this existence, the implications of disaster lurking in the near future. The poet reminds us that the gold-hall Heorot is destined to be burned down in a future fight between Hrothgar and his son-in-law Ingeld. Scyld may, in the opening lines of the poem, rescue the Danes from their unhappy lordless state, but Beowulf right at the end leaves the Geats similarly lordless, exposed to all the dangers of a small unprotected nation with powerful and hostile neighbours. When the poet describes peace or harmony he uses some such phrase as 'at that time' to remind us how precarious and transient it was to prove. Nevertheless, these hints, though present, are not in the first part of the poem overwhelming. In the latter part of the poem they become so. There the treasures described are not glittering and pleasure-giving, they are buried in the earth, rusty and useless: 'the riders sleep, the heroes in the grave; there is no sound of the harp nor joy in the courts as there once was.' The poet has lightly sketched in the historic background to his story, but in the last third of the poem he stresses it more and more. The background of war between Swedes and Geats is steadily and ominously built up until we know unmistakably that after Beowulf's death the Geats will take their 'morning-cold' spears in hand against the Swedes for the last time.

The poet leaves us with three impressions: firstly, of the transience of every earthly good except that reputation for courage or heroism or wisdom, which will linger long after the death of a man or extinction of a tribe or ruin of a great king's hall; secondly, of the harsh duty of man, in full knowledge of impending death and disaster, to fight with what courage he can; and, thirdly, some of the bright quality of the heroism itself. It is not the *Beowulf* poet but a later one, the poet of the *Battle of Maldon*, who is commonly held to have outlined the heroic ethos most exactly. He describes a minor battle between Anglo-Saxons and Viking invaders in which an 'old retainer' urges on his comrades, knowing that a Viking victory is imminent: 'Thought must be firmer, heart must be braver. / Courage must be greater, as our strength grows less.' The Viking enemies, as part of the same Germanic world, would doubtless have approved the sentiments.

The story behind *Beowulf* occurs in other places. Two of the Norse sagas, the saga of Hrolf Kraki and the saga of Grettir, have monster-killing episodes which clearly go back to the same source or tradition as the one in *Beowulf*. Grettir, an Icelandic outlaw, has a fight with Glam, one of the terrifying 'walking-dead', and a subsequent fight with two trolls, one male and one female, all of these very reminiscent of the fights in *Beowulf*. The greater interest of Hrolf Kraki's saga is that the monster-killing there is fitted into the same historical context as the one in *Beowulf*. There, too, a Geat visits the court of the Danish king to rid it of a monster that has previously been plaguing it. It seems oddly clear in both this saga and *Beowulf* that the historical context is real enough, only the Geat adventurer is a fiction, and it is surprising to find the same blend of history and fantasy occurring in contexts so widely separated. Yet the tales are linked by many curious and trivial details, though neither of the Norse versions deals with the material as anything other than a good story. It is only in *Beowulf* that a good story is transformed into one of the finest epics of Germanic literature.

It is of course interesting to see that once again the literature of the Germanic world is linked, that the same traditions, the same figures of history and legend turn up in places and centuries as diverse as eighth-century England and thirteenth- or fourteenth-century Iceland. But it is also of some significance to note that the greatest poem of Anglo-Saxon literature deals not with England and the English, but with Danes, Swedes and Geats. The Anglo-Saxons took time to think of themselves as a nation separate from their Continental background, just as the Icelanders in their remote island recorded far more of the history and legends of the north than any people of mainland Scandinavia. When in the eighth century a churchman, Alcuin, rebuked these Anglo-Saxons for their passionate love of secular literature, he asked them sternly, 'What has Ingeld to do with Christ?' Ingeld, a remote figure in a remote Germanic tribe of the sixth century, means little to us. But, clearly, for the English of Alcuin's day he could be used to symbolize the vividly exciting world of Germanic legend, the cultural inheritance of the northern world.

2
THE GERMANIC
TRIBES
IN EUROPE

H. AMENT

'Think of all that Clovis achieved, Clovis, the founder
of your victorious country, who slaughtered those rulers who opposed him, conquered hostile
peoples, and captured their territories, thus bequeathing to you
absolute and unquestioned dominion over them! At the time he accomplished
all this, he possessed neither gold nor silver.'

Gregory of Tours
The History of The Franks

About 590

The endless waves of barbarian invaders that swept through the former territories of the Roman Empire were without permanent cohesion or political organization. Even the grouping into tribes was a loose one, capable of dissolving and recombining in a way that makes neat historical analysis impossible. The names by which they were known – Franks, Alemanni, Burgundians, Visigoths, Saxons, Frisians, Thuringians – were mostly given them by their enemies. Attempts to classify them through jewellery-types, burial customs or pottery have met with only limited success. The picture, therefore, is bound to be a rather confusing one, until the sudden crystallization of a powerful state around which, henceforth, the whole development of the Germanic peoples was to revolve: the kingdom of the Franks.

How did this small and unimportant tribe set out on a rise to power that was to lead to the domination first of France (the Merovingian state) and then of much of western Europe (the empire of Charlemagne)? The immediate answer seems to lie in the chance conjunction of two exceptional personalities – Childeric and his son Clovis. When the name of Childeric first appears in the annals, 469, the Franks occupied the area that is now north-western France. Childeric himself ruled a small domain around the city of Tournai and was aiding the Romans in their fight against the Saxons and Alans. By the time he died, in 482, he had evidently established an authority that he could pass on to his fifteen-year-old son. In 486, the young Clovis defeated the last of the Roman commanders in Gaul at Soissons. Further victories followed over the Thuringians, the Alemanni and the Visigoths. In 496, Clovis married Clotilde, daughter of the king of the Burgundians, and became a Catholic. The Merovingian dynasty was secure. (The name comes from Childeric's half-legendary father, Merovech.)

The grave of Childeric was discovered by chance in 1653. It was extremely rich, containing jewellery, a battle-axe, two swords and a spear, buckles, a crystal ball, horse-harness, gold and silver coins and a hundred gold bees, originally sewn to the king's robe (they were copied by Napoleon on his own regal insignia). Nearly all this treasure was stolen from the Imperial Art Gallery in Paris in 1831 and never seen again. The only important items left were fragments of two swords with gold and inlaid garnet ornament. In the arrangement shown here (*opposite centre*), the hilt is that of a double-edged sword (*spatha*), the scabbard that of a single-edged (*sax*). Fortunately the other objects had been drawn and published (by an Antwerp physician, Jean-Jacques Chiflet). Four pages from the book are reproduced alongside the swords. One shows signet rings, including the famous 'Childerici Regis'/ a cast of this still exists. The others illustrate bracelets, brooches, buckles and a brooch thought at that time to be a writing instrument. All the ornament tends towards the late Roman orientalizing taste, not the Germanic – an indication of courtly preferences. (1–5)

On previous page: decorative panel from
Linon, in France. In the centre is the face of
Christ, around him the Chi-Rho symbol,
and on each side the Greek letters Alpha
and Omega. (1)

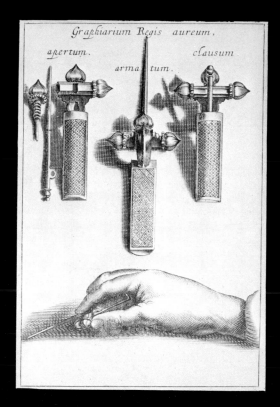

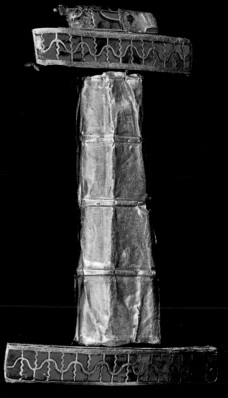

Annuli aurej.

Sarda.

Aureus totus.

SIGIL CHILDIRICI REGIS   CHILDIRICI REGIS

Sapphirus.

Aurum.

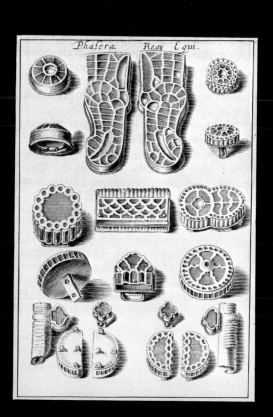

Phalera Regij Equi.

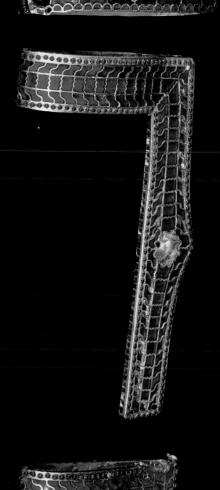

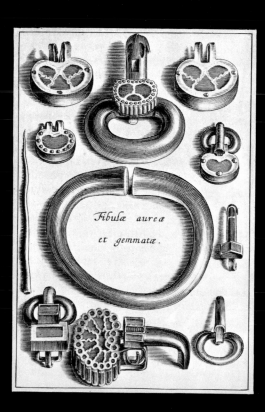

Fibulæ aureæ
et gemmatæ.

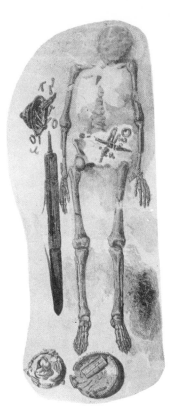

Warriors were buried with their weapons and sometimes their horses, women with their jewellery. Two drawings of male graves as they were opened at Selzen, Germany (*above* and *below*), show how goods were arranged round the body; a horse's skull is next to the right foot of the lower skeleton. (8,9)

A princely grave near Pouan, in France, yielded two swords, belt-buckles and jewellery (*above*). The scabbards have been restored and refitted with their cloisonné ornament. It is possible that the man buried here had been killed in the great battle of the Catalaunian plain against the Huns in 451. (6)

Cremation was practised, often at the same time as inhumation. *Left*: a cremation urn from the cemetery of Wehden. (7)

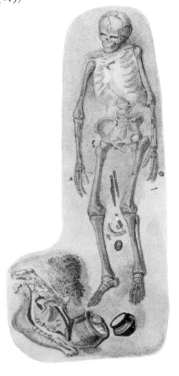

Beneath Cologne Cathedral two royal graves were excavated belonging to a young woman and a six-year-old boy. They contained not only weapons and jewellery but furniture and utensils of various kinds. The bucket (*right*) and small helmet (*far right*) were found in the boy's grave. The pendant triangular mounts round the rim of the bucket contain embossed faces strikingly like classical theatrical masks, but on the plates that secure the handles there is an animal ornament in late Roman tradition. Some jewellery from the woman's grave is shown overleaf. (10,11)

The humbler classes were buried with an assortment of offerings – pots, glass, necklaces and drinking horns. This group (*below*) is made up of objects from several graves in northern France and the Rhineland of the fifth and sixth centuries. (12)

Queen of the Franks

'Regine Arnegundis' is inscribed on a ring found in the rich burial beneath the abbey church of Saint-Denis, near Paris. From the position of the skeleton, traces of fabric and the surviving jewellery, it was possible to make a detailed reconstruction (*left*). On a red woollen cloth, she lay dressed in a long tunic of violet silk, a silk gown with gold-embroidered cuffs, linen stockings and leather slippers. Arnegunde was probably the wife of Clovis's son, Chlotar I. (13)

Krefeld-Gellep on the lower Rhine has yielded a rich grave whose goods included saddle-harness (*below*) of gold set in cloisonné garnets. At the back it had been fixed by pins to something made of leather. (14)

Who was the princess buried next to the boy at Cologne? The headband (*opposite top*) of gold wire (originally woven into the fabric, here restored with new backing), with a jewelled pin in the centre, was a common gift of bridegroom to bride. And it is known that Visigarde, wife of King Theodobert, died soon after her wedding about 540. The body wore a necklace and gold chain (*opposite centre*), fastened at the shoulders by disc-brooches and bearing a Byzantine coin of Theodosius II, and two brooches (*opposite below*) that probably held a mantle round her hips. (15–18)

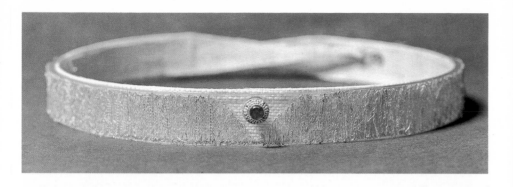

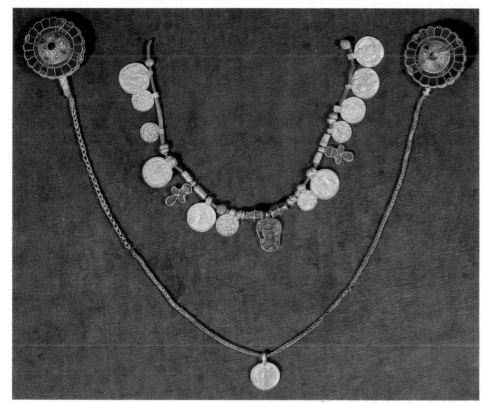

Women's graves customarily contained jewellery, some of it of extreme richness. These two brooches are from an Alemannic cemetery at Wittislingen. The upper one is a rich example of a type common all over northern Europe; the lower perhaps looks to Byzantium for its inspiration. Four double-headed serpents in cloisonné are looped to form a quatrefoil against a gold filigree background. (19,20)

The Christian hope

'In hunc titulum requiiscit bene memorius Badegiselus presbiter qui vixit in paci annus xxxxx feliciter' ('In this grave rests in good memory the priest Badegisel who lived happily 50 years in peace'); a seventh-century tombstone found at Mainz. (21)

Christ's image forms the centre of a superb decorative panel found at Linon, in France (*above*). In the hollow spaces are the Greek letters *Alpha* and *Omega*, with the *Chi-Rho* symbol in between. Three sections of the outer ring contain pairs of boars' heads which can also be read as human faces. (22)

Paganism and Christianity were probably not so far apart in the minds of a seventh-century Frank as they seem to us. On a Rhineland tombstone of about 650 (both sides shown *left*), the dead man is preyed upon by a double-headed serpent; he carries a sword in one hand and is apparently combing his hair with the other. On the reverse is the transfigured Christ surrounded by rays of light. *Opposite*: a funerary stele of a warrior from Hornhausen, Germany. (23,24,25)

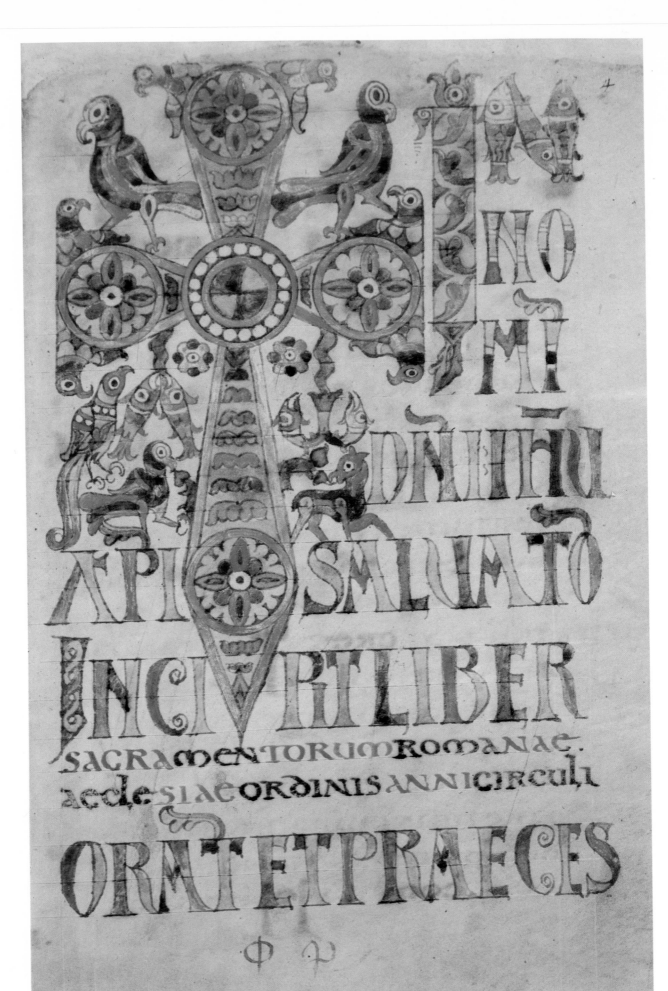

IN NOMI
NE DNI NRI
IHV SALVATO
INCIPIT LIBER
SACRAMENTORUM ROMANAE
aeclesiae ORDINIS ANNI CIRCULI
ORM ET PRAECES

Φ P

THE GERMANIC TRIBES IN EUROPE

AT THE BEGINNING of the fifth century AD, the most important section of the Roman Empire's central European frontier, the late Roman *limes* running the length of the River Rhine from Lake Constance to the North Sea, was officially intact. As recently as the year 395/96, the imperial commander-in-chief Stilicho had superintended defence works. In the province of Germania I (formerly Germania superior) these works were intended to check the invasion of the Alemanni, who were settling to the east of the Rhine, and were meant to have the same deterrent effect on the Franks in lower Germania (Germania II). Stilicho even succeeded in signing treaties with the Franks; that was why in 401 he thought it safe to withdraw strong contingents of troops from the Rhine frontier to Italy to fight the invading Visigoth Alaric. The Franks did fulfil their treaty obligations by fighting the Vandals, the Suebi and the Alans who crossed the Rhine from the east at Mainz on the last day of the year 406. But Stilicho's action, although purely pragmatic, marked an historic turning-point, as subsequent events were to show. The Rhine frontier, held with such energy by the Romans since the days of Augustus, could never again be consistently defended; and the power of action passed increasingly into the hands of the Germanic tribes.

Six tribes

The Franks. At the beginning of the fifth century the mass of the Franks were probably settled on the east bank of the Rhine. The name Frank, implying such characteristics as 'bold, brave, fierce', had been applied since the middle of the third century to Germanic tribes to the east of the lower Rhine who had banded together against the Roman Empire. Their general aim was to share in the wealth of the Roman province, by means that varied from occasional raids to peaceful settlement in imperial territory. The Roman reaction was correspondingly varied, ranging from bitter enmity to trustful collaboration. While the Emperor Valentinian after 369 called himself Francicus (Conqueror of the Franks), another Emperor (Constantine) had coins minted around 342 to celebrate, as a great political achievement, the settling of Franks on imperial soil. Such settlements had occurred as early as the 290s; but their great historical impact came principally in the fourth century, when Germanic, especially Frankish, groups made their homes in northern Gaul. They might be called *laeti*, *dediticii*, or *foederati*, but the intention was always the same: by the cultivation of fallow land the Romans hoped to increase both the taxable wealth of the province and its military strength. The intensity and extent of Germanic settlement in Gaul can be measured quite precisely through an examination of burials. The Germans shared with the Gaulish Roman provincials the practice of providing the dead in their graves with vessels for food and drink; but they also gave weapons to the dead warriors and brooches to the women. The form of this jewellery found in the women's graves is unlike any in the Roman region, but closely resembles finds from Germania, east of the Rhine. Germanic graves of this kind are not infrequently found in the

◁ **The bizarre fantasy** displayed by Merovingian illuminators surpasses even those of Northumbria and Ireland. Precedents in late classical art are rare, and in Germanic non-existent. It has been suggested that the style looks to the eastern Mediterranean and the Coptic art of Christian Egypt. And unlike such manuscripts as the *Book of Kells* (p. 108) and the *Lindisfarne Gospels* (p. 80), the text and pictures are here clearly by the same hand. Shown *opposite* is a page from the *Sacramentary of Gelasius*. Top left is a cross divided into foliated patterns. The arms end in birds' heads and two more exotic birds perch to left and right. From the cross hang the Greek letters *Alpha* and *Omega* composed of fishes! To the right the text begins with the words IN NOMINE, but the N of IN also consists of brightly coloured fish. The manuscript was produced between 750 and 770 and is now in the Vatican. (26)

northern provinces of the Roman Empire, between the Rhine and the Seine, and even in less dense concentrations (much less dense as far as women's graves are concerned) in the north-west of Gaul, to the west of the Seine.

No sites of dwelling-places of these Germanic colonists have yet been found; we can only draw conclusions from their cemeteries. On this evidence, the newcomers seem to have become very largely assimilated into the existing settlements, but occasionally they also founded their own. In the Franks' area of origin to the east of the Rhine, on the other hand, the sites of a few settlements have been found, peasant houses built with a wooden framework (e.g. at Westick near Unna), but graves are virtually unknown.

Groups of Franks also established themselves early on in the region near the frontier. This move was more like territorial possession than was the settlement of *laeti* and *foederati*, directed by the Romans, in the interior of the province. In 355, for instance, the Emperor Julian retrospectively approved the much earlier settlement of Salian Franks in Toxandria (northern Brabant). In the fifth century, the acquisition of territory by conquest began to be commoner than by settlement. In 459 Cologne, the capital of lower Germania, was taken by the Franks after a long siege; and in 476, when the rule of the Roman Emperors came to an end in the western part of the Empire, a broad belt of land in the former Roman province, from Cologne and Mainz in the east to Cambrai and Tournai in the west, was already under Frankish control.

The Alemanni, the second-largest group of Germanic tribes along the Rhine frontier, behaved in a far less expansionary way in this late phase of Roman rule; their conquests of Roman territory already lay two centuries behind them. This was another group built up by tribal alliances. In their case it probably happened around the turn of the second and third centuries in the interior of Germania, among Germanic tribes (principally groups of Suebi) of the Elbe region; and the alliance first came to notice in 213 in battles along the upper German *limes* near Mainz. After years of increasing violence one great invasion of Roman lands succeeded in the years 233 to 235; a further raid in 259/60 permanently dislodged the troops of the Roman *limes* from their emplacements. The land bounded by the Rhine, Lake Constance, the River Iller and the Danube was thenceforth occupied and colonized by the Alemanni, who set up the first Germanic tribal state on Roman territory. Because of the origins of the Alemannic tribe, this state consisted of many individual domains; only at the end of this period, in the second half of the fifth century, did centralized power develop in the hand of a king.

Archaeology has recovered some objects from this early period of Alemannic settlement. They come

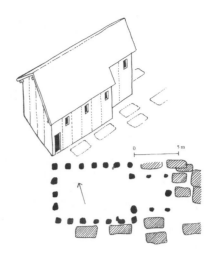

Reconstruction and plan of the seventh-century church and graveyard at Staubing, near Weltenburg on the Danube. (3)

mostly from inhumation burials, though cremation was also practised, as it was probably the ancestral burial custom of the Alemanni. The grave-goods, where they occur, are essentially the same as among the Germans of northern Gaul: the men receive weapons as funeral gifts, the women brooches, and both sexes are also provided with various vessels, in keeping with their personal wealth. There are obvious connections with the central German homeland of the original Alemanni in the design of individual objects – for instance in the disc brooches of the woman's grave at Spielberg near Erlbach, and in certain other details of burial customs, such as the bronze or silver arrowheads placed in men's graves as symbolic weapons. The Alemanni moving into the previously Roman region seem to some extent to have fitted into the established framework of settlement, partly by using existing Roman roads. At the same time new rural settlements were also founded, built entirely of wood (for instance at Sontheim in the Stubental). A number are fortified hill settlements. At the Round Hill near Urach, the summit and the gentler parts of the slopes were intensively occupied from the end of the third century onwards. The summit was encircled by a wall, clearly defending the home of some princely personage. The surrounding population was mostly engaged in business, crafts and trade, so the settlement must have had the overall character of a town.

The territorial boundaries set for the Alemanni by the late Roman Danube-Iller-Rhine *limes* remained unchanged in the fifth century. Even after the virtual abandonment of the Rhine frontier soon after 400, there was no movement westwards (into Alsace), although there had earlier been isolated military raids into the area (357, battle of Strassburg). Only in the east do graves of Alemannic type indicate that they advanced along the Danube to the region of Regensburg and Staubing.

The Burgundians. In the wake of the westward movement of 'Elbe-Germanic' groups (Alemanni), the east Germanic Burgundians from the Oder region also began to migrate, and as early as the third century established themselves at the rear of the Alemanni. The old imperial boundary, the Upper-German-Rhaetian *limes*, probably served as the frontier between Alemanni and Burgundians. Again in the wake of other tribes moving westward – the Vandals, Suebi and Alans – the Burgundians were able to cross the Rhine in 406. Here they were soon pressed into service as *foederati* by the Romans in the defence of the Rhine frontier. In the year 413 we hear that the Burgundians were allotted homes 'on the Rhine'; later legend named Worms as the centre of this area of Burgundian control, but there have been no specifically Burgundian archaeological finds in the area.

In 435 the Burgundian king Gundicar attacked the neighbouring Roman province, Belgica I; he was defeated by a Roman army under Aetius. In the following year, Hunnish mercenaries completed the work of destruction; the king's family was killed along with 20,000 Burgundians. In 443, Aetius resettled the remnants of the people in Sapaudia or Savoy, a region on the eastern slopes of the Swiss Jura around Lake Geneva. A few finds in this region tell of the Burgundians of the period; this very small enclave became the starting-point for a remarkable regeneration of the tribe that had been so badly decimated in 435/36. As early as 451 a Burgundian contingent fought with heavy losses on the side of the Romans (under Aetius) and the Visigoths against the Huns. In 456 we hear once again of a Burgundian king, and in the following year the Burgundians expanded westwards, occupying large areas of the province Lugdunensis I. The capital Lyons soon afterwards replaced the old royal seat of Geneva as the main residence of the Burgundian kings. By the end of the western Roman Empire, further expansion to the north and west had increased Burgundian dominions.

The Visigoths. In this way the Burgundians had become neighbours of the Visigoths, the only tribe which had not moved into this area by a direct route from the interior of Germania. Their eventual allotment of land in south-west Gaul in 418 brought to an end a migration which had lasted more than a century and had taken them through the Balkans, Italy and the Iberian peninsula. The Visigoths were given large sections of the province of Aquitania II along with a few neighbouring territories, among them that of the future capital Tolosa (Toulouse); it was a fairly wide strip of land along the Atlantic coast between the Loire and the foothills of the Pyrenees. They at once sought access to the Mediterranean, but only won it in 462 with the conquest of Narbonne; with that, the way was clear for the incorporation of the entire province of Septimania. At the same time in the interior of Gaul, after wearisome battles, the province Aquitania I in the Massif Central area was conquered. A peace treaty signed with the Emperor Julius Nepos in 474 confirmed the Visigoths' possession of the whole area between the Loire, the Rhône and the two coastlines. Their kingdom, including the large areas they had gained since the beginning of the 50s in the Iberian peninsula, was one of the most important power centres in the west at the end of classical antiquity, and appeared as such to the Visigoths' contemporaries.

We should bear this in mind when searching for archaeological traces of the Goths' long residence in south-west Gaul. Apart from two silver brooches from the dubious complex of finds at Herpes, there are no traceable remains of the Visigoths from all the Gaulish territories they lost to the Franks in 507. Even in areas which were under the Goths' control for a longer time (Septimania), finds of a Germanic nature which can be dated to the fifth century are extremely rare (one instance is the grave at Valentines).

One grave which came to light in 1842 near Pouan 6 (Aube) is of interest in this connection. The warrior buried there was provided with two swords, a two-edged *spatha* and a one-edged *sax*. The hilts of both weapons were covered in gold plate and decorated with gold and cloisonné work; even the blades bear cloisonné decoration (garnets set in gold cells). A belt-buckle in cloisonné work, more massive gold buckles from the warrior's trappings, and some jewellery – a necklet, an arm-bangle and a finger-ring, all made of gold – complete the burial. They are comparable, in more ways than one, to the funeral gifts of King Childeric, but they are older and can be dated soon after the middle of the fifth century. Considering the site of this find – in the neighbourhood of Troyes and certainly not far from the probable site of the battle in 451 – one cannot disregard the opinion of the nineteenth-century researchers who thought they had found here the tomb of the Visigoth king Theodoric, who fell in the battle with the Huns. The modern view is that this is uncertain and even improbable, since the Goths did not generally place weapons in their graves; nevertheless, this tomb undoubtedly looks like the resting-place of a princely person of Germanic origin, and one who might have played a leading role in the turbulent events of the fifth century in Gaul.

The Saxons. When we turn to the Saxons, we find fewer written sources but more material remains. They were settled in the region of the Elbe and Weser estuaries, and along the lower courses of these rivers. Between them and the Roman Empire lay the Franks, so that the only way for the two to come into contact was through sea expeditions, mainly to Britain and secondly to the north coast of Gaul. Roman writers first mention these raids in 286. The origins of the Saxons are obscure, but undoubtedly they came into being as a result of the same tribal groupings that produced the Franks and the Alemanni.

Cremation of the dead was the general practice of the Continental Saxons until the end of the Roman Empire, and the characteristic form of cemetery is one containing urns, often in their thousands. These cemeteries began to appear as early as the first century AD and some of them were in use until the tenth century. From the fourth century onwards, isolated burials of bodies occur; in the early Middle Ages they predominate, until finally all graves are inhumations. Four of the many cemeteries deserve special mention: Westerwanna because of the size of the urnfield (some 3,000 graves excavated), Mahndorf because it is so well documented, Issendorf as an example of a recent investigation and Liebenau because of its particularly good state of preservation.

Of the urns, the most striking and characteristic type from the late Empire period is a vessel overloaded with somewhat baroque decorations, bulges, knops and stamps. Other common finds, though they do not occur in every burial, are articles of dress like brooches or parts of belts, and small utensils. These remains tell of intensive contacts with the Roman province; apart from straightforward imports like complete military belts decorated with chip-carving (a shallow facetting of the surface to give a glittering effect), we find native forms under strong Roman influence, for instance the supporting-arm brooch. There are also many examples of a type of brooch (the equal-arm brooch) which is quite unknown in the Roman province but which illustrates late Roman techniques of chip-carved bronze-work so perfectly that we must seriously consider the possibility that Roman craftsmen were working in the Saxon tribal area. More archaeological material survives from the Saxon heartland between the lower courses of the Rhine and Weser than in other areas in north-west Germania, which are poor in remains but were certainly not uninhabited during the late Roman Empire.

We know a lot about the community life of the Saxon tribe, thanks to exemplary excavations at Feddersen Wierde and Flögeln. Feddersen Wierde is an artificially built-up settlement mound in low-lying coastal marshland, which was liable to flooding. The site was occupied from the first century BC until the fifth century AD. At its greatest extent, the settlement consisted of at least twenty-eight courtyards radiating from a central open space. One of these enclosures has been identified as a chieftain's house because of its size and isolated position and its special type of construction. The similar settlement of Flögeln is still being excavated.

Both settlements were abandoned permanently in the middle of the fifth century. The same is true of other settlement sites and many cemeteries. What is the explanation? Surely it is the emigration of the Saxons to England an event well authenticated historically. After the legions left Britain at the beginning of the fifth century, the Saxons were able to intensify and expand their earlier attacks in that direction; and during the first half of the fifth century they moved to England wholesale, though in several stages. An archaeological map for the second half of the fifth century, compared with the distribution map of the urnfields over the old Saxon lands, shows how this emigration depopulated the coastal part of the Saxon heartland.

The Thuringians. The migrations of the third and fourth centuries, concluding with the departure of the Vandals, Suebi and Lombards at the beginning of the fifth, had greatly reduced the Germanic population of central and eastern areas of middle Europe. Only one Germanic tribal state of real political importance developed to the east of the Alemanni, Franks and Saxons during the fifth century, that of the Thuringians. The name occurs for the first time about 400, when it is clearly connected with the Ermunduri, a tribe which had been settled since the early days of the Empire in various places to the north of the Danube, along the upper part of the River Main and in the region of the River Saale. The Ermunduri who remained in the interior of Germania formed, together with other small tribes and tribal offshoots – such as the Angles and Varni – the new large tribe of the Thuringians.

In the course of the fifth century, the Thuringians seem to have expanded their dominions considerably. In the end their realm extended southwards behind the Alemanni as far as the Danube and to the north encompassed the whole strip of land between the Elbe and the Frankish tribal area. There are even indications that the former Saxon and Frankish areas of settlement on the North Sea coast came under Thuringian rule, after the Saxons' tribal organization on the Continent had collapsed with their migration to Britain, and the Franks had moved on towards Gaul, largely abandoning the area of the Rhine delta. At the same time the scarcity of archaeological remains shows that this extensive Thuringian realm can have been only thinly populated; not until the beginning of the early Middle Ages is this area (at least the Thuringian heartland, in what is now central Germany) represented in archaeological terms as befits its political significance.

Comparing the situation at the beginning of the fifth century with the conditions prevailing in central and western Europe in 476, one is led to regard the western migrations of the Germanic tribes as the historically most significant event in that period. By then the lines of military defence established along the Rhine and Danube and on the coasts of Britain and Gaul had long since been abandoned. Visigoths, Burgundians and Franks in Gaul, Saxons and Angles in Britain, had set up

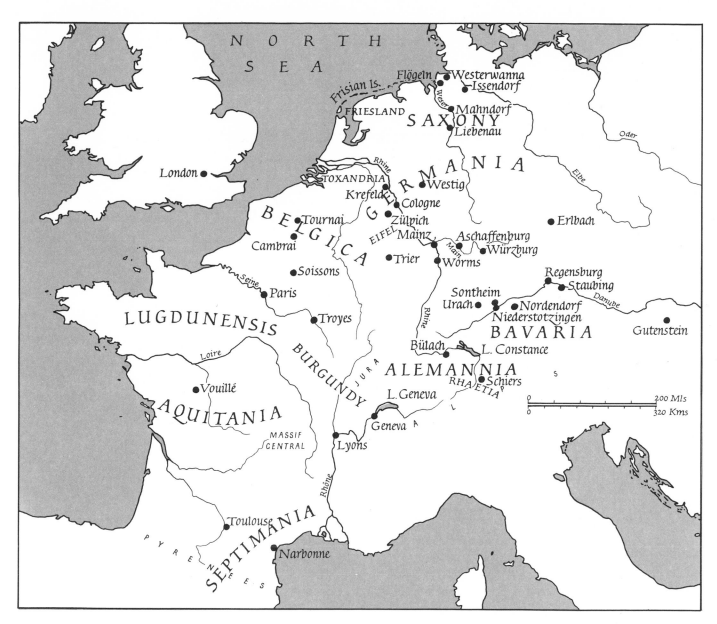

their own governments; the Alemanni had expanded their sphere of influence to Rhaetia, Because of these migrations extensive areas in the east had been more or less emptied of Germanic tribes.

In northern Gaul, there still existed after 476 a kingdom in the tradition of the Roman state. This was ruled by a man called Syagrius, a son of the Roman commander Aegidius. He was the first to challenge the Frankish power that was now vigorously expanding, on the threshold of a new era.

A new state: the Merovingian kingdom

In the crucial year 476 a minor Frankish king ruled over a small area in northern Gaul that was probably not much more than the city of Tournai and its immediate hinterland (Civitas Turnacensium). His name was Childeric, and from his domain was to rise the most

powerful state of early medieval Europe: the kingdom of the Franks, soon to become that of the Merovingians and finally that of Charlemagne.

With Childeric the royal race of the Merovingians steps out of the darkness of myth into the light of history. Around the years 469/70 we find him mentioned as an ally of the Romans in battles against Saxons and Alans in the area of Orleans and Angers. He died in 482. By a remarkable stroke of fortune, this ruler, who began the history of the Frankish kingdom, still exists archaeologically for us today. In 1653 his tomb was discovered near Saint-Brice, a church set outside the walls of the medieval city of Tournai on the northern bank of the River Scheldt. Most of the rich contents of the grave was recovered, but very little of it remains today. Among the king's grave-furniture 1-5 were first of all his weapons: a two-edged sword with a gilded hilt and a single-edged sword (*sax*), a javelin (*francisca*), lance and shield. The two swords in particular, richly decorated with gold and garnets, far excel in value and quality all other known weapons from this period. The equipment of the armed warrior is completed by the bridle of his horse; indeed the animal itself seems to have been buried with the king, for there are reports of a horse's skull having been found near by.

Two items serve to indicate the different sources from which the ruler drew his power. The golden wrist armlet, although rare, has widely scattered counterparts in Germanic graves – for instance at Pouan, also the grave of some very high-ranking person; the gold armlet was obviously a widely accepted token of rank in the Germanic world. The golden ceremonial brooch, however, was part of Roman official dress, probably offered to Childeric as a Roman ally, together with a cloak (*paludamentum*). A gold signet-ring, inscribed CHILDERICI REGIS, clinched the identification of the person buried at Saint-Brice.

We may take Childeric's tomb as an example of the burial practices followed by almost all the Germanic peoples of central and western Europe during the following century. Bodies were buried in cemeteries, the graves being laid out in rows west to east; weapons were put in men's graves, jewellery in women's, and vessels – no doubt for food and drink – as well as small utensils, were provided for both sexes. The dead were buried in the clothes they had worn during life, complete with jewellery; a custom, however, which was not purely Germanic, nor indeed invariable among the Germans. The excavation of thousands of these aligned graves provides us with an immense wealth of archaeological remains from Germanic Europe in the first two or three centuries of the Middle Ages; and that wealth can make valuable amends for the generally meagre written sources.

Childeric's son Clovis brought Frankish power to its first peak by subjecting all the Frankish dominions to his own authority, and greatly expanded the area of Frankish rule at the expense of other tribes (Visigoths and Alemanni). His first attack was launched against the final remnants of Roman rule in Gaul: in 486/87 he beat the *Rex Romanorum*, Syagrius, in a battle at Soissons and then pushed on to the Seine, and later to the Loire. Archaeological finds tell us that this expansionist movement was accompanied by at least a partial settling by Franks of the conquered lands. The distribution area of the characteristic 'aligned' cemeteries (whose graves are always endowed with the Germanic type of weapons and decorative accessories) extends as far as the Seine. Beyond that river only quite isolated graves were furnished in this way. Cemeteries here contain graves with only simple jewellery and perhaps some pots, apart from articles of dress. By parallel with

graves in the Alpine and Mediterranean regions, such burial places – the largest and best-known, with over 800 graves, is at Isle-Aumont (Aube) – can be ascribed to a native, Romance people. In certain cases it can even be seen that migrating Franks and indigenous Romance peoples have used the same burial ground, and so presumably lived together as well, sharing the same settlement (Dieue-sur-Meuse, Moselle). On the evidence of the grave-goods, there would seem to have been no Frankish migration across the Seine. The expansion of Frankish power into this region must be seen as a political and military act, probably carried out by a small élite of aristocratic warriors. This is particularly true of the area ruled by the Visigoths in south-west France. In the conflict with the Franks, beginning in the middle of the 90s and ending with the battle of Vouillé in 507, the Visigoths lost their possessions in Gaul with the exception of a small area of land in the northern Pyrenean foothills and the province of Septimania on the Mediterranean coast.

Clovis's second great thrust beyond the boundaries of Frankish territory was aimed south-eastwards at the Alemanni, whose lands stretched in the north to the River Main: the cosmographer of Ravenna described Aschaffenburg and Worms as Alemannic at the end of the fifth century. It seems the Alemanni were advancing even further, for their first clash with the Franks occurred at Zülpich, north of the Eifel mountains. In the decisive battle of 496/97 (the battle after which Clovis was converted to Christianity) the Alemanni, now under their own king, were defeated. In 507 Clovis crushed the last flare-up of resistance. The Alemannic centres of government were demolished; the early Alemannic citadel on the Round Hill at Urach, for example, was destroyed by fire. Even more than the traces of burning, the many valuables hidden and never retrieved by the inhabitants bear dramatic witness to its violent destruction. After 507 the northern Alemannic area seems to have come under Frankish rule; later territorial boundaries at least suggest this. The southern part of Alemannia, however, remained independent for a time under the protection of the Ostrogoths.

It was the Ostrogoths, too, who continued to guarantee the effectiveness of the Rhine frontier. The upper Rhine still separated Germanic from Romance settlement areas, as it had done in late antiquity. The steady development of the burial grounds of the citadel of Kaiseraugst demonstrates most clearly the undisturbed continuance of established communities in the former province. Only with the decline in the power of the Ostrogoths do circumstances change. In 536 Clovis's grandson Theudebert gained control of the rest of Alemannia, and from now on an Alemannic migration took place – perhaps under Frankish protection – to the strip of land south of the upper

Rhine, extending into central Swiss territory. This is demonstrated by the incidence of cemeteries with aligned graves, in no way different from those of the Alemanni to the east of the Rhine.

The policy of conquest introduced by Clovis was vigorously and successfully continued by his sons and grandsons. Childebert and Chlotar subjugated the Burgundians in several campaigns between 523 and 532, while Theuderic and his son Theudebert put an end to Thuringian autonomy between 529 and 534. Theudebert also exercised authority over the lands north of the Alps, which until then (like southern Alemannia) had obviously belonged to the Ostrogothic sphere of influence. In this area, already partly settled by Alemanni, the Bavarian tribe was now growing – the youngest of the great tribes of the age of migration. Its nucleus would seem to be a Germanic group which had moved from northern Bohemia, descendants of the Marcomanni whose graveyards can be traced until the early Merovingian period but then disappear completely. The migration of this group into the northern Alpine foothills, and the gradual emptying of an eastern strip of the Thuringian tribal area, are the last acts in the westward movement of the central European Germanic tribes. In this way, from the third decade of the sixth century onwards, all the Germanic tribes between the Alps, the Pyrenees and the North Sea were united in a single Frankish kingdom. Only the Frisians and Saxons on the North Sea coast retained their independence. Thanks to the rich archaeological inheritance of burial gifts, a custom generally practised until the end of the seventh century, we have a clear and varied picture of the different cultures within this extensive realm.

The western areas, which had remained free of intense and widespread colonization by Germanic settlers, show correspondingly few Germanic influences. This is particularly true of the former Visigoth territory of Aquitania. The Visigoths in their time had contributed little of Germanic character to the pattern of remains in this area; the Franks who ruled from 507 onwards had equally little impact. The burial customs continue to show Romance characteristics: burial in costume with all its main elements, especially buckles; a preference for sarcophagi, the form and decoration of which followed their own line of development from the basic form of late antiquity. Weapons and brooches of Frankish type, on the other hand, are extremely rare. Things are no different in the north-west of Gaul, north of the Loire and west of the Seine; indeed, apart from the sarcophagi, the same can be said of the archaeological remains in Burgundian tribal territory. Both before and after the loss of their independent state, the Burgundians generally kept to Romance burial customs. In the most recently investigated cemetery, that of Monnet-la-Ville, anthropological evidence provides

the only proof of the existence of a Germanic element in the population.

The picture is different in those areas which experienced Germanic settlement of a territorial nature. The Frankish tribal area between the Seine and the Rhine, like the Alemannic, Thuringian and Bavarian territories, has typically Germanic cemeteries with aligned graves containing numerous weapons, jewellery and vessels. Even here, however, there is Romance influence, and not only in the occurrence of entirely or partly Romance necropolises. In the course of the Merovingian period the Germanic population increasingly turned to the simple southern burial rites. This process began in the west, in areas with a very large non-Germanic element in the population, and from there spread eastwards. The custom of placing weapons in the graves, for example, was largely abandoned as early as 600 in the area of modern France, a good fifty years later in the Rhine region, and not until the beginning of the eighth century among Alemanni and Bavarians to the east of the Rhine. Admittedly some factors counteracted this move towards genuinely Mediterranean burial customs. In the east of the Merovingian kingdom indigenous and essentially pagan customs repeatedly asserted themselves and even gained ground in the late Merovingian period: horse burials, cremations, burial mounds and so on.

Two tribes remained outside the Merovingian state: the Saxons and the Frisians. We have seen how the emigration of the Saxons in the course of the fifth century created a power vacuum which favoured the expansion of Thuringian rule to the North Sea coast. Subsequently, however, there was a Saxon revival; their tribal organization was even reinvigorated, apparently by the leadership of a population group which had come from the north. As early as 530 Saxons are found to be useful allies of the Franks in battle against the Thuringians, gaining considerable lands in the process. Thereafter, however, the relationship between Saxons and Franks remained tense in the Carolingian period, as a result of constant Saxon pressure on the north-east border territories of the Franks; in the area of modern Westphalia this pressure actually led to Saxon territorial gains. Their furthest advance was marked by the conquest of the Frankish district of the Boruktuari, south of the middle part of the River Lippe, in the years around AD 700. At the same time the Saxons were also exerting pressure in northern Hesse.

This Saxon thrust southwards resulted in an emigration from the lands of the North Sea coast. The Frisians extended their area of settlement eastwards and northwards along the coast as far as what are now known as the North-Frisian Islands.

We can see reflected in the archaeological remains the importance of the Frankish kingdom as a political and cultural point of reference for the Saxons. The increase of inhumation burials in graves aligned west to east shows how the old customs of the Merovingian kingdom were adopted – slowly and with visible hesitation. At the same time, however, such pagan customs as cremation, horse burial, mound-burial and grave circles continued in use for a long time; even in the late Merovingian period they spread into the areas under Frankish rule on the lower Rhine and into northern Hesse. The assimilation process was probably most quickly and thoroughly completed in the realm of costume; Frankish brooches and Frankish buckles are found everywhere among the Saxon grave-goods.

The custom of aligned graves strongly imbued with pagan elements persisted among the Saxons into the ninth century. Its end is clearly linked with the incorporation of Saxony into the Frankish kingdom and its ensuing conversion to Christianity – both results of the Saxon wars of Charlemagne from 772 to 799.

The social order

The establishment of the Germanic states in western and central Europe on the ruins of the old Roman Empire marked the beginning of a new social order; this still contained elements of tribal structure, but there was an increasing emphasis on class hierarchy which was to lead eventually to aristocracy and feudalism. Archaeologically such trends are best illustrated by those burials distinguished by unusual richness of grave-goods and traditionally known as 'princely tombs'.

One example: the grave (numbered 1782) discovered in 1962, during the excavation of a big Romano-Frankish graveyard at Krefeld-Gellep on the lower Rhine. The occupant of this grave had been given a complete set of weapons; a gilded helmet, a sword decorated on the pommel with gold and precious stones, a short dagger and battle-axe, three different spears and a shield. Costly trimmings from saddle and bridle were found, as well as a snaffle covered in gold and silver. The tableware also seems to have been well suited to one of high rank: a drinking-bowl and a handled vessel of glass, three large bronze bowls, a small, inscribed bronze pot, a spit for roasting, two knives with golden grips and a silver spoon. The sumptuous contents of the tomb are completed by items of personal apparel; a purse-frame decorated with garnets, a massive gold belt-buckle and a gold ring with a classical gem.

But the social rank of the man buried in this grave is shown not only by the abundance and value of his gifts. In the course of the excavations, it became clear that this grave was also the first and oldest of those in this particular part of the cemetery. What is the significance of this? It can only mean that the man buried here was a great leader, the founder of a new settlement. His successors – perhaps his descendants – were similarly honoured. Four other graves of rather later date have also been discovered, whose riches were once comparable with his, but these were looted in antiquity. Their sheer size, however, is impressive: the largest chamber was 6.8 metres long, 4.5 wide and 5.0 deep. The natural supposition is that what we have here are the tombs of a princely family.

This assumption is confirmed by the fact that the circumstances observed in Krefeld-Gellep are repeated in numerous other cemeteries with aligned graves. Many cemeteries were founded by the initial laying down of outstandingly rich burials (Güttingen and Lavoye, for instance). In several places it is clear that a small group of people retained the role of chieftain within a settlement for several generations. In the cemeteries of Rübenach and Schretzheim, for instance, graves of a particular kind are distributed all over the cemetery, representing the various phases of its use. Finally, the ruling élite is most clearly separated from the rest of society where its graves are not in the community's aligned graveyard, but form a separate necropolis on its edge (Kirchheim im Ries) or even in another place altogether (Niederstotzingen).

What is exemplified in these burial customs – the pretensions to leadership, the sense of special identity, the family tradition – all corresponds to the attitudes of an aristocracy; this is why archaeologists have adopted the term 'nobles' graves' for burials of this kind. At the same time it must be remembered that for the historian the nature of the Merovingian aristocracy is by no means settled. But we are not going against the archaeological evidence if we conclude that Merovingian communities were generally organized from the top, just as the state as a whole was organized from the king downwards. Childeric's grave surpassed even the richest of the 'nobles' graves' in the scope, combination and quality of its grave-goods. Even if the signet-ring had not been found, one would have had to speak here of a 'king's' rather than a 'noble's tomb'.

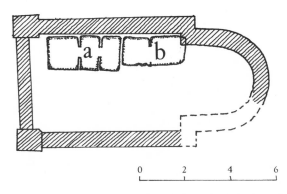

In the centre of the atrium of the first Cologne Cathedral stood a small chapel containing the bones of a woman (a) and a boy (b). The site lies beneath the choir of the present cathedral. (4)

Two other royal burials are known and must be briefly described. The first, identified by the inscription on a gold ring as that of Arnegunde, the wife of the Frankish king Chlotar I, was discovered under the basilica of Saint-Denis, near Paris, in 1959. The grave was furnished with splendid items of apparel, with two cloisonné enamel disc brooches, gold earrings and hairpins, a heavy silver belt-buckle, a large jewelled pin and rich silver trimmings from the straps of the shoes and leggings. By the time she was buried, however (about 570), the number and value of burial gifts seem to have been declining in the western part of the Frankish kingdom. This is shown not only by the poor provision of vessels (there was only one small glass bottle); but even more importantly by the fact that the jewellery has been made up with false pieces, which can hardly have represented the queen's most precious possessions.

No such considerations apply to two graves discovered (also in 1959) under Cologne Cathedral. The burial place was originally the centre of the atrium of the first cathedral on the site, and the bodies were those of a woman and a six-year-old boy. Precious jewellery, weapons, vessels, utensils and furniture were provided in abundance. Both graves seem to have been dug at the same time. The date, calculated on the basis of coins and analysis of tree-rings, was around 540. We do not know the name of the woman and child, but Cologne was then the capital of the Merovingian kingdom, so presumably they were members of the royal family.

The tombs of members of the ruling class can fairly easily be distinguished by the range and quality of the grave-goods, and the special construction and position of the graves. This is true also of the independent estate owners, who in the rural communities are quite clearly distinguished from the other members. An analysis of the lower social classes is more difficult; but again the differences in the range and type of burial are great enough to show that here too Merovingian society was by no means homogeneous.

The community and economic life

How would the occupation of an area by Germanic peoples affect the way of life within the community? In some parts of the former Roman provinces rural settlements prevailed over urban. Countless new rural communities were founded, unconnected with the previous Roman settlement of the land. In the place of stone-built estate-houses provided with heating systems and a piped water supply came farmsteads built of wood, isolated or in groups, always near a plentiful natural water-source, a stream or a spring. The preference was for areas naturally favourable to cultivation – valleys, open countryside with fertile soil and a mild climate. Only during late Merovingian times and later did people move to cultivate the higher, less hospitable lands.

Dwelling-houses were one storeyed and rectangular, supported by rows of posts dug into the earth. Around them were grouped large numbers of what are called sunken-floored buildings, small structures dug into the surface of the ground, with low walls and a tent-like roof. They served for the storage of supplies or as workshops. Besides all this there were small granaries on stilts, wells, fences and paths. So far, we know of no stables in the Merovingian area; stock was either not kept indoors at all, or was not in the immediate vicinity of the dwelling-houses.

Such settlements varied considerably in size. We learn this less from the few actual settlements that have been excavated than from the far better known graveyards, whose size obviously depends directly on the population of the settlement to which they belonged. Judging by these, there must have been isolated farms as well as proper villages, but most common probably were medium-sized, hamlet-like groups of farmsteads. From the distribution of the cemeteries we also learn that settlements were fairly numerous, but widely scattered; so the early medieval picture may have been not unlike the scattered settlement of Roman times. The modern pattern of many long-settled landscapes with their large villages is only the result of a movement towards concentration in the later Middle Ages.

Naturally this form of land settlement could only take over where the Germanic element in the population was sufficiently strong. The largely Romance western areas not only retained and developed rural settlement on the model of the *villa rustica*; they also retained towns. It is quite clear that the civic continuity of the ancient Roman towns was ensured primarily by the successors of the provincial population, however few they may have been; this was true even of those on the banks of the Rhine and Danube, but it is even more true of those in the interior of the old provinces. Here the Church, upheld at first mostly by the Romance peoples, played a significant role. A Roman town like Trier might, in the early Middle Ages, temporarily disintegrate into a series of agrarian settlements; but town life was maintained here in the neighbourhood of the cathedral: the starting point for a new blossoming in the Middle Ages. For the Germanic newcomers also clearly recognized the political and economic value of towns as a type of settlement and were at most alien, but never hostile to it.

Just how alien, however, can be seen from the fact that towns found favour in the Frankish kingdom east of the Rhine only in the later period. The early Alemannic citadels of the fourth and fifth centuries, seats of government with town-like characteristics like the Round Hill at Urach, remained episodes. New development took off from exactly the same point and often at exactly the same place. From the late Merovingian period onwards, large fortified installations were built in many places in the area east of the Rhine; this was by no means merely a reaction to an external threat (as Büraburg and Kesterburg in north Hesse around AD 700 were a response to Saxon raids). Such places seem to have been conceived above all as a political focus for the surrounding territory, with the role of an economic and ecclesiastical centre following almost inevitably. When Boniface established a bishop's see in Büraburg in 742, the place became known as *oppidum* (town); and the see of Würzburg, established at the same time, shows a development which leads in a direct line from a *castellum* (fort) to the medieval town.

The economy of the Germanic tribes during the early Middle Ages was determined, like so much else, by traditions already established before the takeover of Roman provinces. In farming, animal husbandry seems to have had pride of place. This is suggested both by the earliest Germanic legal codes (the *Lex Salica*, for instance, contains elaborate clauses about cattle stealing) and by the clear dependence of the rural settlements on an abundant water-supply which must be related to the requirements of livestock. The pig was the most important animal in the Frankish settlements (Brebières, for instance) and this is well illustrated in the regulations of the *Lex Salica*. In other environments, other husbandry was practised: in the Alpine region cattle, sheep and goats predominated (at Schiers, for instance). The crops grown were varied, but presumably corn was the most important.

Spinning and weaving work was carried out without great specialization, by women, while simple iron tools or leather articles were produced by the men. R. Christlein has recently shown that the simplest economic step is the production of goods in and for the use of one household. The next step would imply specialized trades working for the wider needs of a rural community, like the village smith or the miller, and at an even higher level there must also have been major trades supplying the surrounding countryside from some centre (a court or a town) with rather more valuable products: weapons and belt mounts, jewellery of plain or average quality, pottery vessels and carved wood, probably sold directly to the customer without a middleman. We can judge the extent of such trading areas from the distribution of objects bearing the same stamp and therefore originating from the same workshop – pottery and jewellery for example. Where the distances are greater, we must allow for the intervention of a merchant; in this way Rhenish glasses came to Alemannia, Mediterranean bronze dishes to the Danube, and wine was carried from the central Rhenish area to the Rhine delta.

In those cases where the trade allowed, travelling

craftsmen must be envisaged. A number of graves containing metalworkers' tools bear this out. A grave at Poysdorf in lower Austria, for instance, contained two moulds of brooches of a type which could be made by a travelling smith without a fixed workshop.

One final illustration of trading methods in the early Middle Ages is provided by the small balances which quite often appeared in Merovingian men's graves. Such scales were used to weigh precious metals, particularly gold and silver coins, which were the accepted medium of payment.

Paganism and Christianity

In the decisive battle with the Alemanni fought by Clovis in 496/97, in the fifteenth year of his reign, the king vowed that he would convert to Christianity if the victory was his. When he was baptised, a couple of years later, his example was followed by thousands of Frankish chieftains. This spectacular event began the conversion to Christianity of those Germanic tribes, like the Franks, which had their roots in the barbaric areas to the east of the Rhine. (The east German tribes of the Burgundians and Visigoths had already become Christians before they settled in Gaul.)

The conversion of those central European Germanic tribes which sooner or later formed part of the Merovingian kingdom seems to have been quite peaceful. Such is the impression conveyed by the archaeological remains. Finds of a decidedly pagan character are rare and remain completely isolated; they seem to be individual statements, rather than expressions of a communal religion. By contrast, in the numerous finds of common Christian significance, there is a sense of generally understood conventions which arises from widespread shared convictions and religious rituals. In this context, the image on the gold plate of a brooch from Pliezhausen (in the district of Reutlingen) stands alone on the Continent: it shows a mounted warrior, overriding a vigorously struggling opponent, receiving help from a divine-demoniacal figure who guides the victor's spear from behind. Similar, but still more detailed, images from Scandinavia help us to understand the pagan character of this pictorial motif, 'supernatural powers bringing victory'. Much the same can be said of the image of the 'wolf-warrior' on the sword scabbard from Gutenstein (in the town of Sigmaringen) or that of a 'weapon dance' on a plaque from Obrigheim in the Palatinate. The runic script on the reverse of a square-headed brooch from Nordendorf in Bavarian Swabia is indisputably pagan – the three gods Woden, Donar and Loki are named – but there is hardly any other inscription with such a firm pagan statement. Christian relics, on the other hand, are plentiful. Countless objects of secular use, such as pieces of jewellery or belt-buckles, were hallowed by the addition of Christian symbols. The

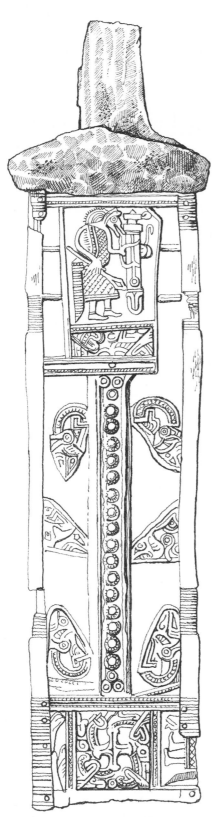

Sword scabbard from Gutenstein, Germany, ornamented with the mysterious figure of a 'wolf-warrior' near the hilt. The exact meaning is lost, but no doubt the appeal was to supernatural powers who bring victory in battle. (5)

frequent occurrence of so-called 'gold foil crosses' in the Alemannic region demonstrates the adoption of a Mediterranean custom; at burial, a cross of precious metal was fastened to the shroud of the dead person. In the Rhineland, the custom of gravestones, traditional from the late Roman period, flourished again, giving abundant expression in words and symbols to Christian spiritual values. Not only were churches everywhere built near settlements, but Merovingian aligned graveyards even produce Christian monuments of wood or stone.

The flaw in this picture of a populace closely bound to Christian beliefs is not so much the few explicitly pagan remains of the type described above, but the frequent evidence of superstitious practices, e.g. the excessive use of amulets, many of which have only the most distant Christian connections. The recurrence of ancestral, essentially pagan, burial customs – the cremation of the corpse, the digging of a circular ditch and the heaping-up of a mound to mark the burial place, and the sacrifice of the horse at the burial of a lord – also emphasizes a surviving pagan tradition.

Later on, such customs even gained ground in the eastern areas of the Merovingian kingdom; they were strongly adhered to by the one Germanic tribe at this time which still clung to paganism and practised those very rites. It took Charlemagne's mission to the Saxons, undertaken with military support in the last decades of the eighth century, to remove this focus of paganism; and it took the much more peaceful missionary activity of the Anglo-Saxon Wynfrith (Boniface) about the middle of that century to bring back the inhabitants in the east of the Frankish kingdom to a purified form of Christianity.

Arts and crafts

The Germanic art of the first millennium AD began very much under the influence of Roman art, or rather of certain forms of Roman art; for clearly architecture, sculpture and painting did not sensibly affect the artistic creativity of the Germans. The influence was felt in more modest crafts by the men who made brooches, belt-buckles and pieces of jewellery. Often the basic form was drawn from a Roman design and preserved in essence, but with obvious changes which proclaim the desire for a different style.

Such a development began at the end of the fourth century. It was a movement away from Roman origins, leading to the most characteristic and specific form of artistic expression, the Germanic animal ornament. This is derived from the animals which occur chiefly on the borders of provincial Roman chip-carved bronze plates: beasts of prey, sea creatures and all kinds of fabulous beasts, sea-lions, griffins and the like. As we have already seen, the form and technique of Roman chip-carved bronze belt-plates found remarkable

Part of a belt mount from Obervorschütz, Germany, with a more diagrammatic rendering separating out the animals that make up the ornament. Mouths, eyes, legs, bodies and tails form semi-isolated elements, but are combined in a highly sophisticated decorative style. (6)

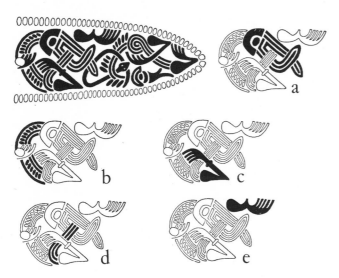

Detail from a gold-foil cross from Hintschingen, Germany, showing Germanic animal ornament. The left-hand animal is analyzed into its component parts in the five smaller drawings. The head (a) consists of a heavy semicircular eye-socket with an oval eye; from this project the two jaws, represented by triple lines, the upper one straight, the lower bent upwards at a right angle and crossing it. Behind the head is the neck (b), a curved beaded band contained within single and double lines, leading to the foreleg (c) – a pear-shaped thigh bone joined by a sharp angle to the shin; this has a cuff-like projection before the foot, which ends in four toes. From a point between the neck and the thigh bone, the body of the animal (d), consisting of a triple line, reaches diagonally upward to the jaws, crossing over the lower one. At the upper end of the body, though not connected to it, is the hind leg (e), which likewise consists of a pear-shaped thigh, a sharp angle and a foot, this time with five toes. (7)

favour in the Germanic world; among the Saxons, for instance, works of this kind were produced in a style indistinguishable from provincial Roman products. Side by side with this perfect reproduction, there also began in the first half of the fifth century a reworking of the design in the indigenous style – not only in the north where the Sösdala style was starting to develop, but also on the Continent. This trend is best illustrated by a piece of metalwork that came to light a few years ago at Obervorschütz in northern Hesse, far outside the *6* area of the Roman Empire. It is a well-known type of late Roman belt mount otherwise found only to the west of the Rhine. The animals on the edge and in the centre of the piece, however, are stylized in a quite un-Roman manner: the individual parts of the body are clearly separated from each other, so that the animal, whatever it is, seems put together from a series of details – mouth, eyes, leg, body, tail – in a cumulative process. However, the excellent quality of the workmanship and its costly material (silver-gilt) demonstrate that it is the product, not of incompetent imitation, but of a conscious will and style. Thus H. W. Böhme: 'The division of these animals along the upper edge into separate, individual parts of the body, and the already advanced stylization of the animals more realistically portrayed in late Roman art – these can be seen as elements of a new artistic conception.' Böhme dates the find from Obervorschütz 'immediately before the transition to artistic creation in the Germanic Animal Style I'.

In fact, works like this, stemming from Roman arts and crafts, herald a form of artistic expression which was to appear for centuries on countless small decorated objects in the Germanic world. The details produced by breaking up individual animal figures were abbreviated into signs recognizable to an informed – but only to an informed – public. The rules of composition were artistic, not anatomical. Only by analyzing each image and reassembling the parts, as it *7* were, letter by letter, can the unpractised observer gain an insight into the image's meaning. It is in fact a process akin to reading: the details (hoof, jaw and so forth) correspond to letters, the individual animals to words and the animal compositions, each within a self-contained area of decoration, to sentences.

On such a high level of perception, we can set high standards of quality: how has the available surface been filled, what is the rhythm of its design? How great is the refinement in choice of subject and composition? This refinement consisted first and foremost – since the elements of the picture were heavily standardized – in constructing the individual animal; and this was done in the most fanciful way possible, so that it was usually quite unrealistic. New possibilities opened up in the course of the sixth century, when interlacing entered the Germanic Animal Style (Style II), a motif derived from Mediterranean art, accepted largely through the influence of the Continental Germanic tribes. The individual animal, previously a self-contained image, could now be so dove-tailed with the other elements of the picture that even the expert must have found it hard to encompass the whole figure at a glance. Again a detailed reading process was necessary to pursue the convolutions of the animal's body through the interrupted and interwoven lines, and so to track down the animal in its artistically arranged concealment. At a superficial glance, it seems merely a pleasing ornament; in reality, despite the formal limits of its basic convention, it is a highly complex and deliberately obscure design, the meaning of which could be revealed only by intellectual effort. To modern observers, understanding usually ends at the correct 'reading' of the ornament, while its true significance almost always remains obscure.

In animal ornamentation the Germans had found their own appropriate form of artistic expression. It was used wherever they settled, from Scandinavia to Italy. Outside the Germanic world it made no impact; it was ethnic art in the strictest sense of the word, an art which could hardly be understood, let alone enjoyed by any other people. The Germanic tribes on the mainland at least maintained this art form until the end of the Merovingian era; and even in the early Carolingian period it was not completely forgotten.

A second area of artistic creativity should also be mentioned, in which the Germanic peoples in the Migration Period and the early Middle Ages produced high-quality works of a type that was all their own. From eastern, possibly Iranian, sources a style of decoration had spread to the west in which multicoloured effects were achieved by inlaying variegated stones in cells on a metal surface. This style of decoration had found favour in the Roman Empire, principally in relation to the technique known as cloisonné, in which the whole decorated surface was divided up into small cells filled with coloured semi-precious stones or glass; it was also popular among the neighbouring barbaric peoples to the north. Through the westward movement of Germanic, Hunnish and other groups in the course of the fifth century, the tribes of western and central Europe became more familiar with it. From the fifth and sixth centuries onwards numerous cloisonné-decorated objects are found: women's jewellery, belt decorations, even weapons of particular value. The objects found in Childeric's grave show all the important applications of this decorative technique; the objects found here are in technical and artistic terms among the highest achievements of this type of ornament. Of a similar standard in the field of women's jewellery are the pair of bow brooches from the lady's tomb beneath Cologne Cathedral and also (from as late as the seventh century) the bow brooches from the

Liturgical chalice, signed by the seventh-century goldsmith, St Eligius, formerly in the convent of Chelles, in France. Bowl, stem and foot are decorated with the cloisonné technique. (8)

woman's grave at Wittislingen. Such objects must certainly be considered as special commissions; but the two disc brooches from Queen Arnegunde's tomb represent a type rich in variety. It is characterized by narrow cells which divide the surface into small and colourful segments; and it demonstrates the last artistic refinement of cloisonné technique, its final impetus in the second half of the sixth century.

Later on in the Merovingian era, this method of decoration disappears, to be replaced by a related style, also based on a polychrome technique and likewise rooted in the arts and crafts of the Migration Period. It is known as *cabochon* decoration: separately set, polished, coloured convex stones are arranged in a regular pattern to contrast generally with a gold background, often decorated with filigree patterns. The large numbers of gold disc brooches represent the best examples of this work. The cloisonné technique, however, was still cultivated in the seventh century by the best artists of the time. The saintly goldsmith and bishop Eligius (died 660) used this technique to decorate his many masterpieces, though unfortunately none of them survives in the original. They seem, however, to have been in the Mediterranean rather than the German cloisonné tradition.

Classical traditions of art, especially in stone sculpture and architecture, were further cultivated, particularly in the west of the Merovingian kingdom, with an abundant new flowering in the Carolingian Renaissance. In these media there were few instances of Germanic innovation, and unlike animal ornamentation and cloisonné, an individual style was not formed. Germanic art during the early Middle Ages was caught in an area of tension between Christian-Mediterranean influences and traditional Germanic forms of expression; this situation is perhaps best illustrated by a decorative panel found in 1885 at Linon (Puy-de-Dôme), one of the most outstanding works of Frankish art. Its basic form is an open-work Chi-Rho monogram of a kind commonly found in the Mediterranean area, and particularly the Byzantine world, with abundant variations and differing functions. The design includes the letters *Chi* and *Rho*, enclosed by an outer ring (such as a garland, for example), the letters *Alpha* and *Omega* hooked on to the lines of the *Chi*, and a strong emphasis on the straight lines for the sake of symmetry, so that the part of the *Rho* which turns to the right – here formed like an R – is positively stunted. In a normal Mediterranean panel, the upper surface is smooth, the effect that of a silhouette achieved by a strong contrast between light and dark. This Frankish object is quite different. The sharp bony relief of the upper surface produces a lively play of light and shadow, the inlaid red garnets contrasting with the gold background in which they are set. The power emanating from the haloed face in the centre of the panel is complemented by the rhythmic effect of the animal ornament in the outer area. Three pairs of boars' heads form the outer ring. The hooves which are set directly against them are so shaped that they can also be seen, together with the eye setting of the animal heads, as a human face. Alternating with these masks are intertwined pairs of animals heraldically arranged on the remaining three lines. In this work, measuring only 6.3 centimetres in diameter, the somewhat dry form is clearly perfected and brought to life in a highly artistic fashion, and its expressive power enormously increased. The Linon piece above all others demonstrates clearly the special character and expressive capacity of Germanic art, in direct comparison to that of the Mediterranean.

This symbiosis of immigrants and natives, Germans and Latins, in the area of the former Roman provinces was decisive for the character of the age, and for that of the succeeding era. The spiritual encounter between these two peoples gave birth to the culture that was characteristic of the Middle Ages. The beginnings of this process can already be clearly recognized in the early Middle Ages. The Germanic character was best able to assert itself in the life of the settlements. Everywhere that German settlements grew up, even in areas that had once been Roman, the pattern of habitation is still decisively affected by that development. Villages today, for instance, can usually be traced not to Roman, but to Germanic roots. In the spiritual sphere, however, the culture of the Mediterranean world, based on Roman foundations, proved for the most part to be dominant. Christianity rapidly supplanted the pagan beliefs of the Germans, and their ancestral law was finally abandoned in favour of Roman legal standards. In art, too, we can see how specifically Germanic taste gave way gradually to Christian-Mediterranean perception. But one feature did remain. In women's dress, the Germanic brooch was abandoned, but an element of costume with Germanic roots was preserved throughout the whole of the Middle Ages in the form of the chatelaine; likewise in many other ways Germanic and classical traditions combined to form a new whole.

If we compare the situation at the start of the fifth century with the position of the Germanic tribes of central and west Europe in the seventh and eighth centuries, we can see the far-reaching changes wrought in the intervening period. The Roman Empire, that fateful power with which the Germans of antiquity had to come to terms either peacefully or in battle, no longer existed. On the territory of that Empire, new, Germanic states, including the Frankish kingdom with its increasingly open imperial ambitions, had come into existence. Admittedly the geographical expansion of the Germans had lagged far behind that of their political power; but a considerable area of land to the west of the Rhine and the south of the Danube that had been Roman had become permanently Germanic. At the same time, settled land in the east had been abandoned; in eastern central Germany, in Bohemia and Moravia, migrating Slavs replaced Germanic inhabitants, and a picture emerges of a westward displacement of the area settled by Germanic peoples.

3

THE ANGLO·SAXON SETTLEMENT OF ENGLAND

CATHERINE HILLS

Before the Romans withdrew from Britain, Saxon pirates were already menacing the southern shore. After 410, the attacks multiplied and groups of immigrants from what are now Jutland and Schleswig-Holstein began to occupy the south-eastern part of England. Within a relatively short time they dominated the whole country south of Scotland and east of Wales.

This much is certain. But the details of the whole process are still largely a mystery. Who exactly were the Angles, the Saxons and the Jutes? Where did they live before the migration? Was the settlement peaceful or violent? How did the newcomers relate to the native Britons? What sort of social, economic and religious community did they establish?

By the eighth century the darkness has lifted. Written sources become plentiful, both works of scholarship, such as Bede's *Ecclesiastical History*, and a large corpus of poetry including *Beowulf*. Evidence from material remains increases and we have the first stone churches. Rounded history becomes possible.

But for the 'lost centuries' of Anglo-Saxon England, which are indeed those during which England itself was born, we must depend on the objects and sites recovered by archaeology – each one itself a small mystery until placed in its context and interpreted. Comparison with Continental finds may tell us about the movement of peoples; imports from distant countries speak of trade; grave-goods and funerary practices can give insight into religious beliefs;

excavations of long-vanished houses provide information about village life and agriculture. It is a work of dogged patience and mostly unspectacular results, but from time to time the routine is suddenly illuminated by a discovery that is totally unexpected and startling in its splendour. Such a moment came in July 1939, when the Sutton Hoo ship burial was unearthed in Suffolk, once the territory of the East Angles.

Here was the burial of a great leader, almost certainly a king (though in fact the body was missing – perhaps lost in battle or buried elsewhere). In a boat about twenty-four metres long had been placed a magnificent treasure: several Byzantine bowls, silver spoons inscribed 'Saulos' and 'Paulos', Gaulish coins, a helmet and sword, possibly from Sweden, and many pieces of gold and garnet jewellery that were probably made locally. The burial, with its mixture of Christian and pagan features, is datable to the first half of the seventh century. Its implications are still being assessed, and the meaning of some of the objects remains doubtful. The piece shown here (*opposite*) is made up of two separate parts which were not originally thought to belong together. The top is a beautifully modelled bronze stag standing on a ring of twisted iron wires supported on a short bronze pedestal. Below this is the upper end of something variously called a 'whetstone' or 'sceptre', a smooth stone bar about sixty centimetres long with four surfaces carved at the ends into faces. Suggestions are that it symbolizes the power of the being as provider of swords or as wielder of thunderbolts. (1)

*On previous page : detail from one of the
Witham pins, among the masterpieces of
Anglo-Saxon metalwork. The design uses
strange winged bipeds lost in a maze of
interlacing lines. (1)*

Traces of migration

Rome was the model to which barbarian culture aspired and it is often difficult to decide at what point the transition from 'Roman' to 'Germanic' occurred. The early fifth-century buckle and counter-plate of bronze inlaid with silver found at Mucking, Essex (*far left*), is of a type normally associated with the late Roman army. Yet it was found in a Germanic grave in an Anglo-Saxon cemetery and is decorated in a style peculiar to south-east England. Did it belong to one of the earliest settlers or to a Germanic soldier serving in the Roman army? Was it made by British or by Saxon craftsmen? *Left*: the gold and garnet buckle found in the grave of a chieftain at Taplow, Buckinghamshire, was made about two hundred years later than the Mucking buckle and is purely Germanic in style. The disintegrated ribbon interlace is hardly recognizable as zoomorphic: it has come a long way from the naturalistic beasts still visible along the borders of the earlier buckle. (2,3)

Virtually identical equal-arm brooches have been found at Haslingfield, Cambridgeshire (*above*), and Anderlingen, near Hanover (*below*). Both date from the fifth century, powerful evidence for a connection between the two areas. (5,6)

Saucer-brooches with scroll decoration have also been found in England and Germany. This example (*above*) comes from a cemetery at Westerwanna, south of Hamburg. (4)

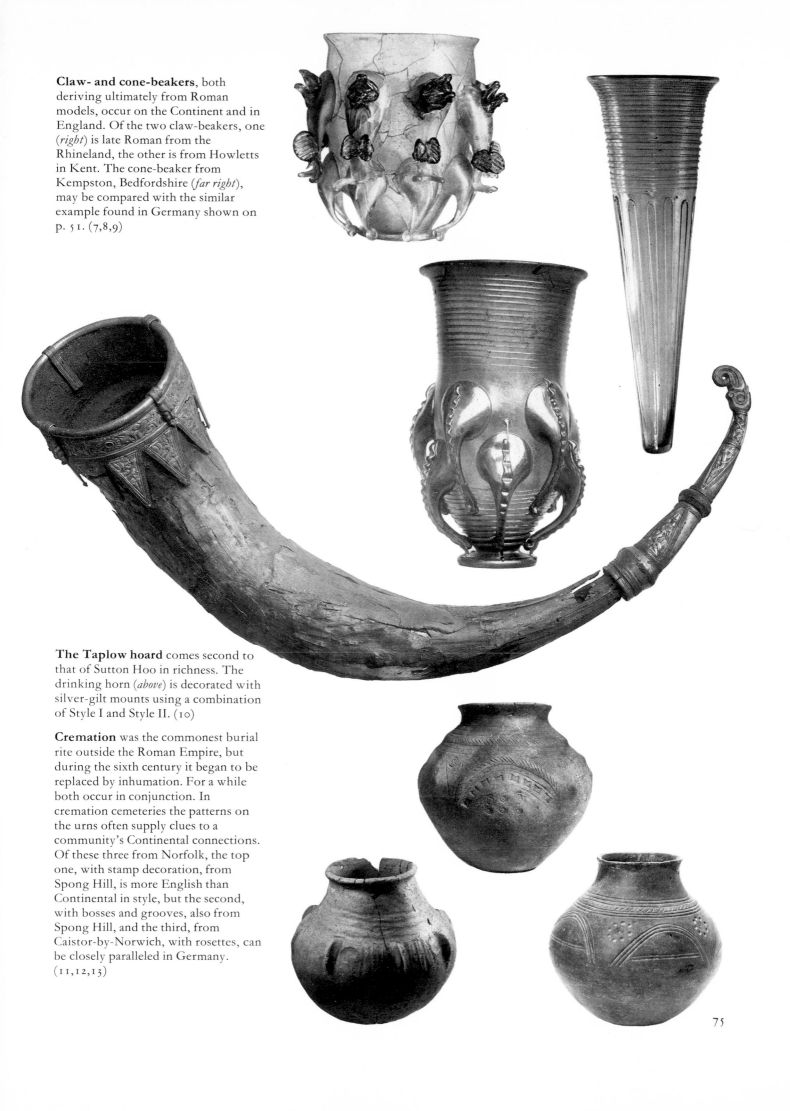

Claw- and cone-beakers, both deriving ultimately from Roman models, occur on the Continent and in England. Of the two claw-beakers, one (*right*) is late Roman from the Rhineland, the other is from Howletts in Kent. The cone-beaker from Kempston, Bedfordshire (*far right*), may be compared with the similar example found in Germany shown on p. 51. (7,8,9)

The Taplow hoard comes second to that of Sutton Hoo in richness. The drinking horn (*above*) is decorated with silver-gilt mounts using a combination of Style I and Style II. (10)

Cremation was the commonest burial rite outside the Roman Empire, but during the sixth century it began to be replaced by inhumation. For a while both occur in conjunction. In cremation cemeteries the patterns on the urns often supply clues to a community's Continental connections. Of these three from Norfolk, the top one, with stamp decoration, from Spong Hill, is more English than Continental in style, but the second, with bosses and grooves, also from Spong Hill, and the third, from Caistor-by-Norwich, with rosettes, can be closely paralleled in Germany. (11,12,13)

The goldsmith's art

The Kingston brooch (*left*) is among the finest pieces of Anglo-Saxon polychrome jewellery, a style which flourished between 550 and 700. Found at Kingston Down, in Kent, it is decorated with filigree and semi-precious stones – garnet, lapis-lazuli and cuttle-fish shell – set in gold and silver cells (cloisonné). (14)

Square-headed brooches seem originally to have been a Scandinavian type, which became popular in England around the end of the fifth century. *Below left*: a brooch from Empingham, in the area of Mercia. *Below*: a set of jewellery, including a square-headed brooch and belt-buckle, from Berinsfield, Oxfordshire, showing them as worn; the strings of glass beads are held by saucer-brooches on the shoulders, not round the neck. (15,16)

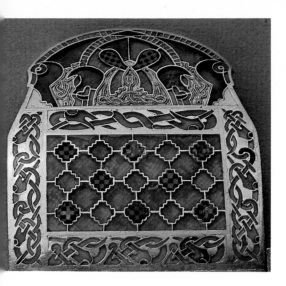

Shoulder clasps with cloisonné ornament formed part of the Sutton Hoo treasure (*above*). At the top are two semi-naturalistic boars making a symmetrical pattern, while round the edges there are interlaced beasts. (17)

A stylized animal fixed to a shield, from Bergh Apton, Norfolk. Shield trappings are not very common and may indicate their owners' high rank. (18)

The Witham pins are a set of three linked pins fixed to small discs, found in the River Witham in Lincolnshire, dating from the eighth century. This enlarged detail (*right*) shows part of one of the discs, with ornament made up of strange creatures enmeshed in continuous interlace. (20)

The minute scale of much Anglo-Saxon jewellery makes it virtually indecipherable. *Above*: an enlarged detail from the rim of the Taplow horn. The motifs are so stylized that they have become abstract. Note the hand with outstretched thumb and the 'helmet'. (19)

Anglo-Saxon landscape

Offa's Dyke (*left*) remains a monument to the power and resources of Anglo-Saxon England. It was built as a bulwark against the Welsh by King Offa of Mercia, who reigned from 759 to 796, the dominant personality of his age. (21)

Yeavering (*below*) in Northumberland has been identified as the site of the Northumbrian capital, *Ad Gefrin*, mentioned by Bede. The foundations of halls, an amphitheatre and possibly a temple have been uncovered. (22)

Churches survive in substantial numbers from the eighth century onwards, but the scale is small (partly because the more important churches and cathedrals have been rebuilt and enlarged many times), and since they are mostly in remote rural districts, the workmanship is often not sophisticated. The church at Deerhurst, Gloucestershire, is perhaps the best. The fluting and entablature of these windows (*right*) are obviously classically inspired; the triangular heads are an Anglo-Saxon speciality. (26)

The classical tradition nourished not only metalwork and manuscript illumination but almost every other art and craft as well. The vine-scrolls inhabited by animals on the Bewcastle Cross (*above right*) clearly belong to the same world as the ivory panel (*above left*) from the throne of Maximian at Ravenna. (23, 24)

At West Stow, Suffolk (*right*), a group of sixth-century farmhouses has been reconstructed on the original site. (27)

Porchester, in Hampshire (*above*), was a Roman fort, built to defend the coast against Saxons. Part of the enclosure became a Saxon village. What we see there today are the Roman walls, with the castle and monastic church built by the Normans. (25)

Excavations at Chalton, Hampshire (*right*), have exposed the foundations of Anglo-Saxon houses, each divided into two with a separate door to each part. (28)

THE ANGLO-SAXON SETTLEMENT OF ENGLAND

MODERN BRITAIN is a mixture of races, a mixture where elements have been growing more heterogeneous for thousands of years. There have been immigrants in search of a better life, refugees from religious wars and victims of political persecution. To find a people who actually conquered the country we have to go back to the Normans. But the Normans themselves were a mixture, descendants of Scandinavians who had settled in northern France among a population that was already a blend of Germanic Franks and Gallo-Romans, and cousins of those Norsemen who had invaded the north and east of England in the ninth century. None of these folk movements – important and far-reaching as they were – has left such obvious traces on the future as that which took place during the fifth century AD, when the peoples who came to be called Anglo-Saxons crossed the North Sea. The largest part of Britain is still called England, and we speak English, a direct descendant of the Germanic language which was brought to Britain by the fifth-century settlers. These peoples are the subject of this chapter.

Tribal ancestry: Angles, Saxons and Jutes

Our knowledge of the Anglo-Saxons, both in their

◁ **The final glory** of Anglo-Saxon England was its superb manuscripts, of which only a tragic few survived the Viking attacks and the vicissitudes of a thousand years. The provenance and dating of these books, nearly all copies of the Gospels, are matters of some complexity, and the mixture of stylistic elements – Celtic, Germanic and classical – makes it difficult to classify them with exactness. We can be sure, however, that most of them were produced in the *scriptoria* of the great monasteries of Northumbria and Ireland between the seventh and the ninth centuries. The most famous of all, the *Lindisfarne Gospels*, can be dated to about 700. This 'carpet page' (*left*) incorporates a cross outlined against a background of interlace so dense that the eye can hardly decipher it. Later ages looked back incredulously to such books and said that they were the work not of men but of angels. (29)

Continental homelands and during and after their settlement of England, depends very largely on archaeological evidence. A few documentary sources should, however, be mentioned, although there has not always been agreement as to their value or as to the significance of the information they contain. Tacitus, at the end of the first century AD, and Ptolemy, in the middle of the second, both list north German tribes and suggest geographical locations for them. Both mention the Angles, although unfortunately they do not seem to put them in quite the same place. Only Ptolemy mentions the Saxons, who, he thought, lived somewhere in the region of modern Holstein. The Angles probably lived to the north, in the Jutland peninsula. It seems to have been the Saxons who made the greatest impression on the later Roman Empire: the system of defences along both sides of the Channel was known as 'The Saxon Shore', presumably because the defences were designed to protect Britain and northern Gaul from Saxon pirates.

By the fourth century, the Saxons had probably moved and expanded south-westwards along the North Sea coast, perhaps absorbing an earlier people known as the Chauci.

One problem in interpreting early written sources is that we do not know what the authors understood by the tribal names they used, and we certainly do not know what the peoples concerned themselves meant by them. A tribal name might begin as the name of a small clan and then, with political or military success, be extended to cover various other, previously separate, groups. Alternatively, groups once affiliated might be separated and realigned with others. After the late fourth century we are dealing with a period in which there was a great deal of movement, of small war-bands and family groups as well as of whole peoples and tribes. It was a situation too fluid for us now to determine precise definitions of ethnic, social or political groupings, which probably were not clearly defined at the time. Our most important written source for Anglo-Saxon history up to the eighth century is the *Ecclesiastical History* of the Venerable Bede, written at Jarrow, completed in AD 731. At the beginning of this work Bede describes the ancestry of the English as it was known to him. He says that the peoples of England were descended from the three most formidable races of Germany: the Saxons, Angles and Jutes. The Saxons came from Old Saxony, now Lower Saxony, the coastal region of northern Germany; the Angles from Angeln, probably the eastern part of Schleswig-Holstein; and the Jutes from Jutland. Parts of these regions, according to Bede, remained depopulated to his own day. The sixth-century Byzantine historian Procopius said Britain was peopled with Angles and Frisians. His contemporary, the British writer, Gildas, did not concern himself with the detailed origins of the barbarian invaders, while the other major English source, the Anglo-Saxon Chronicle, depends partly on Bede for its earliest sections. Much ink has been spilt over the degree to which these sources, together with other odd scraps of information from Continental writings, can be reconciled with each other and with the archaeological evidence.

Archaeology provides the excavated remains of buildings and graves. Until recently, most of our information came from cemeteries, but there are now a number of substantially excavated settlements, which have begun to balance the picture. During the fourth and fifth centuries the predominant burial rite in northern Europe outside the Roman Empire was cremation, and this was also the rite practised by the earliest settlers in eastern England. Most cremations were contained in pots, usually decorated with patterns which vary from region to region, and which change over the years so that they are very useful indicators both of chronology and of social groupings. Inhumation was not entirely unknown, and was adopted by Germans who settled in or near the Roman Empire, where it was the normal practice. During the sixth century, both in England and apparently in northern Germany, cremation began to give way to inhumation; and in England this process was accelerated once the conversion to Christianity had begun in the seventh century. Pagan inhumations provide a great deal of information about jewellery and weapons because these were often buried with the dead. Pots, 7,8,9 glass vessels, and bronze bowls or cauldrons were also put in the graves of richer individuals. Sometimes fragments of fabric, stuck to the back of brooches, allow some reconstruction of clothing, while the bones themselves give us information concerning the physique, disease and age at death of the population.

Using this evidence, it seems that at least some credence can be given to Bede's account, even if he does give a simplified picture. In the region between the Elbe and Weser river mouths, south of Hamburg in Lower Saxony, many cemeteries of the fourth and early fifth centuries are known from excavations. The best known has been the one at Westerwanna where over four 4 thousand cremations were unearthed before the First World War. More recently, near Stade at Issendorf, six thousand cremations have been excavated, while Liebenau, not far from Hanover, is an interesting site which includes the funeral pyres as well as the actual burials. Some of the most characteristic types of pottery, and the metalwork found in the pots, can be paralleled in England. For instance, one popular pattern found on pottery includes a rosette motif set within zig-zag or arched lines. Many examples of this pattern can be seen in the Elbe-Weser cemeteries and it can also be found in Norfolk, at the cemeteries of Caistor-by-Norwich and Spong Hill. One pot from 11,12,13 Caistor has a face mask which is so similar to a mask on a pot from Wehden that it has been suggested the same p.50(7) potter made both, so that either the pot, or more probably, the potter, must have travelled from Germany to England. Similarly, a round brooch found at Spong Hill has a pattern of four masks within a border, a pattern found almost exactly repeated on three brooches from Mahndorf, near Bremen. Other types of brooch were popular on both sides of the North Sea. There are round brooches with spiral scroll patterns and 'equal-armed' brooches which also have 5,6 scroll patterns as well as animal borders.

If we consider the Angles, it is again possible to discover a distinctive culture in the region Bede suggests, or in fact in a somewhat larger region, centred on Angeln, which includes parts of Mecklenberg and perhaps the Danish island of Fyn as well as much of Schleswig-Holstein. Characteristic pots from this region have a decoration which consists of contrasting horizontal and vertical lines or grooves, horizontal around the neck of the pot, vertical grooves or bosses across the shoulder. The pots tend to be shallower, wider vessels than the Elbe-Weser pots. Grave-goods include sets of miniature shears, tweezers and razors (which also occur in the Elbe-Weser region, but less frequently), and cruciform brooches. Again, many parallels for these can be found in England. In particular at Caistor-by-Norwich there is a series of 13 pots, all of the classic Anglian type, which suggests a direct connection. Cruciform brooches became one of the most popular ornaments of the fifth and sixth centuries in England, especially north of the Thames.

A rough division between north and south, Angle and Saxon, can be made in England on the basis of inhumation grave-goods: women of the 'Saxon' south of England and the Thames valley preferred round brooches, while in East Anglia and the Midlands cruciform and other types of bow brooch (as well as simple annular brooches) were more common. 'Anglian' women fastened their sleeves with metal

clasps and had cloaks pinned with large bow brooches. Unfortunately this distinction belongs to the sixth century, not to the fifth. Archaeology cannot yet distinguish clearly between the various peoples who came to England in the very early stages of the migrations.

In some places it seems as if there may have been settlers who were already of mixed origins when they arrived. At Spong Hill, a cemetery in central Norfolk, the fifth-century material displays a mixture of pottery and metalwork traditions which derive from various

parts of northern Europe including southern Scandinavia. A similar mixture is observable in Germany, at Issendorf. It may well be that in some regions movement had already by the beginning of the fifth century produced a mixed culture on the Continent, so that, when some of the people from those areas moved to England, they brought the same mixed pattern with them. There must be some reason for the later dichotomy between Angle and Saxon: perhaps it lies in the ancestry of the eventual ruling clan rather than in any actual original ethnic difference between the

11,12

83

mass of settlers in different parts of England (although one would not expect this to affect general patterns of female dress).

In the fifth century, if not later, there are traces of several other peoples and traditions. The most important group is the Jutes, said by Bede to have occupied Kent and the Isle of Wight, together with part of Hampshire. These areas did have a common and distinctive culture, distinguished by very rich jewellery and weapons, with close affinities to contemporary material from the Rhineland. Because of this, it was for some time thought that the 'Jutes' were in fact Franks. However, this rich culture belongs to the later sixth and seventh centuries and so must have developed after the initial phase of settlement. It is now clear that there are similarities between pottery and metalwork from Kent and from Jutland, although so little has been published from Jutland that it is unwise to be dogmatic. There seems no reason to doubt that early settlers in Kent could have had southern Scandinavian ancestry. There are also fashions in brooch types and in ornament which seem to develop first in Denmark during the fifth century and then to spread to eastern England. This suggests continuing contact. In fact, the quantity of material which can be closely paralleled between England and northern Germany and Denmark now suggests that the period of the migration must have lasted for some time, during which there was communication across the North Sea. Only later, during the sixth century, did England develop separate regional identities and traditions although, as we have seen, their German origins were still remembered in the eighth century.

Other peoples of whom there is some evidence are the Frisians, Alemanni, Swabians and Franks. The Frisians occupied the coastal regions of the Low Countries and Germany as far as the Weser, as well as some of the islands. They may themselves have been partly absorbed into the 'Saxon' culture sphere during the fifth century, and some settlers who eventually arrived in England may have used Frisia as a temporary or more long-lasting base. The fragments of records which relate to a Jutish chief named Hengist suggest just such a sequence. This man came first to Frisia, and then, if he is the same person, to Kent, where his treachery to his British employer Vortigern is well known from Gildas and Bede.

Alemannic leaders from southern Germany, presumably leading units of their own men, were recorded in Britain during the fourth century as part of the Roman army. The presence of Swabians, also from central or southern Germany, is thought to be indicated by the place-name Swaffham, found in Norfolk and in Cambridgeshire. Neither group has left any other traces. It is possible to detect other traditions as well. Both in England and in the Elbe-Weser region there is a

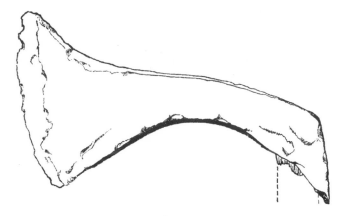

A '*francisca*', or throwing axe, from Howletts, Kent; it would have had a short wooden handle on the right. The name seems to indicate that it was associated with the Franks. (3)

characteristic late fourth- early fifth-century type of pottery, which includes vessels with sharp faceted carinations and pedestals. This appears to derive from third-century west German fashions. The tendency towards wider, shallower bowls apparent at Issendorf may owe something to the central and eastern German 'bowl urn' tradition.

The presence of the Franks, once they are no longer identified with Bede's Jutes, is more controversial. Their origin seems to be as obscure as those of other Germanic tribes and it is not clear whether, before they became partially assimilated to late Roman culture, they were culturally distinct from other tribes, for instance from the Saxons. They settled first in the Low Countries and then moved south into the Rhineland during the fourth century, still under the aegis of Roman power. Some were probably employed in the Roman army as federates (*foederati*). These were barbarians who were not simply recruited into the regular Roman army and incorporated into its normal structure. Instead, large groups, perhaps whole tribes, agreed to fight for the Empire in return for subsidies in food and money, and for land. They fought under their own leaders and probably retained their own social and political organization, bringing their own women to settle with them in the lands granted to them. They adopted the Roman rite of inhumation but were buried with equipment and jewellery, which was not the practice of the local Christian native population. Most of the objects found in Frankish graves are, however, of Roman manufacture, apart from a few brooches which are of types known otherwise from the Elbe-Weser region. It is therefore difficult to identify a Frankish grave as such when it is found outside the areas known to have been Frankish, since such a burial might have been that of any barbarian using and being buried with the available Roman objects. Furthermore, although it is possible to find in southern England material which has been imported from the Rhineland, there is seldom reason to suppose that this could not have happened in the normal course of trade or exchange; in other words, the movement of the objects does not imply a large-scale movement of people. Yet there are a few English graves whose equipment can perhaps be described as typically 'Frankish': a certain type of throwing axe, for example, is called a *fransisca* precisely because of its Frankish associations. Some English graves contain swords of a type probably made in the Meuse valley. In the sixth and seventh centuries there was clearly very close contact between south-eastern England and the Frankish Rhineland and there is no reason why there should not have been such contact in the fifth century, which might well have involved participation in invasion or migration by Franks.

Migration and settlement

Having discussed who the settlers were, we should attempt to say why they came. Several reasons can be suggested. The Roman Empire and its wealth was an inevitable attraction to the barbarians, while pressure from movements of peoples further east gave added impetus to the westwards surge of those nearest the Empire. In the North Sea coastal regions it seems that the reasons for the migrations may have been economic. During the second to fourth centuries AD many coastal settlements had been built up into mounds (*terps*) in order to avoid the increasingly wet and flooded lower-lying ground level. This process of isolating the settlements on mounds was eventually uneconomic. Neither arable nor cattle farming could profitably continue in the marshy coastlands, and those terps which have been excavated show decline and eventual abandonment during the fifth century. Even sites further inland, such as Wijster in Holland and Flögeln in the Elbe-Weser region suffered the same fate. In the case of Flögeln the archaeological evidence has been supplemented by analysis of pollen found in the soil, which shows that previously cultivated land was allowed to revert to woodland and heath. Some of the population may have moved south, and in a few cases we may simply be seeing part of a process of constantly shifting settlement within a limited area. The abandonment of so many cemeteries and settlements in the coastal regions must, however, surely be partly the result of emigration. Eastern England is not far from the other side of the North Sea even in primitive boats, and the attraction of an agriculturally rich land with an apparently dissolving political and administrative system would have been hard for the coastal people to resist.

There was in any case a tradition of communication between England and the barbarians. Saxon sea pirates had been attacking the coast since the third century (or even earlier) and barbarians had for some years been employed in the Roman army. There had been plenty of opportunity to acquire familiarity with England and to estimate its potential. To begin with, this might not have been such a danger to Rome because troops, even if foreign, were recruited into the regular Roman army and probably rapidly became Romanized, marrying wives in the provinces in which they were stationed or where they were eventually pensioned off. In the fourth century, however, as we have seen, it became more usual for whole units to be employed as federates, who retained a semi-independent status. These units, however loyal some of them may have been to the Empire, were bound to lead to a blurring of the distinction between Roman and barbarian. Barbarians also rose to very high positions within the regular army; Stilicho, who ruled the Empire for some years in the fifth century, was a Vandal, a member of a tribe whose name has become a byword for wanton destruction.

It has been suggested that the existence and distribution of these Germanic soldiers, whose presence is certainly historically recorded, can be traced in the archaeological record. Particularly important in this respect are certain types of belt equipment. During the fifth century – perhaps under eastern influence, perhaps as result of barbarian taste – large and elaborate bronze buckles and other fittings for belts became popular. Most of these have been found in towns, forts or graves along the Rhine-Danube frontier or in frontier provinces such as Britain and North Africa. This distribution suggests a military context since these were the places where the army was stationed. The belts are also so elaborate in appearance that an official function seems very likely. However, we do know that in the late Empire civil servants were entitled to military rank, which would presumably have carried with it the right to the insignia of that rank. It is also not clear that all the belts which have been brought into the argument are military. One small type of buckle, found only in Britain and probably made in the province, has a fragile, delicate plate sometimes decorated with Christian symbols. This kind of buckle has never been found in a male grave and was probably worn by women. Not enough is known about fourth-century civilian dress to be certain of this, but there is at least one third-century sculpture which shows a female figure wearing a belt with a buckle. The larger belts may well have been originally military in function, but when only broken fragments are excavated from an occupation site it is not always possible to say who the last owner was nor why it was lost in that particular place. Pieces of Roman metalwork may have survived in the barbarian world for centuries after the end of the Empire. There are a very few graves in England which do justify the suggestion that they are those of Germanic soldiers. These are the burials containing belt fittings – and sometimes weapons – which occur in cemeteries where they stand out as a distinctive group like the Frankish graves in the Rhineland. A grave at Dorchester on Thames may have belonged to this category, but unfortunately the rest of the cemetery, if it exists, has never been excavated. A cemetery outside Winchester, Lankhills, has produced a group of apparently Germanic settlers who belong to a phase before the breakdown of Roman authority, the mid-fourth century. There are also graves within Anglo-Saxon cemeteries which appear to belong to the earliest stages of the settlement. Several such graves have been found at Mucking in Essex. In this case it is not clear whether we are dealing with the first independent settlers or with an initial group deliberately planted by still-existing Romano-British authorities.

The nature of the migration itself is still in question. It used to be thought that hordes of Saxons overran the country, pillaging and murdering as they went, and that the Britons who were not killed, either emigrated or became slaves. It is true that the word for Briton and for slave, *wealh*, is the same in West Saxon dialect, and some Britons did emigrate to Brittany, Wales and the south-west. However, the size of the population of Roman Britain has recently been reconsidered on the basis of extensive fieldwork, and it seems likely that it was very much larger than had previously been supposed. Natural disasters, plagues and war may have killed many people, but they are unlikely to have left an empty land to be occupied by the Anglo-Saxons. It has also been doubted whether the numbers of the settlers were as large as Gildas's picture of hordes of invading barbarians would suggest. The numbers of a victorious enemy are prone to exaggeration, and if they all had to come, as they did, across the North Sea in small ships, the movement of large numbers of peoples would have been a long-drawn-out and gradual process.

Nonetheless, there are some indications that very large numbers of immigrants did arrive. The number of those buried in the cemeteries, which has in the past been estimated in hundreds, should, in some cases (perhaps in many) be counted in thousands, up to half of which may belong to the first century of the Anglo-Saxon period. We speak today a language which is descended from Old English and not from Welsh. Very few words in modern English can be traced back to a Roman or Celtic root and Celtic elements in place-names are very infrequent in the south and east of Britain. If large numbers of the native population did survive, they were entirely swamped by the culture of the invaders, at least so far as archaeologically detectable aspects of it go. There may have been Britons who continued to live in their farms and villas, maintaining as near as possible a Roman way of life long after much of the country had been settled by barbarians. Such people would have had pottery and equipment which, if excavated now, would appear to be

'late Roman' in date, if somewhat worn. They would have been buried as Christians without grave-goods so that if their cemeteries were ever found they would also be indistinguishable from late Roman graves.

Careful examination of the location of early Anglo-Saxon settlement and place-names suggests that the course of events varied from region to region. In Sussex it looks as if there may have been a division of the land by treaty, since all very early Anglo-Saxon sites lie in a group between the rivers Ouse and Cuckmere, as if the immigrants had been granted that particular area to settle. Elsewhere it has been suggested that the settlers were not allowed to occupy the best farming land, which would mean they were not in a sufficiently dominant position to do as they pleased. However, the settlement sites which have been quoted as examples of settlement on marginal land are not entirely convincing. Mucking, in Essex, may be on a rather barren gravel terrace, but it has a strategically strong position from which the Thames could be observed and perhaps controlled. Chalton in Hampshire is on top of a hill, again a strong position, whether for offence or defence. Whoever settled there was taking a position of some strength, which does not support a picture of refugee peasants allowed to occupy land no one else wanted. The known settlement sites of this period are still so few that no generalization can yet be made.

The Anglo-Saxons did not come into an empty country and the most difficult problem of all is the question of the degree to which they took over existing buildings and property boundaries. Some modern estate boundaries can plausibly be traced back through late Anglo-Saxon land charters to earlier times, although it is a very tentative study. It may be that some properties retained their Roman limits and were taken over as going concerns by incoming Saxons. Buildings may have been reused and patched up for some time. There are place-names which contain elements that appear to incorporate references to surviving Roman buildings or villages. The distribution of some early place-names shows a relationship to the Roman road system which should mean that the roads were still to some extent used and usable, although in general river valleys are a far more dominant feature of any Anglo-Saxon settlement pattern.

Urban sites present a great problem since they have in most cases been occupied for centuries, leaving little of their earliest phases for the archaeologist to discover. Most Roman towns are now, and were in the late Anglo-Saxon period, towns again. It was once thought that the pagan Anglo-Saxons shunned the towns and feared them as the homes of ghosts: an early poem, 'The Ruin', describes the fallen remnants of a city, perhaps Bath, as 'the work of giants of old', a wonder which had lain in ruins already for generations when the poet saw it:

Wondrous is this wall-stone; broken by fate, the castles have decayed; the work of giants is crumbling. Roofs are fallen, ruinous are the towers, despoiled are the towers with their gates; frost is on their cement, broken are the roofs, cut away, fallen, undermined by age. The grasp of the earth, stout grip of the ground, holds its mighty builders, who have perished and gone; till now a hundred generations of men have died. Often this wall, grey with lichen and stained with red, unmoved under storms, has survived kingdom after kingdom; its lofty gate has fallen . . . the bold in spirit bound the foundation of the wall wondrously together with wires. Bright were the castle-dwellings, many the bath-houses, lofty the host of pinnacles, great the tumult of men, many a mead hall full of the joys of men, till Fate the mighty overturned that. The wide walls fell; days of pestilence came; death swept away all the bravery of men; their fortresses became waste places; the city fell to ruin. The multitudes who might have built it anew lay dead on the earth. Wherefore these courts are in decay and these lofty gates; the woodwork of the roof is stripped of tiles; the place has sunk into ruin, levelled to the hills, where in times past many a man light of heart and bright with gold, adorned with splendours, proud and flushed with wine, shone in war trappings, gazed on treasure, on silver, on precious stones, on riches, on possessions, on costly gems, on this bright castle of the broad kingdom. Stone courts stood here; the stream with its great gush sprang forth hotly; the wall enclosed all within its bright bosom; there the baths were hot in its centre; that was spacious . . .

Bede tells the story of St Cuthbert's visit to Carlisle where he was shown the Roman fountain as a marvel rather than as a useful means of distributing water. Although it is clear that buildings were not reconstructed or properly maintained, nevertheless it may not be true that all Roman cities were in fact totally deserted during the early Anglo-Saxon period.

Buildings and pottery of early Anglo-Saxon types have been excavated at Dorchester on Thames and at Canterbury, as well as in London. Some Roman buildings stayed in use well into the Saxon period: when the roof of the headquarters of the Roman fort at York finally collapsed it fell on top of late Anglo-Saxon pottery; this implies that the building may have been standing as late as the ninth century. In the fifth and sixth centuries it does not seem that conditions were settled enough for trade or industry in any real sense and without these urban life cannot really exist. Yet some Roman walled towns may have been occupied by descendants of their original inhabitants well into the fifth century: at Verulamium the construction of a water pipe some time long after the end of the fourth century indicates continuing urban organization. Anglo-Saxon leaders may have taken over the more substantial surviving town buildings as royal residence. Excavation in Canterbury has produced Anglo-Saxon huts of both fifth- and seventh- or eighth-century date. It has been suggested that this represents a break in the sixth century, and that in fact it was only the stimulus of the Augustinian Christian mission after AD 597 which reawakened interest in the site. However, one might equally well explain the archaeological evidence as showing a site which was sparsely occupied, so that areas within the walls were sometimes occupied, sometimes open spaces, gardens or even fields. Bede describes Canterbury as a *metropolis* in the days of Æthelbert (late sixth early seventh century). By this he must surely have meant a place with some urban characteristics. It is difficult to see why the Frankish princess Bertha, who married Æthelbert, and her chaplain Liudhard should have chosen a church in Canterbury as a place to pray unless there was a royal residence there. Augustine need not have chosen Canterbury as the centre of his mission: he had intended to start from London, the old capital of the Roman province and, when he found that was not possible, he might have chosen one of several other towns in Kent if there had not already been a good reason for its choice as the chief residence of the king. Certainly in the later Anglo-Saxon period this town rapidly became so overpopulated that in the ninth century it was necessary to specify in a land grant that houses built on the plot should have about a metre of eavesdrip between them. Bede, writing in the eighth century, could refer to London and to York in terms which indicate some use of these places as trading centres. At Hamwih, near Southampton, excavation has produced clear evidence of trade and industry beginning probably as early as the seventh century. At Winchester there is some evidence for seventh-century occupation and it has been suggested that this was a royal and administrative centre, related to the port and market at Hamwih.

Some Anglo-Saxon genealogies and king-lists are preserved, chiefly in the Anglo-Saxon Chronicle. These seem to show that most of the recorded dynasties began in the later sixth century, that is, long after the original migration. It is clear that there was, throughout the fifth century, a very confused and complex political situation in England. Peoples from various parts of northern Europe settled in most of eastern and south-eastern England in groups of varying sizes. In some areas they were for a time subordinate to the local population, and in others they may have been deliberately invited. It is only during the sixth century that England takes the form in which it was known to Bede, with several large and medium sized English kingdoms.

The Anglo-Saxon village
The settlements of the Anglo-Saxons in England used to be contrasted unfavourably with those of their ancestors on the Continent. During the first four centuries AD, there were, in the Continental homelands

of the Anglo-Saxons, villages of some size, consisting of substantial houses with associated outhouses, granaries and workshops. Most settlements seem to have included a number of separate farmsteads whose buildings often lay within a fenced enclosure, and the whole layout of a settlement usually appears to follow some pattern. The main buildings were 'long-houses', that is, long, aisled timber structures with space for animals at one end, and for humans at the other.

For many years it was thought that the typical Anglo-Saxon dwelling (particularly of the early period) was a hut, the floor of which was sunk into the ground – a sort of pit dwelling. (This kind of building appears on Continental sites where it is usually interpreted as a workshop or other ancillary building.) It was thought that people lived within the pit and, since these were often not very large (only 2–3 metres in length), a picture of the Anglo-Saxon village as a collection of squalid hovels could easily be presented.

27 However, recent excavations have begun to change this idea. At West Stow, the excavator observed in some huts that there were hearths at ground level, not at the bottom of the pit, and also that in one hut which had burnt down, there were loomweights lying on top of what appeared to have been a floor overlying the pit. From this it does seem that, at least on this site, the pit functioned as a cellar rather than as a living space. The hovels are therefore not necessarily so primitive as has been thought. In fact, other kinds of building have now been found. At West Stow again, for example, there are several rectangular ground-level houses, each with its associated group of ancillary huts. At Mucking, perhaps the largest settlement so far excavated, it was thought for some years that the only buildings were the huts, but it is now clear that these were associated with a

28 variety of rectangular structures. At Chalton in Hampshire only three huts have so far been found, as opposed to the large number of substantial rectangular buildings. All these rectangular houses have a family resemblance: they tend to be a double square in shape or slightly shorter and to have opposed doors in the middle of each long side. At one end there is sometimes a partition. The same type of building, only much

4 larger, has been found at Yeavering in Northumbria.

22 This site has been identified as the royal palace of the kings of Northumbria, the *Ad Gefrin* mentioned by Bede as the place where Paulinus once stayed for thirty-six days with King Edwin, preaching and baptizing. A series of large rectangular buildings here was rebuilt on more than one occasion and was associated with a curious structure in the form of a segment of an amphitheatre. This may have had some ceremonial or religious function. One building was interpreted as a pagan temple.

The English buildings do not, however, resemble the Continental structures. There are no English long-

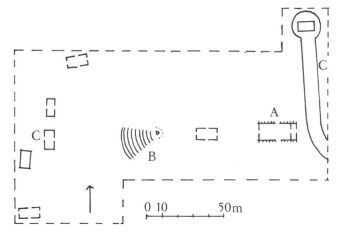

Yeavering, the royal palace of the kings of Northumbria, in the early seventh century. The king's hall (A) has been fairly certainly identified, but the strange structure like part of an amphitheatre (B) is still mysterious, and another rectangular building (C) could have been either a church or a pagan temple. (4)

houses from this period. One possible explanation is that it was no longer necessary to house animals in the milder English climate and that the richer soil put less of a premium on the collection of manure from the animal stalls. Alternatively, the difference in form might be explained in terms of another building tradition, in which case the tradition could only derive from Romano-British buildings and might in some way represent a translation into timber of Romano-British stone. It may be that archaeological concentration on the more glamorous elements of the material culture of the period – towns, forts, villas and roads – has left large parts of Roman Britain untouched. Ordinary rural houses may have been fairly simple stone or even timber rectangular buildings much like the later Anglo-Saxon ones, which may continue an earlier tradition.

Too few settlements have been excavated to allow any generalization concerning their layout and organization. Catholme in Nottinghamshire and Chalton, however, have plans which show them as clusters of several separate units or farmsteads within ditched or fenced enclosures. West Stow also appears to have been a group of small farms. Elsewhere, for instance in Oxfordshire at Eynsham, there may have been a more scattered pattern of buildings strung out over a wide area. So far early Anglo-Saxon villages have not been discovered directly underneath excavated sites of deserted medieval villages, nor have those excavated so far shown continuity from the early to the later Anglo-Saxon period. This suggests a shift in settlement during the Anglo-Saxon period which might be partly explained by the later concentration into nucleated villages of an earlier random, non-nucleated pattern of scattered hamlets and farmsteads.

Provision for death: the cemeteries

The life of the Anglo-Saxons in England has until recently been illustrated mostly by cemeteries, and these are still important sources of information. They have occasionally been found near settlements, as at Mucking, Essex, West Stow in Suffolk and possibly Spong Hill in central Norfolk, but more often cemeteries seem to have been placed at some distance away from their contemporary settlements. This may have been because there was a wish to keep the dead as far as possible from the living, or it may have been that more than one community used the same cemetery. If burial sites were put near the boundaries of the lands of two communities which shared them this would have been convenient for both, and may explain the fact that many cemeteries are on what are now parish boundaries and which might have already been boundaries in the early Anglo-Saxon period. They also often occur on hilltops or on rising ground which is a landmark in the area: Loveden Hill in Lincolnshire is a good example of this.

As has been noted, the size of cemeteries has in the past been greatly underestimated. It used not to be thought necessary to excavate more than a part of a site, so that total numbers and area covered were seldom established. At Loveden Hill over two thousand cremations were excavated and at Spong Hill 1,200 cremations, from what may be between a half and two-thirds of the whole cemetery, have so far been

11,12 excavated. Many of the cremation urns at Spong Hill contain the remains of more than one individual, so that the total population figures will be even higher than would be suggested by the number of pots. Since the cemetery was in use from the middle or possibly near the beginning of the fifth century and does not so far appear to have continued in use long into the seventh century, it covers two hundred years, six or seven generations. This gives us a minimum of three hundred in each generation, allowing for further excavation, but not allowing for the presence of multiple burials. The actual total is likely to have been somewhat higher. There is no reason why some of the other partially

5 excavated cemeteries, such as Lackford, Suffolk, or Sancton, Yorkshire, should not have been of equivalent size or even larger. We are thus dealing with a fairly substantial population.

One obvious source of information supplied by cemeteries is provided by the skeletal remains of the bones themselves. From these bare bones it is possible to learn something about the health and diet of the Anglo-Saxons and to say something about their way of life. Unfortunately many soils are too acid to preserve bone so that some cemeteries provide little or no skeletal material. Cremated bones can never be as informative as a complete and well-preserved inhumed skeleton, but even so a surprising amount of detail can be recovered from a few fragments of burnt bone. As yet there is no published statistical survey of the ages of death or of the incidence of types of disease in Anglo-Saxon England, so that most comments consist of informed guesswork rather than accurate analysis. It is clear that many Anglo-Saxons died before reaching adulthood and it is probable that average life expectancy was far lower than it is today, but as yet there is no definite evidence to show this. Determining the age of a skeleton after 'maturity' is not easy and it may be that there were more very old people than one might expect. The most obvious disease shown by the bones is arthritis, but odd features such as trephination of the skull indicate a fairly sophisticated approach to medicine. At least some of the men were six foot or over, but again there are no overall figures to show how representative that is.

Pagan Anglo-Saxons were buried with their clothes, jewellery and weapons, as well as sometimes with glass or pottery vessels, buckets, or bronze bowls. This is true of cremations as well as inhumations, except that there are very few weapons in cremations. Even if the objects have been burnt or distorted in the funeral pyre, it is often still possible to identify them. The chief drawback to cremation grave-groups is that we do not know what form the funeral ritual took and so we cannot be sure that care was taken to collect all the grave-goods and put them with the bones in the pot. It is clear that not all the bones themselves were collected: most of the skull was usually placed in the pot, otherwise widely varying proportions of the body are found, so that some of the bones must have been left on the pyre or buried elsewhere. At Liebenau, in Germany, where pyres have been discovered, it was found that many of the grave-goods had been left behind although much of the bone had been collected into the pots.

The pots in which the cremations were contained were, in England as on the Continent, highly decorated hand-made vessels, not usually very well fired. This represents a complete break with the Roman tradition in England. In the Rhineland, on the contrary, Roman techniques of pottery manufacture continued unbroken, and wheel-thrown, hard-fired pots were still made. It was probably from the Rhineland that these more sophisticated techniques were reintroduced to England during the later Anglo-Saxon period, but throughout the pagan period it is only in Kent that a few imported wheel-thrown vessels can be found.

We do not really know as yet very much about the organization of pagan Anglo-Saxon pottery manufacture. It used to be stated categorically that it was a domestic product, made by the women of each household for their family needs, but there is as yet little evidence to prove it, and some which contradicts it. Most pots come from cemeteries and it is not yet clear how far they can be regarded as products of a specialized funerary industry. Until more careful analysis of pottery from settlements is available it is impossible to say whether ordinary cooking-pots were simply taken off the shelf when grandfather died, or whether only special pots were used for burials. If the latter were true, then one could be far more confident in interpreting some of the decorative motifs on the pots as having religious meaning.

The clay from which the pots were made usually had various substances mixed in, such as crushed potsherds, sand or organic materials which may have been incorporated together with animal dung. All these substances made the clay easier to work and less likely to break during firing. One study of inclusions of crushed limestone shows that pottery found near Peterborough had been made using stone from Charnwood forest in Leicestershire, and other pottery made with the same material has been found elsewhere. Such evidence hardly supports the idea that this was a very localized, domestic industry. Examination of the pots has often concentrated on their decoration and some of the results of this study also contradict interpretation of pottery manufacture as a purely domestic occupation. The impressions of the same stamp tool used in decoration can be traced from one pot to another, thus identifying the products of the same potter. Distribution patterns for such stamp-linked groups of pots sometimes extend over large areas. Numerous small groups, found at perhaps two or three neighbouring cemeteries, could still be thought of as the results of contacts between a few villages (perhaps as the result of intermarriage), but other groups cannot be explained save as the result of specialization in the production of pots. In East Anglia hundreds of pots from one group, the Lackford-Illington pots, have now been found at several cemeteries and at one settlement site. Another group includes pots from Yorkshire, Lincolnshire,

Pottery of a high order was made for cremation burials, some of it sufficiently individual to be attributed to a single potter. This example comes from Lackford, Suffolk. (5)

90

Nottinghamshire and Norfolk. It is not yet clear whether the potter or his products moved: the difference in clay between some of the Lackford-Illington pots suggests that it was the potter who travelled, finding local deposits of clay wherever he was working.

The jewellery and weapons which have been found mostly in inhumations form the basis for consideration of regional and chronological variation during the fifth, sixth and seventh centuries in England. It is possible to arrange many types of objects according to art-historical principles in an evolutionary series. Fig. 6 shows this sequence worked out for the kind of brooch known as 'cruciform' from its shape. The early versions of this brooch developed from Iron Age 'safety pin' brooches under the influence of more massive Roman crossbow brooches. The spring of the brooch is behind a rectangular plate from which three knobs extend. The two lateral knobs are cast separately and are fastened to a bar which passes through the spring. The catch plate is behind an elongated terminal which takes the form of a horse's head. In later varieties the side knobs are cast in one with the head and become larger and flatter. Excrescences of all kinds appear at both extremities of the brooch and sometimes there are panels of decoration on the end plate. It should be noted that all carefully excavated graves show the brooches worn with the catch plate uppermost.

Similarly, it is possible to trace the development of other brooch types, usually from small simple varieties with elements in their design clearly derived from classical models, to larger ornate and sometimes clumsy creations. As well as cruciform brooches, there are other large bow brooches with rectangular or square head plates ('square-headed' brooches) and there are also smaller brooches which seem to be simple versions of either cruciform or square-headed brooches. The other main form is circular. There are simple ring or annular, flat disc, dished or 'saucer' brooches and others which have separate discs of decorated bronze applied to a plain metal disc. The distinction between 'Anglian' and 'Saxon' women has been mentioned, but even more noticeable is the difference between the jewellery of women from Kent and the Isle of Wight and from the rest of England. Kentish women wore round jewelled brooches made of gold or silver as well as bronze. Coloured glass and garnet inlays combined with various techniques such as niello, filigree and chip-carving to produce rich and varied patterns. The most famous of these brooches is the exquisite Kingston brooch. From Kent there are also gold buckles, clasps and pendants as well as wheel-thrown pots and a great variety of glass vessels.

It is less easy to set weapons into an evolutionary sequence, partly no doubt because they would not change unless methods of fighting changed, and partly

Three examples of cruciform brooches, showing the sequence of development: A, from East Shefford, Berkshire; B, from Barton Seagrave, Northamptonshire; C, from Sleaford, Lincolnshire. (6)

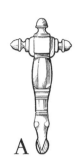

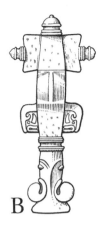

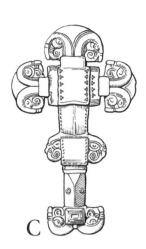

A   B   C

because they were made of iron, which has not always survived in such good condition that we can now say very much about its original form. The iron bosses which strengthened the centre of Saxon shields did develop, becoming taller during the seventh century, and there are perhaps a few distinctive types of spearhead which can be given a rough regional and chronological distribution, while the ornamental fittings of sword scabbards can be related to styles of ornament found on other types of metalwork.

The styles of decoration are as important as the form of the objects in classification. Germanic craftsmen were fascinated by animals, but they seldom represented them realistically. At first they may have copied the stylized but still recognizable lions and hippocamps found on the borders of late Roman belt fittings. Very 5,6 similar animals appear on the borders of Saxon equal-armed brooches and it may be that craftsmen went from Roman workshops to work instead for Saxons in north Germany. Barbarian craftsmen may have been trained in Roman workshops and then returned home to use the Roman techniques they had learned in the production of Germanic brooches. In England there is a small group of metalwork which is decorated with a very distinctive type of animal ornament. All the items in the group are either parts of belt fittings or large quoit-shaped brooches. They appear to have been made in southern England during the early years of the fifth century by craftsmen who had been trained in techniques in use in the workshops of the Rhineland or northern Gaul. It is not clear for whom they were made, whether for soldiers of British or Germanic ancestry fighting for the Romano-British authorities, or for barbarian invaders.

The main types of Germanic animal ornament were defined at the beginning of the century by a Swede, Bernhard Salin, who gave them the numbers by which they have been known ever since. His Style I is usually carried out in chip-carving. This is a high-relief technique, where the pattern, although cast, looks as if it has been chiselled out like wood-carving. This accentuates the disjointed character of the beasts portrayed, who often have a head, a hand or claw and a hip as their only obvious attributes, together with various schematic parts of the body which are not shown in any normal anatomical articulation. Sometimes there are anthropomorphic masks or heads, including the curious type of head in profile which led one scholar to rename the style 'helmet style'. Hands with out-turned thumbs derive ultimately from representations of the Roman imperial *gestus*. Salin's Style II is characterized by its flowing rhythmic p.68(7) appearance, produced by the intertwining of sinuous snake or ribbon-like animal bodies. Again there is no attempt at anatomical accuracy. Most animals have elongated jaws, eyes and a head indicated by a rounded or angular ribbon, and one or two limbs. Style II beasts are seldom chip-carved, but instead are carried out in techniques such as filigree wire which is suited to the production of flowing ribbon forms, although Style II beasts in gold and garnet cloisonné occur elsewhere.

For a long time it was thought that Styles I and II were strictly consecutive and they have often been used in chronological discussion. Style I was equated approximately with the sixth century, Style II with the seventh. While there is still perhaps some truth in such a view there are also problems. The evolution of Style I from late Roman border animals seems to have taken place during the fifth century and to have become popular in England at the same time as the arrival of the square-headed brooches, originally a Scandinavian type. This may have been around the end of the fifth century but there is no very firm date for it. Style II was believed to have developed under the influence of Byzantine interlace patterns which it was thought were transmitted to northern Europe only after the Lombards' arrival in Italy in AD 569. However, in graves north of the Alps attributed to the Lombards before they moved to Italy, and dated to the sixth century, there was metalwork decorated in a style not unlike Style II. Rich Frankish graves found in Cologne p.53–55 Cathedral and the abbey of Saint-Denis, near Paris,

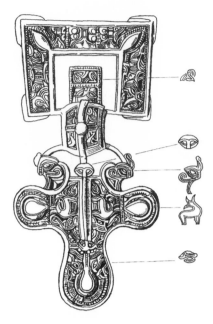

Square-headed brooch from Ragley, Warwickshire, illustrating the animal style that has been called Style I. Some of the animal motifs used are picked out for clarity at the side. (7)

contained objects decorated with interlace. One of these graves, at Saint-Denis, contained a ring inscribed with the name Arnegunde. This may identify the grave as that of a Frankish queen who died in 569. Some of her ornaments were decorated with curious intertwined animals which again look more like Style II than I. It has already been pointed out above that some techniques of metalworking are more suitable for the production of one style than the other. There is a regional bias, in that in England more Style II ornaments have been found in Kent than anywhere else, save for the royal burial of Sutton Hoo in Suffolk. In much of the rest of England it may be that craftsmen continued to produce Style I long after the Kentish goldsmiths had turned to Style II. This is a fundamental drawback to reliance on typology as equivalent to chronology. There is no real reason to suppose that fashions changed universally and suddenly in early Anglo-Saxon England. No one could afford to change their brooches every year: they probably lasted a lifetime or more. Some parts of England were much more exposed to foreign ideas and stimulation than others, and some regions were richer than others. It is also perhaps unwise to see a typological evolution as even and gradual. There might have been sudden rapid change at some periods and stagnation at others. A great many of the minor variations are more likely to reflect the imagination or taste of individuals than differences in date of manufacture. Some differences in ornament might have been related to the status of the woman with whom they were buried. It might have been the custom for married and unmarried, rich and poor women to wear distinctive types of jewellery, so that contemporary burials of women of different status might contain brooches which appear typologically different.

Status certainly is reflected in male equipment. Many male graves may not be immediately recognizable as such because they contain no weapons, except perhaps a knife. Probably only some classes of men were allowed to bear weapons and perhaps not all of these could afford to bury their fathers' weapons in their graves. In the later Anglo-Saxon period we hear of a sword which was an heirloom. It had originally belonged to King Offa of Mercia in the eighth century and two hundred years later Prince Athelstan left it in his will to his brother Edmund.

The spear was the weapon in widest use, accompanied often, but by no means always, by a shield. Axes are seldom found and there is little evidence for bows and arrows although it is assumed that these were in use. Swords are rare and in general their presence in a grave is taken to mean that the person buried was a man of some standing in the community. Sometimes status can be inferred from the position and arrangement of the grave within the cemetery. Some cemeteries in Kent and in East Anglia contained graves which had been surrounded by a circular ditch, either the foundation for a palisade or the limit of a mound. In some cases, even if the grave does not appear very rich in absolute terms, if it is compared with other graves from the same cemetery it can be seen that it was relatively distinctive within its own cemetery. A grave with a sword might not have belonged to the most important person in a Kentish community where there were several nobles, but in East Anglia it stands out as so unusual that any such grave can be seen as that of the local chieftain.

Imported bronze and glass vessels are signs of individual prosperity whether they arrived in the course of trade or as gifts from one king or chief to another. It is not likely that there was any very organized trade between England and the Continent during the fifth and sixth centuries, but the presence of a few imports, such as wheel-thrown vessels and glass in Kent, and ivory in East Anglia, suggests that the lines of communication had not been entirely broken. It used to be thought that the Rhineland was the most important source of foreign ideas and goods, but now the part played by France is becoming more apparent. In the later seventh and eighth centuries much of the trade of the port of Hamwih seems to have been with France. By this time there was also direct communication with the Mediterranean, inspired by the Christian mission.

The clearest demonstration of the hierarchical nature of early Anglo-Saxon society is given by the rich ship burial found at Sutton Hoo, on the Suffolk coast near 1,17 Woodbridge, in 1939. The wealth of this grave is such that it can only have been that of a royal personage – it is the richest such grave found in Europe – and it has been most often identified as commemorating King Rædwald of East Anglia, who died in or around AD 627. The material included a Byzantine bowl, spoons inscribed with the names 'Saulos' and 'Paulos' (which were perhaps connected with Christian baptism), coins from Gaul, and a helmet and shield which may have come from Sweden, as well as gold and garnet jewellery made by English craftsmen. It has been variously suggested that this was a cenotaph, the body having been lost in battle or given Christian burial elsewhere; a cremation, perhaps represented by a few possible bone fragments found on top of the Byzantine bowl; or that it was a normal inhumation, but the bone had completely dissolved in the acid soil conditions.

We know very little of the ritual connected with any of the pagan burials discussed above. Our only description of a funeral comes from the epic poem *Beowulf*, which was probably first written down in the last years of the seventh century or during the eighth century, but which describes events which belong to a much earlier period. At the beginning of the poem we are told of a hero, Scyld Scefing, whose body was laid in his ship and sent out to sea. The Sutton Hoo ship burial, although on dry land and not at sea, might represent a version of this ceremony:

> *His own close companions carried him*
> *down to the sea, as he, Lord of the Danes,*
> *had asked while he could still speak.*
> *That well-loved man had ruled his land for many years.*
> *There in the harbour stood the ring-prowed ship,*
> *the prince's vessel, shrouded in ice and eager to sail;*
> *and then they laid their dear lord,*
> *the giver of rings, deep within the ship*
> *by the mast in majesty; many treasures*
> *and adornments from far and wide were gathered there.*
> *I have never heard of a ship equipped*
> *more handsomely with weapons and war-gear,*
> *swords and corslets; on his breast*
> *lay countless treasures that were to travel far*
> *with him into the waves' domain.*
> *They gave him great ornaments, gifts*
> *no less magnificent than those men had given him*
> *long before, when they sent him alone,*
> *child as he was, across the stretch of the seas.*
> *Then high above his head they placed*
> *a golden banner and let the waves bear him,*
> *bequeathed him to the sea; their hearts were grieving,*
> *their minds mourning. Mighty men*
> *beneath the heavens, rulers in the hall,*
> *cannot say who received that cargo.*

Otherwise, we know virtually nothing of pagan religion. Because literacy arrived with Christianity and was for long the province of the clergy, our records of paganism are very few and probably biased. The names of a few gods and their festivals are mentioned by Bede, and Augustine in letters to Pope Gregory mentioned with some horror practices of the heathen English such as eating horseflesh and marrying their stepmothers. The new religion destroyed almost all trace of the old.

Augustine's mission

In the year 597 St Augustine arrived in England to preach Christianity to the heathen English. The conversion was no more sudden and rapid a process than the migration had been, although it is similarly sometimes used as a fixed point in archaeological dating. We have an unusually detailed account of its course because the main purpose of Bede's *History* was precisely to describe how England became Christian. It was a process much bound up with politics, for the conversion of a king would determine the conversion of his followers and allies, and it would depend partly on his relations with other rulers, pagan or Christian. Some conversions followed marriage, as did Edwin of Northumbria's when he married the daughter of the by then Christian king of Kent. Northumbria's Christianity, however, perhaps owed more to the mission of Irish monks than to Augustine and his successors. King (later Saint) Oswald had been brought up in exile in Scotland where he had become a Christian. Some kingdoms, such as Essex, were converted during one reign, only to lapse with the succession of a pagan king. Rædwald of East Anglia thought it prudent to put up an altar to Christ in his pagan temple, in case he was an important god after all. If Sutton Hoo is Rædwald's burial it could be seen as displaying such mixed ideas. The Christian spoons and crosses on some of the bowls could be seen as signs of Christianity, and if the body was missing perhaps it was because it had received Christian burial elsewhere. On the other hand, the whole assemblage and the fact of burial in a ship is a purely pagan rite. Some kings remained pagan well into the seventh century: Penda of Mercia, in spite of a Christian son and an alliance with the Welsh Christian king Cadwallon, remained a stubborn pagan until his death (which was in 655 according to Bede).

The conversion brought with it an influx of new cultural stimuli from several directions. The Roman mission itself came directly from Rome and opened the way to Mediterranean culture. There were also missionaries from Gaul during the seventh century: Felix, who preached in East Anglia, and Agilbert in Wessex. These men must have brought with them books and possibly liturgical vestments and chalices which might have been copied by English craftsmen. Anglo-Saxons themselves went to the Continent in search of inspiration. One of the most famous travellers was Benedict Biscop (died 689), a Northumbrian who went to Gaul to find stonemasons and glaziers capable of building churches since those skills were unknown to the English at that time. Evidence of the results of his work can be seen at Monkwearmouth (founded 674) and Jarrow (founded 681) where excavation of the early monastic sites has produced not only stone buildings and fragments of sculpture but also window glass, amongst much other material. The influence of classical design can be seen most clearly on the carved stone crosses (or 'roods') which are such a feature of the Early Christian period in northern England. Many of these are decorated with a pattern of vine-scrolls, often inhabited by animals or birds. This is an idea taken from 23,24 classical sources but adapted and altered by the Northumbrian sculptors. They were less successful with figural scenes, although it must be remembered that the present battered and worn condition of many of these crosses does not do justice to their original state, which may have been much more finished than now appears. It was presumably such crosses which inspired one of the most poignant of all Anglo-Saxon poems, 'The Dream of the Rood', where the cross itself speaks in most moving terms:

As a rood was I raised up; I bore aloft the mighty King, the Lord of heaven; I durst not stoop. They pierced me with dark nails; the wounds are still plain to view in me, gaping gashes of malice; I durst not do hurt to any of them. They bemocked us both together. I was all bedewed with blood, shed from the Man's side, after He had sent forth His Spirit. I have endured many stern trials on the hill; I saw the God of hosts violently stretched out; darkness with its clouds had covered the Lord's corpse, the fair radiance; a shadow went forth, dark beneath the clouds. All creation wept, lamented the King's death; Christ was on the cross.

The best-known products of the Northumbrian renaissance, as it has some reason to be called, are the illuminated manuscripts. These owe more to the Celtic than to the Roman missionary impulse, although of course ultimately the inspiration for Celtic monasticism lies in the Mediterranean. These manuscripts used to be thought of as purely Irish in character, but they are now more commonly described as Hiberno-Saxon, in recognition of the considerable part which the English craftsmen themselves contributed. The figural scenes in these manuscripts are clearly copied from classical models, with more or less success. It is in the interlaced 29 patterns of the initials and the 'carpet page' that the Hiberno-Saxon artist really came into his own. The intricate and convoluted patterns of animals and interlace which appear on these pages are very reminiscent of the earlier pagan craftsman's delight in complexity and tortuous animal design. When direct comparison is made between panels on one of the earliest and most famous manuscripts, the *Book of Durrow*, and some of the Sutton Hoo cloisonné

ornaments, they can be seen to belong to the same tradition. The skills which in the pagan period had been used for personal adornment were now being used for the glory of God instead.

The formation of the English state

When Bede wrote, England was divided into a number of petty kingdoms, sometimes known as the Heptarchy because of the seven most significant and long-lived of these: Kent, Sussex, Wessex, East Anglia, Mercia, Northumbria and Essex. These kingdoms themselves incorporated various smaller groupings, some of whose names are preserved in a document relating to Mercia known as the Tribal Hidage recently attributed to the years 670–690. This is probably an early tax register and it lists a number of peoples who had by the time of compilation been absorbed into the Mercian kingdom. Northumbria was also originally divided, into Deira and Bernicia, and 'Norfolk' and 'Suffolk' presumably preserve a division of East Anglia into north and south. Lindsey (approximately modern Lincolnshire), between Mercia and Northumbria, belonged to both the larger kingdoms in turn before being absorbed into Northumbria. First one and then another of the major kingdoms had ascendency and this may be reflected in the title 'Bretwalda' which Bede gives to various kings. These may have been in a sense overkings. The first one recorded is Ælle of Sussex, but the South Saxons do not otherwise play a very prominent role in history. Æthelbert of Kent and Rædwald of East Anglia, whose lives were partly contemporary, are both said to have been Bretwaldas, but it is not clear whether this means simultaneously or consecutively. According to Bede, the Northumbrian kings during most of the seventh century were the foremost, but Bede may have been biased in his sources, since he was writing in Northumbria, and Mercian records might well have been inclined to give more prominence to their king Penda. In the eighth century, Mercia clearly did become the leading kingdom under two strong kings, Æthelbald and Offa. Lesser kingdoms such as those of the Hwicce in the Severn valley and the Magonsaete in Herefordshire were first absorbed, and then it was the turn of major kingdoms such as Kent and East Anglia. Offa is remembered now for his creation of a visible boundary between England and Wales, Offa's Dyke. If he had had 21 successors of comparable stature, and if Mercia had not so rapidly succumbed to the Viking invasions, a unified English state might have developed with Mercia as its nucleus. As it was, it was the West Saxon kings, Alfred and his descendants, who won back England from the Danes in the east and the Norwegians in the north-west. It was Alfred who was first described as 'king over all the English'.

4
THE CELTIC CONTRIBUTION:PICTS, SCOTS, IRISH AND WELSH

JAMES GRAHAM-CAMPBELL

'*Because of its high mountains, deep valleys, and extensive forests,*
not to mention its rivers and marshes, Wales is not easy of access. The Britons who were
left alive took refuge in those parts when the Saxons
first occupied the island, and they have never been completely subdued
since, either by the English or the Normans.'

Gerald of Wales
The Description of Wales

About 1200

The north-western fringe of Europe – Ireland and most of Scotland – was never conquered by Rome and remained outside both the Roman Empire and the area of Germanic settlement, inhabited by its indigenous Celtic peoples. Although not immune to classical influences, they were politically and culturally somewhat isolated until the great flowering of the Christian Church in Ireland and north Britain, which began in the seventh century. Their history before that depends on sketchy and often hostile sources and is only now being gradually transformed through archaeological research.

Among these northern peoples, the Picts received some of the worst press from Roman historians, and are still the most obscure. Few sites have been excavated, or indeed identified. The romantic rock of Dunottar, Kincardineshire (*opposite*), is known to have been a Pictish stronghold (it is mentioned in the Irish *Annals* as having been besieged in 681) but the buildings on it now are much later. (1)

On previous page: openwork plaque showing
the Crucifixion, from Clonmacnoise. (1)

Patterns of settlement

Cashels are forts with dry-stone walling characteristic of western Ireland, though difficult to date. Originating in prehistory, they continued to be built during the Early Christian and Viking periods, enclosing the farmsteads of wealthy land holders. This one (*left*) is in Co. Clare. (2)

A Pictish fort with timber-laced walls once stood on the promontory of Burghead (*below*) in the Moray Firth. (3)

Raths and crannogs are two common forms of Irish defensive works. The first (*below left*), near Dungiven, Co. Derry, has earthen walls, the second (*below right*), in Lough Enagh, is a partly or totally artificial island. (4,5)

Along the length of western Britain Celtic settlements show how the earlier population maintained its position after the coming of the Saxons. Cadbury Castle (*above left*) was an Iron Age hill-fort refortified in the fifth or sixth century – by whom? Arthur has been seriously suggested.

Dumbarton Rock (*above right*) was a stronghold of the kings of Strathclyde; it was besieged and captured by the Vikings in 920. *Below*: Dunadd, citadel of the once-powerful kingdom of the Scots, Dalriada, dominates the Crinan Isthmus, in Argyll. (6,7,8)

Cross-currents

The remnant British after the Anglo-Saxon invasions still produced works that are characteristically Celtic rather than Germanic. Among their specialities were ornamented vessels known as hanging-bowls which were highly prized even by the Anglo-Saxons. *Right*: a mount from one of three such bowls in the Sutton Hoo ship burial. *Left*: a Pictish silver bowl from the St Ninian's Isle treasure, ornamented with animals like those on the reliquary shown below. (9,10)

In the Book of Durrow (*opposite*), written in the 670s, spiral motifs, stylized animals and curvilinear interlace – features from both Celtic and Anglo-Saxon art – are imaginatively united. (12)

The Monymusk reliquary (*below*) was made in Pictland in the eighth century, to hold relics of St Columba, with interlace and animal ornament inspired by Northumbrian art. (11)

Standing stones

An age-old tradition of erecting standing stones on graves or sacred sites can be traced in many parts of the world. In Celtic areas the continuity between prehistory and history is particularly clear. *Left*: three memorials with ogham inscriptions, the first from Church Island, Co. Kerry; the second, with bilingual (ogham and Latin) inscription, from South Wales; the third, also bilingual, from Ivybridge, Devon, commemorating three Irishmen. (13, 14, 15)

Pictish stones, many of them pre-Christian, carry a wealth of symbolic imagery but its meaning remains tantalizingly enigmatic. Are these designs the same as the tattoos with which the Picts are said to have decorated their bodies? Shown here (*left*) are a stone from Glamis, both sides; (*above*) one from Dunnichen and (*above right*) one from Nigg, now fully Christian and comparable to Irish crosses. (16–19)

Irish Christian stones range from the simplicity of that at Kilnasaggart (*left*), Co. Armagh, marking a burial ground given by 'Ternóc son of Ciarán the Little to St Peter', to the complexity of the North Cross at Ahenny (*above*), whose details and bosses seem to imitate metalwork. The scene on the base, though comparable to certain Pictish carvings, defies explanation. (20, 21)

Two masterworks

The Ardagh chalice consists of a silver bowl and foot linked by a gilt-bronze stem. Around the bowl runs a girdle of filigree-ornamented panels of the most exquisite workmanship. Underneath the foot (not visible in the large picture but shown *far left*), is a circle of similarly fine patterns whose details (a small section of its middle ring is illustrated next to it) repay almost endless enlargement. (22,23,24)

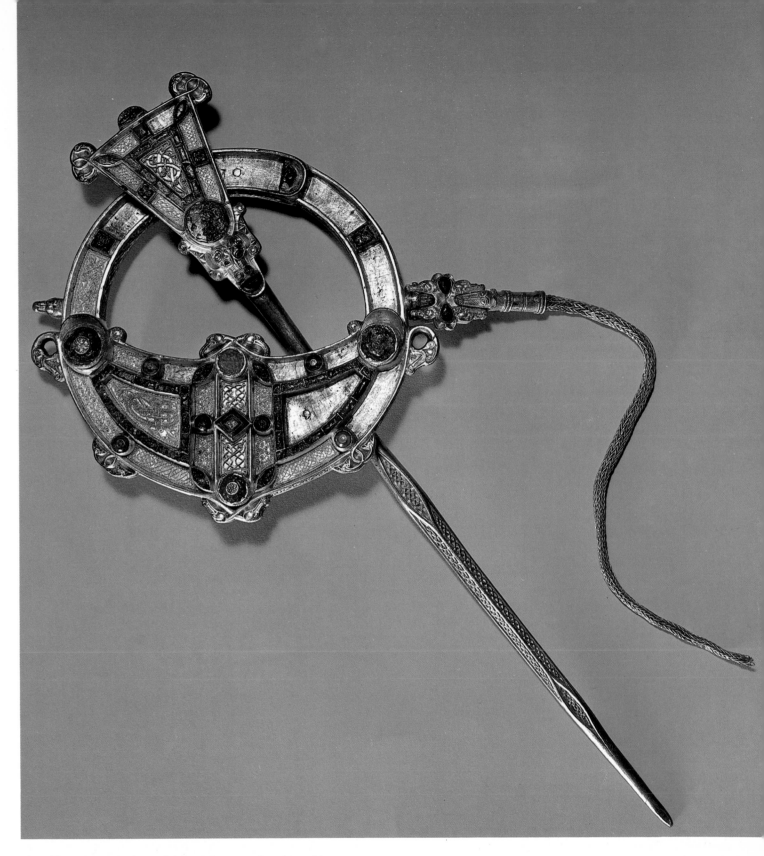

The 'Tara' brooch shows Irish craftsmen using the gold
filigree and other metalworking techniques of the Anglo-
Saxons and far surpassing them. It is of bronze with thin
gold overlay. The triangular top of the pin ends in an animal
head. The circular rim of the brooch frames numerous
panels filled with minute filigree work, with settings of glass
and amber. (25)

The human figure plays a relatively minor role in Celtic art, which excelled in abstract pattern. But where they occur, these faces often gaze at us with an expressive individuality.

Monasterboice, the Cross of Muiredach (*above*): in the centre of the cross-head is the Last Judgment, Christ holding a cross in one hand and a flowering bough, symbol of the resurrection, in the other, with the blessed on the left, the damned on the right. Above him is the meeting of St Paul and St Anthony, below, the weighing of souls. On the shaft are the Adoration of the Magi (with a mysterious fourth figure), and Moses striking the rock. (26)

From the Calf of Man, an island off the southern tip of the Isle of Man, comes a fragment of an altar (*left*) bearing a highly stylized crucifixion. (27)

Clonmacnoise, the Cross of the Scriptures (*right*): on the cross-head, the Crucifixion; on the shaft, the Arrest, the Flagellation and the Soldiers guarding Christ's tomb. (28)

The bronze bowl from which this mount comes was taken from Ireland by a raider and buried in a grave at Myklebostad, Norway. Irish metalwork was coveted and eagerly acquired by the Vikings. (29)

An abbot, from White Island, Lough Erne. (30)

St Matthew's symbol – a man – from the *Book of Durrow* (*right*) has a cloak made up of tiny squares rather like the body in pl. 29. (31)

Three soldiers from a Pictish gravestone found on Orkney carry long spears and square shields. (33)

A lady accompanied by trumpeters takes part in a hunt (*left*); the scene is as mysterious as most Pictish reliefs. It comes from Hilton of Cadboll, Ross-shire. (32)

108

The supreme achievement

In the manuscripts produced by their monastic *scriptoria* in the seventh and eighth centuries, Britain and Ireland created works that have never been surpassed in world art. During this period, Ireland, an outpost on the edge of civilization, assumed an important role in the spread of Christianity, sending missionaries and scholars to England and to what is now Germany and central Europe.

The Book of Kells may have been begun in Iona and taken unfinished to Kells in Ireland early in the ninth century, to escape the Viking raids. It is a large and splendid copy of the Gospels, with a wealth of ornament and illustration including several full-page pictures. St John (*left*) is portrayed sitting on a low chair holding a book in one hand and quill-pen in the other. Behind his head is a radiant nimbus and the whole page is framed with a series of rectangular panels filled with ornament that recalls contemporary metalwork. A curious detail is the figure who seems to be standing behind this frame, his feet and hands protruding at the edges but his head sliced off by nineteenth-century trimming. (34)

The MacDurnan Gospels (*right*) were produced later in the ninth century. The elements of the frame and the figure are comparable to those of *Kells*, but it is more crudely drawn, with a free-hand approach and less concern for detail. (35)

Strongholds of the Church

The early monks included both those who wanted the life of an active community and hermits who sought remote places. *Left*: Illauntannig, Co. Kerry, a monastic cashel with beehive cells and rectangular chapels. *Centre left*: the monastic enclosure of Moyne, Co. Mayo. *Below*: the remains of beehive huts on the rock of Skellig Michael, one of the remotest and best preserved of the early monastic settlements. (36,37,39)

St Ninian's cave, a few miles from Whithorn, is traditionally associated with the first Christian missionary to Scotland, in the fifth century; it was used as a burial place in the seventh and eighth centuries. (40)

At Clonmacnoise, Co. Offaly (*left*), most of the surviving buildings are medieval, but two outstanding crosses and two round towers are preserved from an earlier date. (38)

Glendalough, Co. Wicklow, retains one of the best-preserved early chapels, known as St Kevin's Kitchen, and a Viking Age round tower. (41)

Glastonbury Tor (*below*) was certainly occupied at an early date, probably though not certainly by monks. (42)

Tintagel, Cornwall (*above*), has been claimed as the earliest British monastery, but excavation has so far not been able to show whether the settlement was monastic. (43)

THE CELTIC CONTRIBUTION: PICTS, SCOTS, IRISH AND WELSH

'THE BARBARIANS push us to the sea, the sea pushes us to the barbarians: between the two kinds of death, we are either slain or drowned.' It was thus that the British leaders described their perilous situation in an appeal for assistance to the Roman commander in Gaul (or so it is recorded by the British monk, Gildas, writing a century later). This appeal, which must be placed in or soon after 446, was in vain, for no help was forthcoming; there followed further losses of land to the Anglo-Saxons. These were men who had come first not as invaders, but as allies paid to help fight off other barbarians – the Pictish, Scottish (Irish), and Saxon raiders who had plagued Britain for generations. Dissatisfied with their rewards, the Anglo-Saxon settlers, who had been joined by comrades and families, rose up in arms against their masters, with the result recorded on the Continent that Britain 'passed under the control of the Saxons'. This was not literally the case, for the north and west in particular had not then been conquered.

Gildas, in highly coloured language, described (or rather imagined, for he was writing of events well before his birth) what followed. It must be remembered that these real and imagined deeds of the Anglo-Saxons were doubly wicked to Gildas, for they were those of pagans against Christians:

Horrible it was to see the foundation stones of towers and high walls thrown down bottom upward in the squares, mixing with holy altars and fragments of human bodies, as though they were covered with a purple crust of clotted blood, as in some fantastic wine-press. There was no burial save in the ruins of the houses, or the bellies of the beasts and birds.

At the time Gildas was writing, in the mid-sixth century, Britain's Roman towns would have been largely 'squalid deserted ruins', but there is no evidence that they had been deliberately gutted by the Anglo-Saxons, as this passage would suggest. Those towns that fell early into Anglo-Saxon hands were simply neglected; those that remained for the while in British hands were gradually abandoned. But it is interesting that from both Silchester and Wroxeter are known late fifth-century memorials to men with Irish names; presumably they were leaders of bands raised for the defence of those cities from among the Irish settlers in western Britain who are described below.

The British checked the Anglo-Saxons in the later fifth century, in a campaign that led up to a major British victory at the siege of Mount Badon. We have no contemporary authority to help us locate Mount Badon, or even to tell us who led the triumphant British forces. As for its date, it took place in the year of Gildas's birth, that is around 500. In later sources it is the name of Arthur that is linked to this victory, 'a link too strong to be seriously questioned' in the words of Charles Thomas. Of a man around whom so much legend has accreted, it is perhaps surprising that virtually nothing demonstrably factual is known. One thing Arthur was not, however, was a king. In the ninth century, he was described as *dux bellorum*, 'Duke [or "leader"] of battles', who fought 'along with the kings of the Britons'. A war-leader then, of whom another was to write fourteen hundred years later: 'It is all true, or it ought to be; and more and better besides.' Would that we could tell.

Gildas writes of the (relative) peace that followed Badon and was enjoyed in his lifetime, but the Anglo-Saxon expansion westwards was inevitably to begin

---

◁ **Iona** keeps its character as a sacred site, though most traces of St Columba's sixth-century monastery have disappeared. But the two crosses of St John and St Martin, which still stand there, were probably erected shortly before the island was abandoned in the face of Viking raids in the early ninth century. That of St Martin, shown here, displays a number of Pictish motifs (e.g. the bosses with encircling serpents) but the shape of the cross as a whole is that used in Ireland. The church behind it is the restored medieval building. (44)

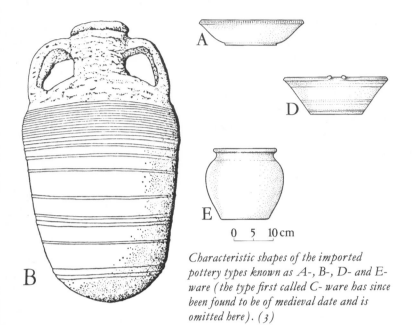

Characteristic shapes of the imported pottery types known as A-, B-, D- and E-ware (the type first called C- ware has since been found to be of medieval date and is omitted here). (3)

again. In 577 the Anglo-Saxons won a battle at Dyrham, capturing Gloucester, Cirencester and Bath, so dividing the Britons of Wales from those of the south-west (who retained their independence a while yet, as is traced below). The story of the north and north-west is also one that will be taken up, but suffice it to say of the Anglo-Saxon kingdom of Northumbria, that that part of it north of the Humber to about Hadrian's Wall (Deira) was among the earliest territory settled by the Anglo-Saxons, while its northern part (Bernicia) was only annexed during the second half of the sixth century.

The Anglo-Saxon settlement of southern, eastern and central Britain, during the fifth to seventh centuries, was thus a complex and long-drawn-out process of variable intensity. The native British population was neither exterminated, nor did it flee *en masse* into the Welsh mountains, but there remains a serious problem of recognizing remnant Britons in the archaeological record, for they did not practise burial with grave-goods, unlike the pagan Anglo-Saxons. It is thus in some Anglo-Saxon graves that a glimpse of British material culture in these areas is to be obtained.

The most important objects of British manufacture that have been found in such fifth- to seventh-century Anglo-Saxon graves are bronze bowls with ornamented mounts, known as hanging-bowls. The mounts, or escutcheons, are usually three in number and are topped with a hook for suspension. The finest escutcheons are ornamented with enamel (and occasionally inlaid with millefiori – multicoloured glass); the patterns consist of curvilinear motifs, arranged as spirals, triskeles and peltas. There were three such bowls in the seventh-
10 century Sutton Hoo ship burial, of which the largest is the finest known example of its kind. The origin of

these bowls lies in vessels made in Roman Britain in the fourth century and it is only reasonable to suppose that they continued to be made in post-Roman Britain, although the centres have not yet been recognized. The techniques required to produce the mounts of these bowls were initially unknown to the Anglo-Saxons, as were the patterns used on them, but were certainly used by post-Roman Britons, as has been demonstrated (for instance) by finds from the excavation of Dinas Powys in South Wales. Hanging-bowl manufacture had certainly spread to Scotland by the seventh century, for an escutcheon mould of that date has been excavated at Craig Phadrig, outside Inverness. In the late seventh and eighth centuries hanging-bowls were also being made in Ireland, probably for the first time, since the claim that the majority of earlier bowls was made there rests on the most circumstantial and inadequate evidence. The Irish bowls have a character of their own and do not turn up in Anglo-Saxon England, but they are found in ninth-century graves in Norway whither they were taken by Viking raiders. Meanwhile the Anglo-Saxons learnt to produce hanging-bowls themselves; one such bowl found its way to Shetland, to be 9 concealed with Pictish silver on St Ninian's Isle at the time of the first Viking attacks.

The fifth to ninth centuries in Britain span the period during which England was settled by the Anglo-Saxons (who are the subject of a separate chapter); the Welsh retained their independence, while the *Scotti* (the Scots from Ireland) first obtained a foothold in Scotland and eventually annexed the territory of the Picts, who dwelt north of the rivers Forth and Clyde. In the ninth century the Vikings established themselves gradually in northern and western Scotland, and also in Ireland (where their settlements were much more restricted); this story is taken up in Chapter 6. These five centuries are known in Ireland as the 'Early Christian period', and elsewhere as the 'early medieval' or 'early historic' period; 'post-Roman' is also a convenient chronological term for those areas that had up until 410 formed part of the Roman province of *Britannia*.

Much of the material culture from these centuries is very difficult to date. Coinage was not used and home produced pottery was extremely simple. In these circumstances, finds of broadly datable imported pottery have assumed overriding importance.

In the fifth and sixth centuries two classes of pottery 3 produced in the eastern and southern Mediterranean were reaching Britain by western seaways. The first class (known as A-ware) consists of red bowls and dishes – tableware in the late Roman tradition – and the second of amphorae (B-ware), large storage jars presumably imported for their contents, which would most probably have been wine, or oil. Of the same date, but seemingly from southern and western France, are grey bowls, including kitchen mortars (D-ware). Most widespread in Britain and Ireland is E-ware, a good quality kitchenware – pots, pitchers, and beakers – also from France (probably Aquitaine); it is of uncertain date-range, but was in circulation in the sixth and, more particularly, the seventh centuries.

A- and B-wares are found mainly (but not exclusively) on aristocratic secular and major ecclesiastical settlements, suggesting that they were expensive commodities. The Mediterranean contacts indicated by this pottery have been seen by Charles Thomas as instrumental in the introduction and spread of monasticism in Britain and Ireland. Atlantic coastal contacts with western France, witnessed by D- and E-wares, are less remarkable and seem also to have involved a limited trade in wine; the growth of these contacts may have some connection with the activities of Irish monks on the Continent from the sixth century. E-ware is the most common of these four classes of imported pottery on insular sites, being found on settlements of very variable social status, and over a wider geographical area, having penetrated well inland in Ireland and Scotland, unlike A, B, and D, which are essentially coastal in their distribution.

Ireland: beyond the Roman Empire

The Roman legions never invaded Ireland, but Ireland was not untouched by Roman influence. Gallo-Roman and Romano-British merchants seem to have travelled to Ireland, if only occasionally. The *Scotti* (as the inhabitants of Ireland at the time were known in Britain) raided the adjacent coasts of the Empire for loot and slaves. As a result of such activities a considerable quantity of Roman material has been found in Ireland ranging from potsherds and coins, through fine metalwork, to the great silver hoards from Balline in Co. Limerick, and Coleraine, Co. Derry. These last are treasures consisting of chopped-up Roman plate and bullion, including officially stamped ingots, which suggests that they may be payments or bribes made by the Romans to maintain good relations and purchase relief from raiding. The best-known result of a raid on western Britain by curragh-borne Irishmen was the abduction, as a young man, of the future St Patrick, carried off to be a slave in the north of Ireland.

The impact on Irish life and culture of these varied contacts with the Roman world was considerable, but in practice it is difficult to disentangle its various strands from those of the immediate post-Roman centuries, when new contacts were established, as a result of Irish settlements in Britain and the arrival of missionaries in Ireland. Influences on objects can be seen in tools and weapons, and in the introduction of new types of household objects, such as barrel padlocks and keys. New personal goods also appear, including toilet implements, but most notably new types of dress-fastener, among which were early forms of the penannular brooch, a type that was to be greatly elaborated by Irish craftsmen. Influences on art can also be traced, such as the integration of 'marigold' motifs into the traditional repertoire of curvilinear patterns composed of scrolls and spirals.

The origins of the Irish ogham alphabet are still p.10(*1,2*) uncertain, but it could have developed only as a result of contacts with the literate Roman world. It uses not letters but groups of short and long strokes, touching or crossing a median line which is usually the edge of the stone or object on which the inscription is cut. The earliest surviving examples of ogham script are on rough memorial stones in southern Ireland, inscribed 13 with the name of the man commemorated and generally some details of his descent, if only his father's name. These earliest memorials are probably pagan, but the majority of the stones will be Christian, some of the later examples being ornamented with simple crosses.

Ireland's greatest debt to the Roman Empire was Christianity, for the initial missions (during the first half of the fifth century) were the work of men of Roman background such as Patrick, and before him Palladius who arrived in Ireland in 431. They were representatives of the Roman Church, Palladius being a Gallo-Roman bishop sent by the Pope to those Irish 'believing in Christ'. The archaeology of the Patrician Church in Ireland is for the most part nonexistent, but the Church established during the sixth century – the period during which 'the battle for people's minds' was fought – was organized on regular late Roman lines. A bishop held authority over a diocese which probably consisted of a petty kingdom, but there was one inevitable modification so far as Ireland was concerned – his seat could not be based on a town, as was the general practice, since Ireland was without urban centres of any kind. But during the sixth century monasticism spread throughout Ireland and before long the organization of the Irish Church had taken on a distinctive character of its own, based on the larger monasteries and their territorial spheres, with bishops losing their administrative functions.

A strong ascetic element was present in Irish monasticism from the beginning, based on that of some of the early fathers who lived far from civilization in the desert; so that in remote and practically inaccessible places we find not only provision for solitary hermits, but also small monasteries with two or three cells that might be better termed 'communal hermitages'. The quest for isolation and the requirements of penance drove Irish monks further afield than the rocky islets off their own coasts, to those of western Scotland, the Northern Isles, and even the Faroes and Iceland where they were the first settlers, to be discovered by the Vikings in the ninth century. It is just possible, as Timothy Severin has recently demonstrated, that St Brendan or some other could have reached America in

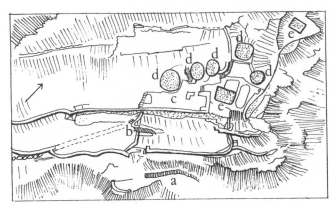

Plan of the monastic settlement on the island of Skellig Michael, off the west coast of Ireland. On every side steep cliffs drop down to the sea: a, steps to sea; b, entrance; c, main enclosure; d, cells; e, oratory. (4)

the type of leather boat that was then available to them for their voyages.

A 'communal hermitage' would possess, within an enclosure, one or even two small rectangular oratories in addition to the living-cells, and a graveyard (perhaps still marked today by the survival of incised memorial slabs). In Ireland, such sites are known mainly in the west where their occupants built in dry stone. Most spectacular of all in its situation and its completeness is 4 *Sceilg Mhicíl*, perched high up on a ledge of the Great 39 Skellig rock, eight miles out in the Atlantic off the south-west of Ireland. It was remote, yet not sufficiently so to have escaped the attention of some early ninth-century Viking raiders.

Sceilg Mhicíl (or Skellig Michael) retains six cells and two oratories with fine roofs of corbelled stone. Of easier access is the little intact oratory of Gallarus on the Dingle peninsula. This has the characteristic rectangular plan, with 3:2 internal proportions; all four walls curve inwards, with the door in the western end and a solitary window at the east. The date of such a simple, if perfect, building is inevitably uncertain and it has been suggested that it may well date to the centuries immediately after our period.

Similar sites and buildings of wood must have existed elsewhere in Ireland. Bede writes that it was the Irish manner to build churches 'not in stone, but of hewn oak thatched with reeds' and an unknown Irish monk in the tenth century, writing of the pleasures of his hermit's hut, says:

...I have a hut in the wood, none knows it but my Lord; an ash tree this side, a hazel on the other, a great tree on a mound encloses it.

Such timber and wattle structures have left no trace above ground. Easier to locate, most clearly from the air, are larger monasteries with their dry-stone or earthen enclosures, such as Moyne, Co. Mayo.

Important foundations like Clonmacnoise, Co. 38 Offaly, founded beside the Shannon in 544, Glendalough in the Wicklow mountains (another sixth- 41 century foundation), and Armagh, where St Patrick established his principal church, developed into monastic 'cities', with populations running into hundreds and thousands, both ecclesiastical and lay, renowned as centres of learning and craftsmanship. Of these only Armagh survived to develop into a modern city, but the cluster of remains at Clonmacnoise (finally reduced to ruins by the English garrison from Athlone in 1552) and those at Glendalough, strung out along its beautiful 'valley of the two lakes', still give some impression of the past size and glory of these great centres of holiness and scholarship.

It is not surprising that they were prime targets for Viking raiders, with large populations to be culled for hostages and slaves, and concentrations of wealth to be carried off, whether in the form of precious objects or more simply as food and drink to supply their forces. The monks had to look to their defences and their enclosures were strengthened. One particular response to this continued threat (in the tenth to twelfth centuries) was the construction of the remarkable stone towers that still remain such a distinctive feature of the Irish landscape. These were certainly used as bell-towers (for hand-bells to be struck from), but their defensive role is obvious from their raised doors and few small windows, except for the standard feature of four larger ones at the top.

Another aspect of the stonemason's craft that survives to us from this troubled period are the High Crosses, those of the ninth and tenth centuries being arguably Ireland's most striking and original contribution to the art of western Europe in the early medieval period. The Irish interest in raising stone monuments may be traced back to the originally pagan ogham stones, whether as pillars or slabs, or as 13 recumbent memorials. Some of the later examples, to be dated to the seventh century, have slightly more elaborate ornament than the simple crosses first adopted in the sixth century, consisting of curvilinear motifs paralleled in the major initials in the *Cathac of St* p.11(5) *Columba* – a psalter traditionally held to be in the hand of St Columba himself, but more probably of early seventh-century date. Human figures make their first, rather tentative appearance in Irish art at this time; a small figure of an ecclesiastic holding his staff on a slab at Ballyvourney, Co. Cork, recalls the treatment of the St Matthew man-symbol in the seventh-century *Book of* 31 *Durrow*.

The free-standing cross does not emerge until the eighth century and the earliest examples of Irish High Crosses appear to be the two at Ahenny, Co. Tipperary. 21 These are derived from wooden prototypes covered in ornamental metalwork, as may have been processional

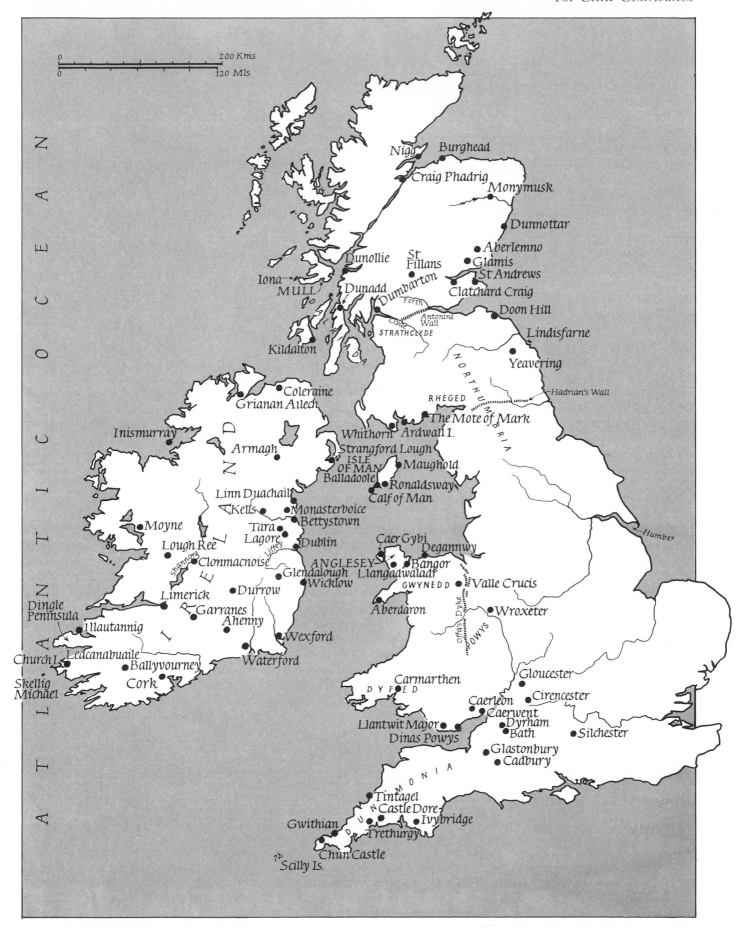

crosses. At Ahenny, the transfer of metalworkers' techniques to stone is seen clearly in the shallowness of the carving and in various details, such as the bosses that imitate metal rivet-heads. The abstract ornament on the shaft and head is that of the metalworker's repertoire.

Development and enrichment of the High Crosses took place during the eighth and ninth centuries with the addition of figure sculpture and scriptural scenes. The so-called Scripture Crosses of the tenth century represent the culmination of this line of development, being (as M. and L. de Paor have written) 'architectural in proportion and composition, with an orderly and systematic iconographic sculptural scheme that is, essentially, a premature manifestation of Romanesque art'. The traveller from Dublin need go no further than Monasterboice, Co. Louth, to find the finest monument of this art. It has a Crucifixion on the east face of its head and the Last Judgment on the west, the panels on the shaft containing scenes from the New Testament below the former, and from the Old Testament below the latter; the whole is topped-off with a carving of a gabled building, having a roof of shingles, recalling the painting of 'The Temple' in the *Book of Kells*. Among the church ruins and round towers of Clonmacnoise can be seen both transitional and fully developed Scripture Crosses, but also impressive are the remains of more than five hundred grave-slabs, many of which are now wall-mounted on the site to form a remarkable *lapidarium*.

Objects of fine metalwork from Clonmacnoise include an openwork Crucifixion plaque and a richly ornamented crozier-head of later Viking Age date. These serve to remind us of the important role played by the monasteries as centres of artistic patronage, where craftsmen were trained and supported, whether as sculptors, scribes and painters, or metalworkers – not to forget their contribution to the literary arts: the nature poetry of Early Christian Ireland has a freshness without parallel in medieval European literature. The most important surviving objects of ecclesiastical metalwork are, however, either chance finds from the countryside, like the Ardagh chalice, which formed part of a hoard concealed in a Co. Limerick ring-fort, or objects that were never buried, being passed down through the ages, often by hereditary keepers charged with the responsibility of their guardianship and maintenance.

Dotted in their thousands across Ireland are the simple circular enclosures, known as 'ring-forts', that contained the farmsteads of the wealthy land-holders of the Early Christian and Viking periods, although some are of earlier date for the settlement-type is one that developed in Irish prehistory. In the west, ring-forts have dry-stone walls and are generally known as 'cashels' or 'cahers', and the remains of structures may

Plan of the stone fort at Leacanabuaile, Co. Kerry. The rampart is ascended at certain points by steps (a). The houses (B) vary in shape and there are two wall chambers (C) reached by passages. (5)

still be visible within, as at Leacanabuaile, Co. Kerry. Elsewhere they have an earthen bank with external ditch and can be known as 'raths'; the buildings within would have been of timber. Not only the wealthy farmer, but also royalty occupied such sites which can vary considerably in size and in the elaborateness of their defences. Double or even triple ramparted ring-forts are known, the largest presumably serving as tribal centres, such as that at Garranes, Co. Cork, in use from the late fifth to the seventh century, but not permanently inhabited.

Ring-forts were largely self-sufficient units based on a mixed agricultural economy in which pastoralism was the dominating element; wealth was measured in cows, and cattle-raiding 'was so common a form of warfare that it must be regarded as no more than a violent and bloody sport' (M. and L. de Paor). Their occupants would have been capable, for the most part, of meeting their own requirements for iron tools, and often for fine metalwork. Otherwise travelling smiths, or the markets at the greater monasteries, would have supplied people's needs. On the other hand, the potter's craft was unknown in Ireland, except in the north-east and even there it cannot be said to have been highly developed.

Closely related to the raths and cashels are 'crannogs', artificial islands situated in lakes or marshy areas and often connected to dry land by a narrow causeway. These too are simple, defended homesteads, occupied by even the highest levels of society. The crannog of Lagore, Co. Meath, is known to have been a royal seat and excavation produced evidence of wealthy occupants patronizing skilled craftsmen, particularly ornamental metalworkers.

The great traditional royal centres of Ireland, such as Tara in Co. Meath, were no more than grassy mounds during these Christian centuries, resorted to for ceremonial purposes. The same might be true of the great stone forts of the west, although these would have retained their defensive function. The fine fort at Grianán Ailech, Co. Donegal, is known to have been a royal seat, destroyed only in 1101. At the opposite end of the social scale one must remember the simple huts and homesteads of herdsmen and coastal dwellers that, for the most part, have escaped recognition.

An artistic flowering: manuscripts and metalwork

The development of Irish art in the fifth to seventh centuries is hard to trace; its surviving examples are for the most part undistinguished, but there are enough simple objects such as dress-fasteners – be they penannular brooches, so-called 'hand-pins', or 'latchets' – and finds of metalworkers' debris (as at Garranes and Lagore) to demonstrate their abilities in bronze-casting, in enamelling, and in the use of multi-coloured glass inlays (millefiori). The patterns are traditional ones drawn ultimately from the spiral and other curvilinear motifs of the late Iron Age art of the Celtic-speaking world, with a few Roman-inspired modifications.

The monasteries, once firmly established and with royal support, required many new types of objects for ecclesiastical use, from display manuscripts to pocket-books, from chalices to croziers, and from crosses to reliquaries, all of which should be elaborately ornamented to the glory of God. There existed therefore new patronage and new requirements on an unprecedented scale. To meet these new and testing demands Irish craftsmen looked around for new ideas and found them in Anglo-Saxon art. The missionary work of Irish monks in England during the seventh century introduced them to cloisonné jewellery and Style II p.77(17) animal-ornamented metalwork, such as that found in the Sutton Hoo ship burial (Anglo-Saxon metalwork of this period does not seem to have found its way to Ireland). In particular, the establishment by Aidan, from the Scottish monastery of Iona, of a foundation on Lindisfarne in the kingdom of Northumbria, brought into being a great Church community linking northern England to western Scotland and Ireland. The free movement of monks led not only to the free exchange of religious objects (particularly books), but also to the actual movement of craftsmen, whether ecclesiastical or lay.

The result was the birth of a new art style in late seventh-century Northumbria. In it can be recognized the contributions of both the Irish and the Anglo-Saxon artistic traditions, mingled with new models introduced by the Roman Church from the Mediterranean. This style, often known as the Hiberno-Saxon style, reached full development with the p.80(29) *Lindisfarne Gospels* of *c.* 700. But the blending of Celtic

and Anglo-Saxon traditions is already visible in the earliest surviving Insular manuscript with full-page illuminations – the *Book of Durrow* from the 670s, which 12 displays a mixture of spiral motifs, stylized animals, rectilinear geometric patterns, and curvilinear interlace. The conception and the script of the *Book of Durrow* owe everything to the Irish foundation in which this manuscript was written and illuminated. This was probably Lindisfarne itself, for it must have been a centre fully exposed to the Anglo-Saxon metalworkers' achievements of the seventh century, a situation that is unlikely to have arisen in Ireland.

Subsequent development of the Hiberno-Saxon style was rapid and can be seen to perfection in the technically brilliant *Lindisfarne Gospels*, or the less well-preserved *Gospels of St Chad* (now at Lichfield). No seventh- or eighth-century manuscript of definite Irish provenance can match this exceptional virtuosity, but this is most probably one of those accidents of survival. On the other hand two or three exceptional pieces of metalwork, ornamented in the fully developed Hiberno-Saxon style, are preserved in Ireland and are clearly of Irish manufacture.

The impact of the Hiberno-Saxon style in Ireland is thus most clearly seen in metalwork. Such important new techniques as gold filigree work, and chip-carving, were borrowed from the Anglo-Saxons and employed with great skill, or even refined to yet higher degrees of excellence. No Anglo-Saxon filigree can match the fineness and control of that on the terminals of the so-called 'Tara' brooch (not from Tara at all, but found on 25 the shore at Bettystown, Co. Meath). The traditional enamel and millefiori designs are converted into rectilinear compartmentalized patterns derived from those of Anglo-Saxon cloisonné jewellery. This development can readily be appreciated by comparing the treatment of the escutcheons of the earlier British hanging-bowls with those made in eighth-century Ireland. Enamel is also seen used in this new way on the handles of the Ardagh chalice.

The Ardagh chalice was found, together with a 23–24 simple bronze chalice and a number of ninth-century brooches, by a boy digging potatoes in a ring-fort where they must have been deliberately concealed. The ornamented chalice consists of a silver bowl and foot, linked by a gilt-bronze stem covered in chip-carved ornament. A girdle around the bowl has a series of gold filigree-ornamented panels, containing interlaced animals or plain interlace, separated by elaborate glass and enamel bosses containing silver grids – a hallmark of Irish craftsmanship in the late seventh and eighth centuries; particularly fine examples are also to be seen on the handles. Beneath the girdle are outlined the names of the Apostles, in the elegant display script used in the *Lindisfarne Gospels*. The foot of the chalice is ornamented both above and below with a remarkable range of techniques; here we find the traditional curvilinear patterns employed within the overall decorative scheme – not abandoned, but relegated to a subsidiary role (as on the 'Tara' brooch where they occur only on the reverse).

Such masterpieces of the jeweller's art inevitably fascinated the Vikings, who treasured some of the pieces
29 that they acquired, by whatever means. It is the Vikings who have been held responsible for putting an end to these exceptional Irish skills, but there is no adequate evidence that objects of such quality were still being produced as late as the mid-ninth century, when the full effects of the Viking attacks were first felt. Such exceptional standards could not have been maintained indefinitely; it was an art that had early reached a peak of intricacy that left it no further scope for refinement. One outcome can be seen in the charming naïvety of MacRegol of Birr's elaborate gospel-book, from the first half of the ninth century. In metalwork repetition and banality seem to have set in before the Vikings arrived. In a curious way they may have provided a new stimulus to the Irish metalworker, for, as a result of their various activities, there were large quantities of silver available for the first time in Ireland.

The result was that during the ninth century a simpler style emerged, making full use of the brightness of plain silver, and eschewing the polychrome approach and surface fussiness of the degenerate Hiberno-Saxon style, elements of which nevertheless continued into the tenth century. The subsequent development of Irish art, injected once again with vitality in the eleventh and twelfth centuries, by an infusion of Scandinavian taste, is beyond the scope of this chapter.

Dalriada, kingdom of the Scots

Recorded tradition has it that, in the fifth century, the three sons of Erc – Fergus, Loarn and Angus – sailed with 150 men from *Dál Riata*, a district of Co. Antrim in the north of Ireland, to invade the west of Scotland. Whatever the exact truth of the story, a limited migration of *Scotti* certainly took place and an Irish-speaking kingdom of Dalriada was established along the coast of Argyll and its islands. Their principal
8 stronghold was Dunadd, a rocky citadel dominating the Crinan isthmus; it was dug over early in this century when few objects that might be thought of as characteristically Irish were found. In particular there was none of the northern Irish pottery that has been mentioned above; indeed the only pottery found
3 consisted of imported D- and E-wares. On the other hand there was plenty of material to demonstrate that Dunadd was occupied during the fifth to ninth centuries, including weapons, tools, ornaments and metalworkers' debris.

Columcille, or St Columba, came to Dalriada with his companions in 563 to serve their faith, and that of their

The Picts were described by Roman writers as painting their bodies ('Picti' = painted men), probably a reference to tattooing. In the seventeenth century the artist John White produced this inventive but completely fanciful idea of how a Pictish warrior might have looked. (6)

fellow *Scotti*, by establishing a monastery on Iona, the small island off the south-western tip of Mull. Other Irish monks established monasteries further up the west coast and in the Northern Isles that in turn served as stepping-stones on the Atlantic voyages of their fellows. Important evangelical work was undertaken from Iona among the Picts, and it was from Iona that 44 Aidan went in 634–5 to establish the monastery at Lindisfarne (also a small island, off the Northumbrian coast) following the return to power of the Anglo-Saxon prince, Oswald, who had been in exile among the Dalriadic Scots. Both in turn were to fall victim to attacks by the Vikings, and in the early ninth century the majority of the monks from Iona withdrew to Kells in Ireland, while others went east to Dunkeld.

Little is known of St Columba's monastery on Iona, although it has been suggested that the stone foundations of a hut on the rock outcrop of Torr Abb, in front of the present Abbey, are those of St Columba's own. The most imposing relics of the early community must date from shortly before its virtual abandonment under the pressure of repeated Viking raids; there are the great free-standing crosses named after St Martin 44 and St John. They have a distinctive character, being quite different in form from the Pictish slabs to be considered below, but the influence of Pictish art is to be seen in their use of large ornamental bosses with encircling serpents. In Scotland such free-standing crosses are rare even in Dalriada, but that at Kildalton, on Islay, is particularly well preserved.

34   The finest example of Hiberno-Saxon art influenced by that of Pictland is the *Book of Kells* – a great display manuscript, written and illuminated in the tradition of the *Book of Durrow* and the *Lindisfarne Gospels*. It has been widely accepted that this magnificent (but unfinished) gospel-book was produced on Iona at the beginning of the ninth century, whence it was taken to Kells at the time of the Viking attacks. Recently Professor Brown has argued that its true date is some decades earlier and that an alternative centre for its production should be sought in eastern Pictland.

In the mid-ninth century Kenneth mac Alpin, king of the Scots, made a move eastwards and established himself in the heart of southern Pictland, at a time when both his own kingdom of Dalriada and the far north of Pictland were losing land to Viking invaders. Kenneth's annexation of Pictland – the details of which are not known – was of lasting importance; it was then that Irish speech became spread across Scotland (developing into Scots Gaelic) and thus the *Scotti* came to give their name to the modern kingdom.

'The Painted Men'

Picti is the term used in Roman writings to refer to the inhabitants north of the Antonine Wall, that is north of a line between the Forth and Clyde estuaries. *Picti* presumably means 'the painted men', referring to the daubing or tattooing of their bodies, and as such is no more than a nickname. The classical writers who tell of the Picts' tradition of tattooing their bodies had their stories very much at second-hand and they cannot be verified. It is most improbable that a Pict looked anything like such a remarkable figure as that conceived 6 by John White, in the late sixteenth century, on the basis of these reports. The fact that we do not know what the Picts called themselves is but one of the many obscurities that still surround them. What is beyond doubt, however, is the severity of the threat that sea-borne Pictish raiders (as well as *Scotti* and *Saxones*) posed to late Roman and post-Roman Britain. It was against them that the defences of Yorkshire had to be secured.

The military aspects of Pictish society have led to one of several breakthroughs in Pictish studies in recent years, in this case as a result of the archaeological investigation of some of their heavily defended strongholds. Excavations of prehistoric forts at Clatchard Craig in Fife and at Craig Phadrig, near 3 Inverness, have produced E-ware among other finds of interest (including the mould for a hanging-bowl escutcheon from the latter site), demonstrating their re-use in the Pictish period. Two of the principal strongholds in Pictland, that at Dundurn, near St

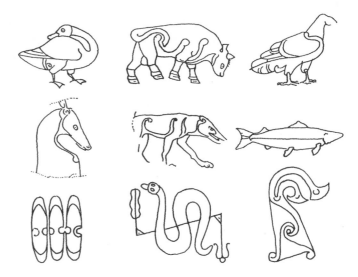

A selection of symbols taken from Pictish stones. Their significance is still largely a mystery. (7)

Fillans, guarding its western approaches from Dalriada, and the promontory fort of Burghead, on the southern 3 shore of the Moray Firth, are now known to have been constructed (and destroyed) within the historical Pictish period, both having great stone ramparts, reinforced by nailed timbers. At Burghead, a large number of stones incised with bull-symbols was found in the nineteenth century, but few survive today.

Such symbol-stones for long formed the only major body of diagnostic Pictish artifacts. They originated in a pagan context, but not necessarily any earlier than the seventh century, and consist of boulders and rough slabs incised with a range of symbols, uniformly 7 stylized throughout Pictland. These symbols include both animals (like the Burghead bulls, but also others such as boars, as well as birds and fish) and a range of abstract symbols among which can be recognized stylized depictions of everyday objects, such as combs and mirrors. The incised symbols generally occur in groups of two to four on what are presumably memorial stones (designated Class I), although their actual significance is a matter of considerable uncertainty and dispute.

Even if pagan in origin, Pictish symbols proved adaptable for use in Christian contexts because Pictish cross-slabs (Class II), which are carved in relief, also made use of them, but generally relegated them to the reverse. In addition there appeared figural scenes, both biblical and secular, and a menagerie of mythical beasts; good examples are to be found on the stone in Aberlemno churchyard, or on the front of that in the garden of the Manse at Glamis (on the other side of 16,17 which are earlier Class I incised symbols). The cross itself dominates the front of the slab and is ornamented with interlace patterns.

Parallels can be drawn between the art of some of the Pictish stones, such as that from Ardross (above), and Insular manuscripts like the 'Book of Kells' (above right). (8)

Apart from the evidence of Christianity offered by the Class II cross-slabs, little is known of the early Pictish Church. Pictland was evangelized from the west, but King Nechtan, at the beginning of the eighth century, turned to Northumbria and the Anglo-Saxon Church for guidance and practical assistance. As a result we find Northumbrian elements entering Pictish art and it is in this context that the *Book of Kells* might have been conceived and executed in Pictland. The Anglo-Saxon version of the 'inhabited' vine-scroll – a running tendril in which beasts lurk and birds perch – appears 32 on such Class II stones as that from Hilton of Cadboll, Easter Ross. Interlaced animals with elegantly coiled hindquarters, such as on the Aberlemno churchyard stone, are also of Anglo-Saxon inpsiration.

The latest Pictish sculpture, before the Scottish takeover, sprouted the bosses with encircling serpents, already noted as appearing on the Iona crosses. They 19 are seen to perfection on the great Nigg slab, or in rather a different context on the ends of an impressive free-standing tomb-shrine at St Andrews. As the ninth century progressed, the use of Pictish symbols faded away.

The use of symbols had not been confined to stone monuments, for they are also found on metalwork, including a number of fine silver ornaments, sometimes inlaid with red enamel, such as a pair of plaques and a 'hand-pin' from a seventh-century hoard found at Norries Law, Fife, and the terminal rings for massive silver neck chains. In fashion among the Picts in the eighth century was a distinctive type of penannular brooch, quite different from those of the 'Tara-type' then in vogue in Ireland. Twelve such brooches formed part of the remarkable St Ninian's Isle hoard.

The St Ninian's Isle hoard was concealed in a wooden box beneath the floor of a small chapel on the tidal island of that name, off the south-western tip of Shetland. It consisted of twenty-eight silver objects and

(inexplicably) part of the jawbone of a porpoise, hidden around AD 800 – no doubt from Viking raiders. Apart from the brooches, the other main group of objects in the hoard consisted of eight bowls of which one was an imported Northumbrian hanging-bowl. The other 9 bowls have been shown by David Wilson to be of Pictish manufacture and two of them are ornamented with friezes of animals whose close relations are to be 8 found on such Pictish Class II slabs as that at Aberlemno, and who share details with those in the *Book of Kells*. In Pictish metalwork their immediate ancestors are to be seen on the front of the so-called *Brechennoch of St Columba*, or Monymusk reliquary, a 11 small house-shaped shrine carved from wood and encased in metal, with enamelled hinge-mounts for a carrying-strap.

Recent excavations on Orkney mainland and in the Hebrides, on North Uist, have thrown some light on the nature and economy of native settlements in these outlying Pictish areas. Settlements at Buckquoy, Orkney, and at the Udal, North Uist, were both taken over by the Vikings in the ninth century and elements of continuity in the material remains found on these sites suggest enslavement of the native population – those, that is, who had not fled or been killed. That the Norse takeover in these areas was far from peaceful is suggested in the Northern Isles by the total obliteration of native place-names, and in North Uist by the construction of a small defensive enclosure at the Udal at that critical moment in the site's history.

North Britons

The British kingdoms that grew up south of the Forth and Clyde in the post-Roman period fell to the Anglo-Saxons of Northumbria in or before the seventh century, with the exception of Strathclyde. Little enough is known of the archaeology of the fifth and sixth centuries in the Lothians and the Borders, but this remained the territory of the *Votadini*, the Roman client-kingdom to the north of Hadrian's Wall in eastern Britain. On Doon Hill, above Dunbar, Brian Hope-Taylor has excavated a native timber hall, set within an enclosure, that was destroyed in the seventh century, perhaps during the Anglian advance for it was replaced by a second timber hall, but of the type then being built at the Anglo-Saxon royal site at Yeavering in Northumberland.

p.88(4)

In south-west Scotland the native kingdoms that emerged during the fifth century were (as in Wales and south-west England) based on the earlier tribal groupings of the Iron Age. The *Damnonii* formed the basis for the kingdom of Strathclyde, among whose earlier kings was Coroticus, or Ceretic, who was admonished by St Patrick for slave-raiding among his Irish converts. Although centred on the Ayr valley, Strathclyde had its major stronghold on its northern frontier at Alcluith, now Dumbarton Rock. Excavations directed by Leslie Alcock revealed traces of a timber-reinforced rampart which had been deliberately destroyed, probably by the Viking force that successfully besieged this citadel in 920. The inhabitants had enjoyed the contents of Mediterranean amphorae (B-ware) and made use of the Class E kitchen-ware; fragments of Merovingian glass were also found and would have been used by jewellers to make beads and inlays for metalwork.

7

3

The other major kingdom of south-western Scotland was Rheged; its boundaries are uncertain, but it stretched across Dumfries and Galloway, with its centre at Carlisle. The Mote of Mark, near Dalbeattie, is one of three major forts within this kingdom that have been archaeologically investigated and shown to have post-Roman occupation, but was itself actually constructed in the sixth century, remaining in use well into the seventh. Much fine metalwork was produced there and the many fragments of clay moulds include some with interlace patterns borrowed from the Anglo-Saxons, who annexed Rheged in the 630s.

A small number of British tombstones of fifth- and sixth-century date, but in the Roman tradition with Latin inscriptions and simple crosses or Chi-Rho monograms, are scattered across southern Scotland and northern England. One such stone at Whithorn, near Wigtown, raised by Barrovadus to Latinus and his young daughter, dates to the fifth century and was found in the cemetery around a small stone oratory which had walls with traces of white plaster. This just might be the *Candida Casa*, the 'White House' (*hwít aern* in Northumbrian English), that gave its name to Whithorn; the chapel was said by tradition to have been built by St Ninian, who went there as a bishop some time in the early fifth century. Eastwards along the coast, at Ardwall Island, Charles Thomas has excavated part of a small sixth- to eighth-century monastic settlement with similarities to those of Ireland.

The separation of the northern British kingdoms from those of Wales must date to the early part of the seventh century, for King Edwin of Northumbria had established his authority west of the Pennines before the 630s when he was able to launch successful attacks on both Anglesey and Man. But there is very little evidence for an Anglo-Saxon presence in Cumbria and Lancashire, which seem to have remained predominantly British until Norse settlement commenced around 900.

Isle of Man

The Isle of Man, like Ireland, escaped the rule both of the Romans and of the Anglo-Saxons, for Edwin's subjugation of the island can have led to no more than a levying of tribute. In fact it was with Ireland that Man had its closest links during the centuries that concern us, and Irish settlement must have taken place (probably in the fifth century), for the Manx language is descended from Irish that had gradually replaced the native British speech. Some of this story can be traced in the Manx series of Early Christian memorial stones, among which are some commemorating men with British names, whereas the use of ogham is also known. A particularly fine, but fragmentary, altar-frontal from the Calf of Man demonstrates the continuing Irish connection, for its depiction of the Crucifixion is closely comparable to eighth-century Irish versions in metalwork. But a cross-slab at Maughold, bearing the words 'CRUX GURIAT', tells another story, for the man in whose memory it was raised may perhaps be identified with the British-named Gwriad, father of a north Welsh king, Merfyn Frych, who acceded in 825. Such monuments also indicate that sculpture was well established in Man at the time of the first Norse settlements in the ninth century, a tradition that formed one basis for the fine series of tenth-century Viking crosses found on Man.

27

Some of the pagan Viking settlers made use of existing Manx Christian cemeteries, such as Balladoole and Balladoyne, for the burial of their dead. Following their conversion, they seem to have taken over the native church organization, making use of the *keeills* – simple early chapels with their surrounding cemeteries. Little enough is known of the settlement-sites of the first Vikings in Man, but even less of those of the pre-Norse centuries. One such has been excavated at Ronaldsway airport, and now Peter Gelling is uncovering, at Port y Candas, the remains of a defended site, of sixth- to eighth-century date, whose occupants possessed E-ware.

Wales and the Irish

The archaeological evidence from post-Roman Wales is extremely limited, apart from a large group of Early Christian memorial stones and a handful of excavated settlements. Roman control and influence had been strongest in the south, with towns established at Caerwent and Carmarthen, but elsewhere the Roman presence had been military in nature. Irish raiding had necessitated extra forts being added to the protective chain in the late Roman period, such as at Caer Gybi on Anglesey, and at Cardiff.

Actual Irish settlement in Wales may have begun during the fourth century – if the established Roman practice of hiring barbarians to fight off barbarians was followed in this frontier area of the province – but it was certainly to happen in the fifth. Again either in the fourth or the fifth century, depending on the interpretation of the documentary sources, a settlement of the descendants of the *Votadini*, from the southern shore of the Firth of Forth, took place in north-west Wales. Under their leader Cunedda, they are said to have driven out the Irish from various parts of Wales.

Irish settlement in both north-west and south-west Wales has left traces in the place-names of these areas but, unlike in Scotland and the Isle of Man, Irish speech never replaced the British of which Welsh is a direct descendant. The fifty or so ogham stones known from Wales represent the principal archaeological evidence for the presence of Irish settlers, together with stones having Latin inscriptions commemorating men with specifically Irish names, on some of which the inscriptions are laid out vertically in the manner of ogham writing. Bilingual inscriptions (ogham and Latin on the same stone) are of particular interest, none
14 more so than that from Castell Dwyran in south-west Wales on which the Latin reads 'MEMORIA VOTEPORIGIS PROTICTORIS', 'the memorial of Voteporix Protector'; for this Voteporix may be identified with the Vortiporius known to have been ruling in the kingdom of Dyfed in the 530s. In north-west Wales, in the kingdom of Gwynedd, there is a Latin memorial preserved in the church at Llangadwaladr on Anglesey to Catamanus (Cadfan) 'wisest, most renowned of all kings'. It dates from the seventh century and employs a curious mixture of Roman capital letters and letter forms derived from the script developed for use in manuscripts. One final royal monument of note is Eliseg's Pillar in the kingdom of Powys. Standing at Valle Crucis, near Llangollen, it was erected in the ninth century by Cyngen to his great-grandfather Elise who had been the chief Welsh opponent of the Anglo-Saxon king, Offa of Mercia. The success of the Welsh in fighting off the Anglo-Saxon advance is expressed
p.78(21) physically to this day in the great dykes of Wat and Offa, constructed by the Anglo-Saxons to serve as the boundary between them and the Welsh.

A memorial stone from Aberdaron in Gwynedd was raised for 'Senacus, priest: here he lies with a host of the brethren', so providing direct evidence for the existence there of a monastery. Memorial stones and documentary records provide virtually our only evidence for the location of early churches in Wales, such as Llantwit Major on the south coast, or the great monastic centre at Bangor. For archaeology has as yet

revealed very little of pre-Norman monasteries and chapels in Wales, and there are no surviving remains of such buildings above ground.

Excavations at a number of pre-Roman hill-forts, such as Degannwy and Dinas Emrys in north Wales (both sites also chosen by later castle builders), have produced indications of post-Roman occupation, including imported pottery. But much more is known of the small fort of Dinas Powys, on a hilltop near Cardiff, that was constructed in the fifth century. Here Leslie Alcock has excavated the traces of two buildings which occupied the space within the defences, and found evidence for agricultural and other activities, including metalworking. The general nature of the material from the site is typical of that found throughout western Britain and Ireland at that date, but scrap-metal and glass fragments to be used in the production of jewellery had been obtained from the Anglo-Saxons to the east, while the presence of the full range of imported pottery demonstrates the site's connections with the western trade in luxury commodities. This then will have been a chieftain's residence of fifth- to seventh-century date. Of ordinary rural and domestic settlements in Wales at this period we still know next to nothing.

The realm of King Mark
During the post-Roman period in south-west Britain there emerged the kingdom of Dumnonia, embracing Cornwall, Devon and Somerset, but gradually shrinking during the sixth to early tenth centuries before the pressure of the Anglo-Saxon expansion westwards. The kingdom appears to have had no permanent capital, but at least one ruler's seat can be identified in Cornwall. The Iron Age fort of Castle Dore was reoccupied and a great timber hall constructed, possibly that used by Cunormorus (or Cynfawr) who was already identified in the ninth century as the legendary 'King Mark'. The fifth/sixth-century memorial stone of his son stands not far away, incised 'DRUSTANUS FILIUS CUNOMORI': 'Tristan son of Cynfawr'. Another Cornish Iron Age fort to have been reoccupied in the sixth century is the massive stone citadel of Chun Castle, where limited excavation has shown that the smelting of tin ore was carried out.

On the eastern boundaries of Dumnonia are situated two Iron Age hill-forts that are greater in size than any other such fortifications known to have been in use in the post-Roman period. Both are called Cadbury, one being sited above Congresbury and the other, Cadbury Castle, by South Cadbury; both have produced 6 material, including imported Mediterranean pottery, that shows them to have been reoccupied in the fifth/sixth century. But the remarkable feature that distinguishes Cadbury Castle from all other such sites is not just its supreme size, but the fact that its uppermost rampart was then refortified in its entirety (a distance of approximately 1,095 metres, enclosing an area of some eighteen acres). The identity of the man who commanded the resources for this massive work is unknown, but it is reasonable to speculate with Leslie Alcock that if any one shadowy figure fits the context better than another, then it is Arthur.

For a limited picture of life at a lower social level in Dumnonia, there is a site at Gwithian, in Cornwall, where Charles Thomas has discovered an undefended settlement of dry-stone huts, with extensive middens that contained a range of native and imported wares. Imported Mediterranean pottery from a 'round' – a type of ring-fort – at Trethurgy shows that at least one example of this earlier settlement-type continued in use into the post-Roman period. Both these sites demonstrate that, at least in the south-west, the ability to acquire imported pots and their contents was not confined to the nobility and the Church.

In south-west England, Christianity survived the departure of the Romans unaffected by Anglo-Saxon paganism, and it will have been in this area that monasticism was first established from the Continent, but of ultimately east Mediterranean inspiration. It has 43 been claimed that Tintagel, in Cornwall, is the earliest known British monastery, with its origins in the late fifth century, but the ecclesiastical interpretation of this site has recently been challenged. It is located on a promontory, cut off by a massive rampart, with 3 structures that have produced A-, B-, and D-wares, indicating fifth/sixth-century occupation (but not all structures at this site are so early). Further debate as to whether this is a monastery or a princely stronghold will have to await detailed studies and new excavations, but even then it may not be possible to resolve the matter with certainty. In the same way it has proved impossible to determine whether the early occupation 42 (with B-ware) on top of Glastonbury Tor represents secular or monastic settlement (although most probably the latter). Excavations at Glastonbury Abbey revealed traces of a large rampart, which enclosed the later Irish foundation that in due course was to become a late Anglo-Saxon monastery of exceptional importance and influence.

A small group of memorial stones in east Cornwall and west Devon suggests that there is some truth behind the tradition of Irish settlement in Dumnonia, but not necessarily direct from Ireland, given the settlement in south Wales already noted. Some of these memorials have Irish ogham inscriptions and others commemorate, in Roman script, men with Irish names. A 15 slab from Ivybridge in Devon was used three times in the sixth/seventh century to commemorate Irishmen: *Suaqqucos* in ogham, *Fanonus* on one side, and *Sagranus* on the reverse (both in Roman script laid out vertically in the manner of ogham inscriptions).

The story would not be complete, even in such brief outline, without mention of the Britons who left Dumnonia in the fifth and sixth centuries to settle in Armorica. Apparently this was a large-scale migration, the reasons for which remain unclear, but pressure from the Anglo-Saxon advance and Irish settlement may have been significant factors. It gave rise not only to the close correspondence between the Cornish and Breton languages, but also left its permanent record in the name 'Brittany' itself.

By the ninth century it was only in Cornwall and Wales that there were Britons free of Anglo-Saxon rule, and those of Cornwall were soon to submit to Wessex. Thus the Anglo-Saxons completed the annexation of all the British lands that became incorporated into the kingdom of England.

Survivals and revivals
The Anglo-Norman takeover of Ireland, even if it did not lead to the subjugation of the entire country, was responsible for a gradual withering of native styles and techniques until waning control by the English, in the later Middle Ages, gave rise to a Celtic revival. The *Book of Ballymote*, for example, compiled about 1390 for a Gaelic lord, includes a tract on ogham among its histories, genealogies, classical tales, poems and legal texts. In addition it has coloured initials which deliberately attempt to copy those of the earlier manuscripts; the animals come to life again vigorously enough, but the intricacies of interlace tend to elude the later medieval artists who lacked the specialized training of their Early Christian predecessors. But copying of earlier works could be carried out with great care and skill; at first sight, the leather satchel traditionally associated with the *Book of Armagh* (although far too large for it) appears to be of eleventh- or twelfth-century date. It is only details of the interlace patterns and animal ornament which cover it (and a clumsy attempt at Gothic lettering) that betray its true date of manufacture in the fifteenth century.

The Celtic revival in medieval Ireland included a strong interest in harp music and two well-known harps may be its finest surviving monument: that in Dublin, traditionally associated with Brian Boru (who defeated the Vikings at the battle of Clontarf in 1014), and that in Edinburgh known as the Queen Mary harp. The pair may have come from the same late medieval workshop, but whether this was in fact in Ireland or Scotland is hard to say, for many early elements had remained current in Scottish art, particularly that of the west Highlands. Two very similar caskets of whale-bone, with bronze locks and mountings, illustrate this well. Known as the 'Eglinton' and 'Fife' caskets, they are decorated all over with interlace patterns and, although it has been argued that they are considerably earlier in date, they seem to be from the fifteenth

The Celtic Revival carried its enthusiasm to lengths which now seem faintly absurd. In 1895, replicas of the Ardagh chalice (discovered about twenty-five years earlier) were put on the market as sugar-bowls, with tongs to match. (9)

century. A similar fondness for interlace is to be found on late medieval stone monuments in the west Highlands and, while the slabs and effigies of this remarkable regional school of sculpture were inspired by Romanesque art, some fourteenth/fifteenth-century free-standing crosses, such as Maclean's Cross on Iona, hark back to the earlier use of this type of monument in the west of Scotland.

Once again, in the mid-nineteenth century, Irish artists were to turn deliberately to the art and architecture of the Early Christian and Hiberno-Romanesque periods for inspiration in their attempt to forge a national art. From the late eighteenth century, Irish antiquarians had been bringing native art and antiquities to wider attention. For instance, as people turned to the High Crosses as a source for monuments and gravestones, they were able to make use of H. O'Neill's *Illustrations of the Most interesting of the Sculptured Crosses of Ancient Ireland*, published in 1857. Manuscripts were ransacked for ideas, patterns from the *Book of Durrow* and the *Book of Kells* being put to many uses from book-illumination to the decorative enrichment of buildings.

Copies of ancient ornaments (often freely adapted) were being produced from at least as early as 1842 by Waterhouse and Company of Dublin, and soon by many others. The discovery of the 'Tara' brooch in 1850, and its acquisition by Waterhouse, gave a tremendous boost to the reproduction business and an imitation brooch of this type was an essential feature of the newly concocted Irish national costume. (In Scotland also, 'Celtic' patterns were freely revived for similar purposes.) The discovery of the Ardagh chalice in 1868 was put to good use, appearing in the 1895

exhibition of the Arts and Crafts Society of Ireland as a sugar-bowl, with matching tongs! Such use and abuse *9* of the Early Christian art of Ireland remained popular to the mid-twentieth century, so that its legacy is still much in evidence today.

Revival and survival of the heroic British past of England has been centred on one figure – that of Arthur, or rather the 'King Arthur' of the prose and verse of Geoffrey of Monmouth, Sir Thomas Malory, Tennyson and many another. Their fanciful elaborations and widespread appeal are not our concern here, but what is of interest is Arthur's early adoption as a hero shared alike by north Britain, Wales and the south where he has become most firmly localized – to the extent that Cadbury Castle has been tentatively identified as the 'Camelot' of the later romances.

The ninth-century *History of the Britons*, attributed to a Welsh monk, Nennius, contains a Latin summary of a Welsh poem listing the twelve battles supposedly fought by Arthur. The poem is of unknown date, just possibly of Arthur's own day, but more likely from the late sixth or seventh century, when there is some evidence that Arthur was already well established as a great British hero. Given the nature of such sources little can ever be resolved about the true character of Arthur and his deeds, but that is of course irrelevant to the telling and retelling of the legend, first fully developed by Geoffrey of Monmouth in 1136.

Certainly the truth will never now be known of the events of 1191 when the monks of Glastonbury claimed to have discovered the bodies of Arthur and Queen Guinevere. With the bodies (whosoever's they were) was a lead cross, illustrated by Camden in the 1607 *2* edition of his *Britannia*, inscribed 'HIC IACET SEPULTUS INCLITUS REX ARTURIUS IN INSULA AVALONIS', 'Here lies buried the famous King Arthur in the isle of Avalon'. The style of this inscription is certainly not that of the sixth century, but neither is it that of the twelfth, for the form of the lettering is tenth/eleventh century – a style that would, however, not have been beyond the capabilities of a twelfth-century monkish forger. Glastonbury has a history of monkish fakes and fancifulness and it is against this background that the claim of Arthur's exhumation must be judged. Is it no more than coincidence that the monastery was badly damaged by fire in 1184 and that funds were short for the rebuilding programme? Such projects have always benefited from a little publicity. . . .

But all these doings are inevitably surrounded by the mists of time, as is so much else encountered in this survey. Despite the limitations of the sources, historical, archaeological and linguistic, they are rich and varied and much work remains to be done on them to further our knowledge of this critical, and perennially fascinating, period in the history of the British Isles.

5·THE SCANDINAVIANS AT HOME

ELSE ROESDAHL

Warriors, adventurers and seamen, the Scandinavians had already established themselves in the lands traditionally associated with them at the time of our earliest written records. The Greek 'Thule' is probably Norway; Ptolemy, Tacitus and other classical writers refer to tribes who lived in Denmark and Sweden. For some of these peoples, the break-up of the Roman Empire was an incentive to migrate to new homes, others expanded from their home base into surrounding territories, while others collected wealth in troubled Europe and returned to Scandinavia loaded with gold. From the first, they seem to have excelled in boldness, initiative and physical vigour, and the period which made the name of the Norsemen famous and feared throughout the known world (*c.*800–1050) was only the climax of a story that began at least five centuries before.

The sites that perhaps give us the most dramatic glimpses of Scandinavian life before the Viking Age are Vendel and Valsgärde, in Uppland, central Sweden. Here, many rich graves have been excavated, datable to a period between the seventh and eleventh centuries. Twenty-five of the men were buried in boats, which immediately suggests parallels with Sutton Hoo. Each grave generally contained cooking utensils, carcases of slaughtered animals, and a wealth of military equipment, including some splendid iron helmets (*opposite*). This one (from Valsgärde) is divided into rectangular panels, like the Sutton Hoo helmet, but the lower half consists of chain mail. The crest and eye-guards are of bronze.

The grave-goods found at Vendel and Valsgärde help to build up a reasonably complete picture of contemporary upper class society in its most important aspects – the warfare that was no doubt an important preoccupation, the feasting and celebrations that provided the highlights of the communal year and the voyaging in boats that were already sophisticated vessels. Of its religious beliefs we know little, but it seems as though men expected the next world to be a continuation of this one, so they took even the tools, clothes and playthings of everyday life into the grave. (1)

On previous page : bronze matrix for
making repoussé panels showing armed
warriors, from Torslunda, on Öland; such
panels were used to decorate helmets. (1)

The age of the migrations

Two golden horns – unique treasures of the period 400–575 – were found at Gallehus, in Denmark, in 1639 and 1734. Tragically, they were both stolen in 1802 and melted down; those illustrated here are reconstructions made from old drawings. The smaller horn has a runic inscription naming its maker as 'Lægæst son of Holte', but the human and animal figures with which they are decorated remain mysterious. The plug on the larger one is a seventeenth-century addition, to make it into a drinking horn. (2)

The weapons of a defeated army were thrown into a lake as a sacrifice to the gods. Three swords with silver hilts, found at Kragehul, Denmark, were deposited in this way (*below*). Caesar reports the same custom in some of the tribes of Gaul. (3)

Gold in surprising quantities gives this early period an exotic richness. A collar found at Färjestaden, Sweden (*below*), consists of five gold tubes linked by panels and filigree gold wire. Such collars are among the most delicately made products of Scandinavian art. (4)

The repoussé panels found on helmets (e.g. that of Sutton Hoo and those from Vendel and Valsgärde) were made by applying bronze matrices (*above* and *below*) to the metal. The youth in the horned head-dress and the man dressed in an animal mask may be performing a ritual dance. All four carry swords and spears and two wear animal-crested helmets. (5,6)

Around the neck of what seems to be the cult image of a god (*above*) is carved just such a collar as the one illustrated next to it. These images are rare. This one was preserved in a bog at Rude Eskildstrup, Sjælland, Denmark. (7)

131

Riches revealed

Most of the gold that has been recovered from the Migration Period was offered to the gods or deliberately hidden in time of war and never retrieved. A hoard of jewellery from Kitnæs, Denmark (*left*), included a square-headed brooch, covered in sheet gold and decorated with filigree and garnets, and many pendants of the type known as bracteates: impressed gold sheets with designs derived from late Roman coins. (8)

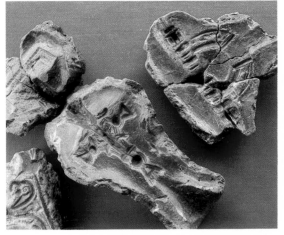

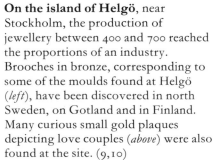

On the island of Helgö, near Stockholm, the production of jewellery between 400 and 700 reached the proportions of an industry. Brooches in bronze, corresponding to some of the moulds found at Helgö (*left*), have been discovered in north Sweden, on Gotland and in Finland. Many curious small gold plaques depicting love couples (*above*) were also found at the site. (9,10)

The goldsmiths could produce filigree thread as fine as a tenth of a millimetre. *Left*: a magnified detail from a collar similar to that shown in pl. 4. (13)

The Snartemo sword (*below left*), made in the sixth century, surpasses all others in its richness and sophistication. At the top of the pommel, which is silver-gilt, two beak-headed creatures face each other; beneath it, three panels in gold contain animal forms so inextricably stylized and twisted as to be hard to recognize. (11)

Art continued to thrive in the later part of the Germanic Iron Age, *c.* 575–800, which is in many other ways a very obscure period of Scandinavian history. So far no coherent account of it can be written. But such splendid objects as the silver-gilt buckle from Åker (*above*) in south-east Norway, from about 600, illustrate the vivacity of design, combining animals, a male face and garnets set in cloisonné. (12)

133

Traces of life and death

The great mounds still to be seen in many parts of Scandinavia probably mark the central points of ancient chiefdoms. The largest, at Raknehaugen, Norway (*above*), apparently never contained a corpse. At Gamla Uppsala (*right*) three mounds held the cremated bones of three men. Kings? Legend supplies many names for them, archaeology none. (14,16)

Stone-built forts, refuges and living quarters for people and livestock in time of danger, were numerous and necessary. The Swedish island of Öland preserves sixteen of them, of which that of Ismanstorp (*above*) best keeps its Migration Period appearance. (15)

A Viking chief after death would sometimes lie in a real ship or in a stone setting shaped like one. Lejre, in Denmark (*below*), is by legend associated with Danish and Swedish kings and also with the story of Beowulf. These remains of a large ship-shaped stone setting are from the tenth century. (17)

A ninth-century house at Hedeby was sufficiently well preserved to allow reconstruction. Built of wattle and daub on a timber frame (*above*), its main room (*left*) had a central hearth and broad benches raised off the earth and lined with planks. The only furniture would be a loom and some chests. (18,19)

From Birka (*above*), on a small island in Lake Mälar, central Sweden, Viking trade reached out to western Europe, Britain, Russia, Byzantium and the Muslim countries. In the tenth century it must have been one of the most cosmopolitan places in the northern world. The town was in the open space by the shore; most graves are in the forest. (20)

Kings and queens

'**King Harald** ordered these monuments to be made in memory of his father Gorm and his mother Thyre: that Harald who won the whole of Denmark and Norway for himself and who made the Danes Christian.' So runs the proud inscription placed by Harald Bluetooth on the largest rune-stone in the world, the Jelling stone (*right*), with the figure of Christ crucified on its main face. The smaller stone was raised by King Gorm in memory of his wife.

At Jelling (*left*) two huge mounds still survive, one containing the graves of Harald's parents, with a church – the stone successor to Harald's wooden original – between them. King Harald consolidated his rule by a series of fortress-villages throughout Denmark, all circular in shape with four entrances, and groups of houses forming rectangular courtyards in the four quarters. This one (*below*) is at Fyrkat, north-east Jutland. (21,22,23)

Queen Thyre, Harald's mother, is associated by legend with the building of the Danevirke (*above*). Archaeology has so far failed to prove such a connection, but her son seems to have strengthened it considerably in the face of serious German threats. The Danevirke is the Danish Offa's Dyke. An earthwork over eight miles in length, it stretches across the neck of Jutland. It was founded in the eighth century but altered many times, and throughout much of Danish history it served as a bulwark against Germany; it was last used in 1864. The Danevirke is here seen towards the east; in the background is the town of Schleswig, the successor of Hedeby. (24)

Crafts and craftsmanship

The most dramatic discovery in Norwegian archaeology came in 1904, when a mound at Oseberg, not far from Oslo, was excavated (*below left*). It was found to contain an almost complete Viking ship, with a wealth of furnishings, many of them elaborately decorated, buried with a queen of the Vestfold royal family about the year 800. Special soil conditions had preserved the wood. Triumphantly it was raised from the earth and transported through the streets of the capital (*below right*) to the Bygdøy museum. Here it joined another Viking ship (*right*) found over twenty years earlier at Gokstad, a few miles further along the same coast. It is from these two ships that much of our knowledge of Viking ships comes. Lightly built, shallow of draught and highly manoeuvrable, they could move under sail or by oars. A replica of the Gokstad ship has been sailed across the Atlantic. (25,26,29)

Complete tool kits recovered from Mästermyr, Sweden (*left*), and Bygland, Norway (*above*), enable us to follow the techniques by which the ships were made. The Swedish chest contained 150 items, including hammers, a riveting block, a nail-making tool, shears for clipping metal, pincers, axes, an adze, a rasp, a morticing saw, a plane, chisels and scales. (27,28)

War and peace: the group of weapons (*above*) brings together a shield, a helmet, four swords, five spear-heads and four axe-heads. Of the swords, the blades were perhaps imported, the hilts of Viking manufacture. *Below*: tubs and other kitchen utensils found on the Oseberg ship. The bucket in the centre (see p. 164) is Irish. (30,31)

The revelation of Oseberg

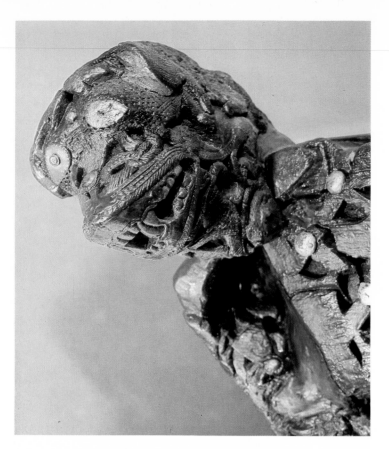

More than a ship came to light at Oseberg: it proved to be an unprecedented collection of Viking art at its most powerful. Most notable was the quality of the woodcarving, both on the ship itself and on the various objects found in it: several beds and sledges, an almost complete cart with its wheels (see p. 156) and other things. *Left*: a monster's head from one of the sledges; clearly intended to be terrifying, its deeper meaning can only be guessed at. *Below*: one end of the Oseberg cart, carved with a scene that may represent the hero Gunnar in the snake-pit (though he is not playing a harp). This cart is elaborately worked to be fit for a queen to ride in, but simpler carts were commonly used. *Right*: a post of unknown use, ending in a ferocious lion's head – the masterpiece of the sculptor who has been nicknamed 'the Academician'. (32,33,34)

An evolution of styles

Small figurines of silver and bronze dating from the Viking Age probably represent supernatural beings but come close to realism in their depiction of dress. The women's robes fall straight at the front, stopping above the foot, but are longer at the back. The two central figures carry drinking horns. (35–39)

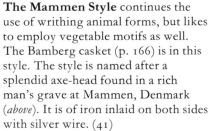

The Jellinge Style takes its name from a silver cup found in the royal burial mound at Jelling (*left*). Its serpentine animal forms have evolved spontaneously from earlier Scandinavian art (see the Oseberg carvings) and were also used abroad in the areas conquered by the Vikings. (40)

The Mammen Style continues the use of writhing animal forms, but likes to employ vegetable motifs as well. The Bamberg casket (p. 166) is in this style. The style is named after a splendid axe-head found in a rich man's grave at Mammen, Denmark (*above*). It is of iron inlaid on both sides with silver wire. (41)

The Ringerike Style returns to almost recognizable animals and birds, but involves them in a jungle of stylized stems and leaves. Notable examples are a series of ships' weather-vanes, such as this from Heggen (*left*); another is the St Paul's stone shown on p. 165. (42)

The Urnes Style represents the last flowering of Viking art, when it was already part of Christendom. Its masterpiece is the stave church of Urnes, Norway (*opposite*), where elongated creatures, some like deer, lose themselves amid an endless interlace of snakes and tendrils. (43)

The earliest Viking coinage was struck at Hedeby in the early ninth century: an animal on one side, a ship on the other. (2)

THE SCANDINAVIANS AT HOME

SCANDINAVIA is almost entirely surrounded by water: to the east and south lie the Gulf of Bothnia and the Baltic Sea, to the west and north the North Sea, the North Atlantic and the Arctic Ocean. By way of the sea the different parts of the area maintained contact with each other. The fringe of islands, islets and skerries along almost the entire length of the Atlantic coast afford protection against ocean storms; and with improvement of ship design, communication became more and more practicable. Thus at the end of the ninth century the Norwegian Ottar, who visited King Alfred's court, told the king that he could sail from his home in Hålogaland in north Norway to *Sciringes heal* (Kaupang) in south Norway in one month, if he camped ashore each night and had a favourable wind each day. From *Sciringes heal* was five days' sailing to Hedeby in southernmost Denmark. Although it was possible to travel by land, such journeys took

◁ **The wealth of the Viking world** is attested both by documentary sources and by archaeological finds. Money came from plunder, from tribute (such as the very substantial Danegeld paid by the English over a long period) and from trade. The total number of English coins so far recovered in Scandinavia is over 42,000. But double that number is the figure for Arabic coins, indicating the vast amount of trade flowing between north and south around the end of the first millennium. Hoards discovered in the Slav lands (illustrated elsewhere, p. 189, 192) make this abundantly clear. Shown *opposite* is a treasure found at Hon, Norway, deposited about 860. It includes a Carolingian trefoil brooch, gold pendants with leaf decoration taken from western European models, many Arabic coins made into pendants, a ring with a Greek inscription and a gold and garnet pendant that must be at least 150 years older than the rest. The story of the Vikings, indeed, demands a wider horizon than Scandinavia alone, and the next chapter will be devoted to their impact overseas. (44)

considerably longer than by sea. Adam, a cleric of Bremen, writing at the end of the eleventh century, said that while it took five days to sail from Skåne (now the southernmost province of Sweden) to Sigtuna in Uppland, the same journey took a whole month by land.

Travelling by land or by sea was risky. The traveller faced piracy, robbery and involvement in wars between different tribes and countries. But, despite such risks, the Scandinavians travelled widely and people from different regions cooperated, solving common problems. In time a distinctive culture – common to much of the region – was evolved, so that foreigners tended to view the Scandinavians as a single ethnic group. This ethnic group was to burst explosively on the rest of Europe during the Viking Age. Five hundred years earlier, however, they were already a force to be reckoned with outside their homelands, some settling abroad and others bringing back to Scandinavia an untold wealth in gold.

The Germanic Iron Age
c. 400–800

The Germanic Iron Age derives its name from the Germanic peoples – including the Scandinavians – who initiated most of the major cultural developments in Europe in the four hundred years after the Roman Empire had collapsed.

The years from 400 to 575 are aptly named the Migration Period: the disintegration of the Roman Empire gave Asiatic and European tribes new opportunities for expansion; many sought their fortunes in far-off lands. Some settled in new countries, others perished, but others returned to their native lands. From Denmark, Angles and Jutes sailed west to settle in England; a Danish king, Cochilaicus, took part in a raid on western Europe in 515, and was killed returning to his ship. Such facts are known, but written information about Scandinavia and the Scandinavians at this time is scanty and chimeric. The literary memorials of the Scandinavians themselves, written in the runic alphabet, are few, lapidary and often difficult to interpret. Those that survive from the early period are rarely more significant than magic formulae; as for example, 'I am called Hariuha, resourceful in danger. I will protect you.' Some inscriptions record personal names, the euphonic woman's name Agilamundo, or men's names, such as Widugastir and Halar.

Symbolic of the Migration Period are the enormous mounds, the largest of which, Raknehaugen in 14 Romerike, Norway, has a diameter of approximately 95 metres. It is 15 metres high, and was constructed from about 80,000 cubic metres of clay, sand and soil, with the addition of 125,000 logs set conically in three layers. It was probably built in a single year, and it has been estimated that it represents the labour of five hundred men working from spring to autumn. The mound was investigated archaeologically in 1939–40, but no burial was found; its date has been established by a scientific examination of the timber used in its construction. It is possible that a burial lies somewhere in the unexcavated portions of this enormous mound; but it may perhaps have been constructed as a cenotaph for someone who had died overseas, or as a symbol of the power of the political or religious leaders of the region. It is sited near a once important artery of communication and it may have marked a place of assembly.

The great effort involved in the construction of Raknehaugen bears witness to the degree of political organization of this region. It is known that Scandinavia was at this period divided into a number of kingdoms and chiefdoms of varying size; rulers were elected from among a number of families who held military and probably religious power. Raknehaugen may have marked the central point of such a chiefdom, just as the man buried with a magnificent gold-hilted sword at Snartemo in West Agder may have been the 11 chief of another Norwegian region.

A third realm was centred on the legendary site known as Gamla Uppsala in the Mälar region of 16 Sweden, which comprises three burial mounds. The first proper archaeological investigations of these mounds took place in 1846. In the bottom of the eastern mound was found a pottery vessel containing cremated human bones and the remains of objects which had also been burnt on the pyre. Excavation of the western mound in 1874 produced similar results. Although most of the objects were so burnt as to be virtually unidentifiable, it was possible by studying them to show that the burials took place in the sixth century, and that the dead had been unusually wealthy. Among the finds were bones of various domestic animals and objects of high quality made from expensive materials. Some of the fragments possibly formed a large gold collar; others perhaps were from gold sword hilts; other fragments may be the remains of a helmet

decorated with figures; and there were glass beakers, gaming pieces and textiles worked with gold thread.

Who were these kings? They have long been identified with Aun, Egil and Adils, known from *Ynglingatal*, the poem from around the year 900 written by the Norwegian scald Thjódolf. This poem identifies the Norwegian kings of Vestfold as the decendants of the Svea kings of Uppsala, and ultimately of the god Odin himself. Several of these kings may also figure in *Beowulf*, the Anglo-Saxon epic poem which is usually attributed to the eighth century (the only surviving manuscript was written down around the year 1000), and they appear again later, in legends associated with Lejre in Denmark, whence the Danish kings sought to trace their lineage. At one time it was thought that these kings lived during a period compatible with the estimated date of the burial mounds in Gamla Uppsala. However, excavations have proved that Lejre reached its peak in the tenth century, and other investigations strongly suggest that many of the named characters were figures from the history of central Europe in the Migration Period, tales of whose exploits were widely disseminated. On reaching Scandinavia, some of these central European heroes eventually became incorporated in the register of the great forefathers of the Scandinavian kings, and their supposed kingdoms were transferred to Scandinavian sites.

It is unlikely that we will ever know who lies buried in the Uppsala mounds, but a description in *Beowulf* gives us some idea of the nature of the funeral ceremonies:

> *And there, on Whaleness, the heroes kindled*
> *the most mighty of pyres; the dark wood-smoke*
> *soared over the fire, the roaring flames*
> *mingled with weeping – the winds tumult subsided –*
> *until the body became ash, consumed even*
> *to its core . . . .*

Many burial mounds of varying size are known in Scandinavia from this period, as well as burials without mounds, and indeed without cremation. The chieftain at Snartemo, whose sword was mentioned above, was not, for example, cremated. The grave-goods found in such burials give us an impression of the tastes and art styles of the period. This is expressed most spectacularly in the gold objects of the Migration Period.

Wealth and war

No other period glitters in quite the same fashion. The gold is rarely found in graves; rather it is found casually in the ground or in peat bogs, where it was either left as a sacrifice to the gods or else was hidden. The gold is often in the form of ingots or bars bent into the form of rings – gold bullion – although some Roman gold coins have also been found. Sometimes the gold was fashioned into elaborate jewellery or used to embellish weapons – a sword hilt or a scabbard for example. The

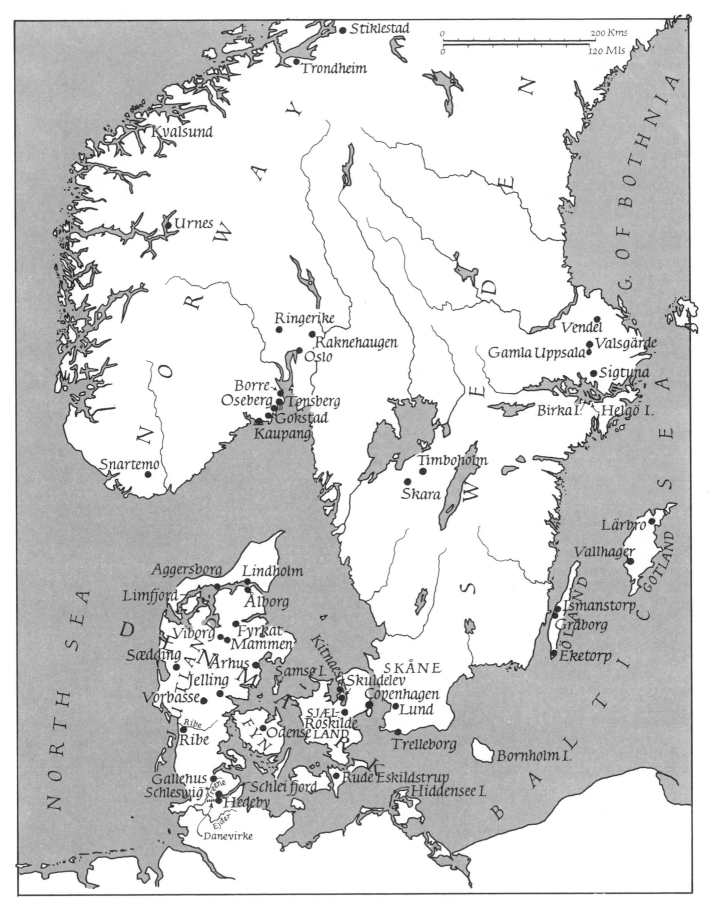

largest known gold hoard was found in Södermanland, Sweden; it weighed more than twelve kilos, but only part of it now survives. The largest preserved hoard from this period is from Timboholm in Sweden: discovered in 1904, it weighs just over seven kilos and consists of gold bullion in the form of two ingots and twenty-six ring-shaped bars. The jewellery of the period often takes the form of large bronze brooches covered in gold foil and decorated with filigree and coloured stones, as, for example, is the case with the 8 Danish brooch from Kitnæs. Some neck rings and collars are, however, made entirely of gold, and on 4 occasion weigh more than a kilo. These collars are among the most delicately made products of ancient 13 Scandinavian art, sometimes comprising as many as seven gold tubes linked by gold mouldings, divided by panels of filigree wire and further embellished with miniature designs representing animals or (less often) human figures. We have already seen that the charred remains found at Gamla Uppsala possibly included fragments of a collar; there is no doubt, however, that 7 the wooden figure of what is perhaps a god, found at Rude Eskildstrup in Denmark, wears a similar collar – suggesting that men did indeed wear collars of this kind.

The most famous finds of this period were the two large gold horns (now destroyed) from Gallehus in 2 south Jutland. The two horns were found by accident in the same field at almost a century's interval, the first (and most complete) in 1639 and the second in 1734. They both created an immediate sensation and were presented to the king. The first horn was published and illustrated as early as 1641 by the celebrated collector and antiquary Ole Worm; the second was published by the archivist J. R. Paulli in the year in which it was found. Together the two horns weighed about seven and a half kilos: Worm gives the diameter of the mouth of the first horn as exactly one Roman foot (29.5 cm) and its length along the outside curve as 71.3 cm. It seems likely that the second horn was originally a little larger. They were probably drinking horns rather than blast horns. Engraved and soldered-on designs of performing animals and human figures decorated the surfaces, but the significance of these scenes remains uncertain. Under the rim of the second horn is the runic inscription 'ekhlewagastir holtijar horna tawido' (I, Lægæst, son [relation?] of Holte, made this horn). In 1802 the two golden horns were stolen and melted down; the nation mourned their loss, and Adam Oehlenschläger wrote a grandiloquent poem to their memory; but they were irretrievably lost, as unfortunately (at a slightly later date) were the casts which had been taken from them. The exact appearance of these horns cannot, therefore, be reconstructed, although Frederick VII had silver-gilt copies made in 1860, based on the old descriptions and drawings, and these replicas, which were later presented to the

Oldnordisk Museum in Copenhagen, give at least a reasonable impression of their appearance.

How did so much gold reach Scandinavia? Much of it came from the tottering Roman Empire, from which the Germanic tribes had extracted enormous sums of money during their raids and migrations. Some of this loot reached Scandinavia, and most of the Roman gold coins (*solidi*) were melted down there. It has been estimated that the amount of gold used to make the gold horns corresponds to approximately 1,650 *solidi*, sufficient to secure the release of about two hundred captured Roman soldiers. The origins of the gold found in the hoards is also illuminated by the Scandinavian bracteates: these round pendants of thin sheet gold 8 were worn as amulets and decorated in the Scandinavian taste. This type of object was new to Scandinavia, and the designs of the earliest bracteates were clearly influenced by the images of the Roman emperor on the gold coins.

Not all foreign contact was, however, the result of war or raids. The small island of Helgö in Lake Mälaren near Stockholm was a major centre of international trade. Excavations have revealed specialized metal-work shops associated with large building complexes, which may also have been farms. Iron- and bronze-workers, as well as goldsmiths, produced artifacts on such a large scale that their works can only have been intended as articles of trade. Objects with designs corresponding to those of the metal moulds on Helgö 9,10 have indeed been found in north Sweden, on Gotland and in Finland. But the goods traded at Helgö would not have been limited to artifacts manufactured on the site – skins and furs are another likely possibility – and the trading connections would have extended far beyond the areas mentioned. The numerous and varied finds from Helgö bear witness to trading relations with areas to the east of the Baltic, with the Continent and with Britain. There are even hoards of Roman gold coins. Helgö was at a peak of activity between 400 and 700, dominating both local and foreign trade in central Sweden; it represented a completely new type of Scandinavian settlement, where large-scale trade combined with large-scale manufacture of something other than agricultural produce. So far Helgö appears to be unique in this period.

A Scandinavian farm usually consisted of a variable number of buildings enclosed by a fence or stone wall. In most cases one end of the principal building would be used for living, while the other end would be used as a byre and perhaps as a barn; such buildings could therefore be of great length. In some cases it is possible to estimate the number of stabled animals by counting the traces of the stalls. One of the farms in the village of Vorbasse in south Jutland housed fourteen 3 large animals, presumably cattle; 8 metres of its total length of 25 metres were used as a byre. The principal building of another farm was 38 metres long: of this a third (at the west end) was used as living quarters, 10.5 metres in the middle housed twenty-two large animals, and the rest was presumably used as a barn. Smaller buildings on the site would have been used for storage and as workshops. In Denmark houses were generally built of wood, whereas in Norway and Sweden local field stone was used to build the walls. The interiors, however, are similar throughout Scandinavia. The roof was supported by two rows of stout posts running the length of the building; transverse partitions often divided the dwelling into several rooms, and there was a hearth in the middle of the floor.

In Vorbasse the farms of this period are grouped around a large open green, giving the appearance of a village with a certain degree of communal organization. It seems that such villages were common in Denmark, whereas Sweden and Norway are characterized by single farms or small groups of farms.

Those who lived on such farms were often wealthy: in the case of a man buried in the Migration Period in central Jutland, it is evident that he appreciated the good things in life and had found occasion to cultivate these interests. His cremated bones were placed in a pot wrapped in a bearskin of which the claws are preserved in the burial; for his enjoyment in after life he had been given thirty-six gaming pieces and a glass beaker (probably from the Black Sea area), inscribed on the rim with an enticing Greek maxim, which reads in translation, 'Drink, and your life will be beautiful'. Two other beakers of this type are known.

The increased prosperity is further indicated by the establishment of many new farms – at least in Norway and Sweden. The area of settlement expanded; all suitable land was brought into cultivation, and new land to the north was colonized; new trade routes from the Trondheim area on the Atlantic coast over the mountains to the Gulf of Bothnia were opened up. Many of these new settlements were on marginal land, and were soon abandoned, but towards the end of the Migration Period changes became apparent even in the old settlement areas. Numerous farms and villages throughout Scandinavia, many of them with a history going back several hundred years (as at Vorbasse and Vallhagar), were abandoned and many burial grounds ceased to be used. The owners of gold hoards were, for one reason or another, prevented from recovering them. These changes have been explained as the result of wars, but similar trends occur over large areas of north-west Europe, and could have been due to alterations in agricultural structure, deteriorating climate or changes in the pattern of trade. It is, further, quite possible that many owners of those hoards which were left in the ground for safety were not killed in their homes, but rather while out looting more gold in troubled Europe.

Long-house at Vorbasse, Denmark. The numbers indicate the separate rooms; the main door is marked with an arrow. Rooms 1–3 are living quarters, room 4 a cattle shed, and room 5 probably a barn or storage space for grain. (3)

There was clearly some unrest, however. Many Scandinavian peat bogs have yielded weapons and other trappings of war, including valuable swords with blades made in Frankish workshops – all sacrificed to the gods in gratitude for victory. A centuries-old custom led them to submerge all the equipment of a defeated army or band of marauders in a sacred lake. Originally all the equipment would be disposed of in this manner, but gradually a more economical system was evolved, whereby only symbolic sacrifices of parts of objects were made, sacrifices of scabbard-mounts, sword hilts, buckles and the like.

The numerous forts built during this period also bear testimony to the unrest and insecurity of the times. Many of these are found far from the nearest habitation on difficult and inaccessible terrain; they were presumably used as places of refuge for people and their livestock during periods of acute danger. The island of Öland in the Baltic, however, exhibits rather different traits. Many of the sixteen round forts on this flat Swedish island are thought to be of this period, others perhaps date from the Viking Age. The largest is Gråborg, which has a diameter of 210 metres. The history of this fort goes back to the fifth century, but it was rebuilt many times and was last used as a refuge by the local inhabitants during a Danish attack on Öland in the seventeenth century.

The fort at Ismanstorp perhaps best retains its Migration Period appearance: it is 125 metres in diameter and encloses the foundations of eighty-eight buildings. Only minor excavations have been carried out here, but investigation of a related fort at Eketorp has produced exciting results. In the fourth century a round structure with an internal diameter of 55–60 metres was built on this site. Inside, and adjoining the circular wall, about twenty buildings were arranged radially, each long wall being common to two buildings with a large open space in the centre. There are no signs of a permanent settlement, and it seems likely that at this time Eketorp was a place of refuge, as so many other fortresses of the period, used only in times of danger. In the fifth century the whole structure was rebuilt, the internal diameter being enlarged to about 80 metres, now enclosing fifty-three buildings, comprising both dwelling-houses and byres. Some buildings were placed radially inside the outer circular wall, while others were clustered together in the centre of the open space. For a couple of centuries Eketorp was a permanent settlement – a fortified village in fact. The similarities between this village and other forts like Ismanstorp are so striking that they must be assumed to be roughly contemporary. Further, at this time a large number of farms on the island (traces of some 900 buildings survive) were deserted. These forts would therefore seem to represent a completely new and original form of settlement, inspired perhaps by the forts of Byzantium, functional and well suited to communal living, and adapted to the conditions pertaining on Öland at that time. This was certainly not a time of peace. Eketorp was abandoned around the year 700 and not rebuilt until the end of the Viking period, from which time it was in use until about 1300.

Stories in stone

During the Migration Period on Gotland, the other large Baltic island belonging to Sweden, a major innovation was the decoration of large limestone flags, which were erected on or near burial sites or by the sides of roads. Such monumental art was new to the island and quite unknown elsewhere in Scandinavia. Some 375 such stones, whole or in fragments, are known, dating from the period *c.* 400–1100. The best of these must rank among the greatest (in every meaning of the word) and most interesting of all the works of art of prehistoric Scandinavia.

The stones of the Migration Period are as much as 3.3 metres high and are shaped like an axe standing on its butt: the long sides curve outwards, and the top surface is convex. The face has been smoothed, and the simple

and strict designs – often consisting of large circles, whorls and spiral patterns set above an elegant rowing vessel – are chiselled out in very shallow relief, the designs being emphasized by paint, of which some traces have been found. When newly painted with what were no doubt striking colours, these large and characteristic stones must have been impressive features of the landscape.

After a period in which the designs on these stones became less skilful, the Gotland monuments reached another artistic peak in the eighth century. Some of them were almost four metres high, and the shape had changed so that the outline of the limestone slab is reminiscent of a sliced mushroom. The ornamental designs are also different, the entire front face being covered with representative scenes, often arranged in horizontal strips. The designs were reserved against a cut-away background and originally picked out in colour.

The meaning of the scenes depicted has been much discussed. Occasionally, as on the Ardre stone, it is possible to recognize episodes from heroic poems and mythology; thus the scene at the top of some stones, which depicts a rider on an eight-legged horse being met by a woman carrying a drinking horn, presumably symbolizes the ceremonial reception at Valhalla, the home of dead heroes. A large ship is often shown at the base, manned by a crew carrying shields and equipped with a large and spectacular sail and a complicated rigging system. This presumably represents the vessel which was to carry the dead from the shores of Gotland to the land of the dead. At Lärbro a stone three metres in height exhibits a drama in six parts, played out above a large ship design. The uppermost design shows a woman flanked by two men wielding swords – presumably the beginning of the story. Below are a

p.18(2)

Inside the second ring fort of Eketorp on Öland – a reconstruction of the scene just before an attack. Cattle and wagons are driven hurriedly inside before the gate is closed, and warriors assemble from the houses. (4)

horse, two swords and two men with their arms upraised, apparently swearing solemn oaths. Next comes a scene showing a man hanged from a tree, surrounded by armed men. Below this is a group of men aboard a boat wielding swords in opposition to another group of similarly armed warriors, who are on foot and are led by a large woman; this perhaps represents a confrontation on a beach. The outcome of this action can be seen in the next scene where warriors surround a man lying on his back beneath a horse with an empty saddle. The ship at the bottom of the stone sailing in heavy seas makes an appropriate close to the drama – the hero bound for the land of the dead.

These stones were raised in the eighth century, when the Migration Period was long past, at the dawn of a period of considerable expansion – the Viking Age. The centuries which separate the two (*c.* 575–800) are in many respects the least known period of Scandinavian prehistory, a period in which a coherent story can only occasionally be glimpsed. The characteristically rich finds of the Migration Period no longer occur, yet the many valuable objects found either casually or in graves 12 – as for example the seventh-century brooch from Åker in south-east Norway – testify to the great wealth of p.68(7) much of Scandinavia. The favoured art styles consisted of abstract animal designs of great complexity and imagination. It is often difficult for the untutored eye to distinguish the details of these animals, with their highly stylized heads, writhing bodies, ferocious jaws and birds' heads.

The graves of Vendel

The centuries which separate the Migration Period and the Viking Age are in Sweden known as the Vendel Period, after the richly appointed boat graves excavated at Vendel in Uppland. The first was founded in 1881 when a wall surrounding the church at Vendel was being enlarged. Of the fourteen closely grouped graves, twelve individuals were buried in boats and two in coffins. All the people buried here were men and are evenly distributed over the period from 600 to 1050. Similar boat burials have been found elsewhere in Uppland and the Mälar region, as for instance at Valsgärde. There can be no doubt that these were burial grounds reserved for the heads of wealthy and established agricultural families of the locality; indeed, the cemeteries were used until the introduction of Christianity.

The rich graves of the Vendel Period are characterized by their ostentatious military equipment. These 1 swords with golden hilts, together with helmets and shields decorated with semi-naturalistic designs, are closely related to the helmet and shield from the famous royal boat burial found at Sutton Hoo in England (see Chapter 3). There can be no doubt that the objects found in Sweden were of local manufacture, for at

Carved stone from Lärbro, Sweden. The elaborate scenes – a drama in six acts – are described at length on this page. Most striking of all is the ship at the bottom, carrying the hero to the land of the dead. (5)

Torslunda on Öland four matrices for the manufacture 5,6 of pressed bronze sheet have been found, which have motifs closely related to those found on the helmets from these sites: it is likely that the helmet and shield from Sutton Hoo were of Swedish origin, forming perhaps part of some great exchange of gifts. Apart from weapons, the boat graves generally contain a generous selection of cooking utensils, whole or half carcasses of slaughtered animals, and such necessities as cups or drinking horns. Horses and dogs ensured successful hunting in the after-life, while the ship, like the designs on the Gotland picture stones, was presumably intended to transport the dead man to his new homeland.

In the graves of the Vendel Period all that is left of the boat is usually an impression in the soil and rows of rivets. But the well-preserved remains of a ship (18 metres long and 3.2 metres wide) were found in a peat bog at Kvalsund in west Norway, where it had been deposited presumably as a sacrifice to the gods. The vessel dates from around the year 700 and unlike earlier ships it has a rudimentary keel, while its comparatively wide hull would have allowed for propulsion by sail. By the eighth century at the latest Scandinavian ships were adapted to carry sails, an essential prerequisite for long-distance voyages. Sailing ships had been known to western Europe for many centuries, but when the Scandinavians finally started to take an interest progress was quickly made. By the eighth or ninth century the Scandinavians had good, manoeuvrable sailing vessels, adequate for use on the Atlantic.

The tools and implements used in ship-building, forging, carving and carpentry now begin to appear in the finds, together with those relating to agriculture, hunting and fishing. In Norway a new custom developed – one which was to last until the end of the pagan era. The dead were no longer merely supplied with weapons, jewellery, fine clothes and playthings: men and women now took with them to the grave the tools used in everyday life. From this period it seems that the Norwegians were prepared to continue their ordinary lives after death, rather than envisaging a constant round of feasting, fighting and hunting. The finds from the graves provide a unique insight into the sophisticated technology of the period, providing us with tools of such perfect form that they were to remain unchanged for centuries. The large number of skilfully made iron objects in the graves implies considerable wealth, skilled smiths and ample iron supplies, a picture confirmed by the evidence of numerous iron-working sites.

p.10(*3,4*) At this time the techniques of writing were also modernized. Runes, the common script of all Germanic tribes, had been current in Scandinavia since the third century. It is not known where runes originated – some scholars have suggested Denmark, which has numerous examples of the earliest runic forms – but it is at least clear that they are derived from one or more Mediterranean alphabets. In Scandinavia the runic script was only slowly replaced by the Latin alphabet after the introduction of Christianity. The runic alphabet or *futhark* (the name is composed of the first six characters of the alphabet) originally comprised twenty-four characters: most inscriptions using this alphabet are very short. In the course of the seventh or eighth centuries in Scandinavia, a simplification occurred resulting in a sixteen-letter *futhark* which was used in two variant forms during the Viking Age. The sixteen-letter *futhark* became widely known and in time it must have been a common accomplishment to read and write in runes. During the Viking Age the runic script was used for all manner of inscriptions on memorial stones, for scribbling on any suitable surface, and indeed for day to day communications which could be cut into a wooden stick (known in contemporary language as a *rúnakefli*).

But in the seventh and eighth centuries only a few initiates had knowledge of runes, and as in earlier times inscriptions often have a magical content. Such an inscription is the unusually long text, written in the earlier *futhark* on the Enggjum stone in Norway: approximately two hundred characters were cut on the underside of this stone which covered a man's grave. The characters are difficult to interpret and were obviously designed to be read only by the dead man. The inscription states, among other things, that it had not been touched by the light of the sun nor cut by iron. It is clear that it was inscribed with some unusual implement by torchlight and carried to the grave at dead of night so that it should not lose its magical properties. Another curious runic inscription from the eighth century has been found in Ribe in Denmark. It is engraved on a portion of a human skull, which has also been pierced for suspension; the person from whose skull this fragment had been taken had, however, been dead for some time before it was used in this macabre way. The inscription is magical and includes the names of three gods: Ulfur, Odin and Hydyr.

Ribe, Hedeby and the Danevirke

Ribe is one of many towns and settlements which flourished in the Viking Age, but had their roots in the eighth century. For many years archaeologists have tried to find the site of Viking Age Ribe, a town which is known from several references in foreign written sources. For many years no archaeological levels of a date earlier than the twelfth century were found. It was thus a matter of some excitement when excavations on the outskirts of the town in 1973–75 revealed a wealth of finds dating from the eighth century, providing unique insights into the prerequisites for the development of such a town – trade and manufacture. The town's position on the River Ribe allowed easy access to the North Sea and western Europe, from which were imported pottery, millstones, glass and the like, and, not least important, twenty-eight tiny Frisian silver coins of the type known as *sceattas*. Only a very few objects from north Scandinavia were found at Ribe, the direction of whose trade was undoubtedly to the south. Among the mass of material found are objects which tell of various crafts and provide information concerning both the techniques of manufacture and the finished products. There were iron and bronze smithies, cobblers' and comb-makers' workshops and a bead-makers' where the local amber was cut and polished, or imported raw glass manufactured into brightly coloured beads. Traces of spinning and weaving were also found here, as indeed they are in every settlement of the period. No true houses have yet been excavated, and there are some who argue that the finds tell of a seasonal rather than a permanent settlement, although this seems rather unlikely. It is clear, however, that Ribe had its origin as a centre for trade and manufacture. The jewellery made by the bronze-smiths was, for instance, in a style which conformed to local taste and must have been intended for sale in a local, or at least in a Scandinavian, market; but the large amounts of imported material must have been paid for with something. What this was is suggested by some thick layers of cattle manure. Until recently Denmark's staple exports have always been agricultural produce and, as the merchants of Ribe were not just middlemen, it seems that agricultural commodities may have been the major exports, were they of live cattle, smoked or salted meat, leather and skins, beeswax or honey. The great monasteries of Europe alone used huge quantities of skins for books, and in the Catholic Church the consumption of wax candles was prodigious.

Other Danish settlements were founded at the same time as Ribe. One of these was Aggersborg, where in the Viking Age the largest fortress of the period was to be built at one of the places where the Limfjord could be conveniently crossed. At an even earlier period both banks on the site of the other major crossing of the Limfjord, near the present town of Ålborg, were settled. The burial ground of this settlement is magnificently situated on the high ground known as Lindholm Høje, with a panoramic view across this important sailing route which links the Baltic with western Europe. The cemetery contains about seven hundred graves ranging in date from the sixth to the tenth centuries.

p.186(4)   Another town, Hedeby, was founded at approximately the same time as Ribe, and was to become the largest and perhaps the most important town in Scandinavia during the Viking Age. Hedeby is situated just to the south of the present Danish-German border, on an arm of the Schlei fjord, which cuts deep inland from the east, and thereby considerably reduces the overland distance to the small rivers Rheide and Treene, which join the River Ejder and run into the North Sea. This was the ideal position for a market and a centre for the transit trade between western Europe and the Baltic. Given adequate facilities for the reloading of cargo, it was possible to avoid the lengthy and often perilous voyage off the west coast of Jutland to the Limfjord. The main route through Jutland from north to south was the Hærvejen or Oksevejen (the military road or the ox road), which passed close to Hedeby, and was the only possible land route to the south: to the west the broad marshy river valleys created an impassable barrier, and to the south it was necessary to pass through a wooded wilderness 20 kilometres in width before reaching the Ejder. On the other side of this river, which in fact formed the border, lived the Saxons and various Slav tribes.

The Hedeby area formed the gateway to Denmark, which in 737 was fortified by a bank and ditch about 4 miles in length and possibly also by another bank and ditch 2 miles long known as Østervold (the East Wall). The system consisted of an earth bank approximately 10 metres wide and 2 metres high, with a wooden palisade on the front face. The date, 737, has been established by dendrochronology, a method of dating by measuring the growth rings in a piece of wood, and comparing them with the growth ring pattern of wood of known date. The historical events which prompted the construction of this extensive fortification are unknown, nor do we know who the builder was, but the system must have been built in the face of a serious threat from the neighbouring tribes to the south.

In time this system of defences (known as the Danevirke) was extended and rebuilt; new stretches of wall were added as others were abandoned, until in the tenth century the whole system extended over $8\frac{1}{2}$ miles. Only rarely do we know exactly when and by whom a particular section of the wall was built, and there is much to learn about this gigantic and complicated structure, one of the largest of its kind in northern Europe; for it is usually impossible to verify the accuracy of the account given by medieval historians. A legend that is particularly persistent links the energetic Queen Thyre with building activities on the Danevirke, but archaeologists have been unable to associate any part of the wall with Queen Thyre's lifetime. The Danevirke served as Denmark's southern bulwark until the political situation in the border-area changed in the thirteenth century; it was used for the last time as a defence by the Danes during the Prussian attack on Denmark in 1864.

The rise of the Vikings
About 800 an increasing amount of information about the Scandinavians begins to appear in written sources, most of which derive from western Europe and were written by people connected with the Christian Church. These historians are almost exclusively preoccupied with incidents of conflict – as for instance the Viking attacks on western Europe or Imperial expeditions against Denmark – or with the endeavour of the Church to convert the pagan Nordic peoples to the true faith. It is these Christian writers who, fearing and despising the pagans and possessing no knowledge of the conditions in Scandinavia, have created the bloodthirsty image of the Scandinavians of the Viking Age still reproduced in popular fiction. The Scandinavians behaved no better and no worse than would any other people in similar

circumstances; they merely remained pagans for a considerable time and had a different culture.

With the advent of the Viking Age, towns and trading centres grew in number, often apparently founded or supported by kings and chieftains. The Danish king Godfred, for instance, destroyed the Slav trading station at Reric, after defeating Charlemagne's Slav allies, and brought the merchants back to Scandinavia to settle at Hedeby. At the same time, according to the historical sources, he built (or enlarged) a fortified bank across the country: this was perhaps the section of the Danevirke over 4 miles in length which is known as the Kovirke. The same king once even dared to threaten Charlemagne that he would conquer his capital city of Aachen. Hedeby expanded and flourished. In the tenth century it was surrounded by a massive bank, enclosing a semicircular area of 24 hectares (approximately 60 acres). This bank was connected to the Danevirke, while a semicircular fortification built of piles protected Hedeby's harbour. Trading connections were far-flung, to both the east and the west, as well as to the whole of Scandinavia. A great variety of goods were manufactured at Hedeby and the traces of many houses have been found, each standing in its own fenced plot. One of these houses is sufficiently well preserved to allow a reconstruction, and has been exactly dated by dendrochronology: it was built in 870 although some alterations were made twelve years later. The building is an ordinary town house, 12 metres long and 5 metres wide, built of wattle-and-daub on a timber frame. There are three rooms: a large central room and two smaller rooms at either end. The room at one end contained an oven for baking bread and was used as a kitchen, whereas the function of the room at the other end is unknown. The main room had a central open hearth and along the walls were low broad benches made of earth retained by wooden planks. These seats, raised above the draughty floor, would have served a multitude of purposes – work, sleep and general accommodation. The only additional furniture would probably be a loom and a couple of chests for storage and sitting. The house was presumably also equipped with textiles, hides and woven rugs. In the eleventh century, Hedeby was abandoned and its role was assumed by the nearby town of Schleswig.

Similar developments can be observed in the Mälar region of central Sweden. At the beginning of the Viking Age Birka (on the small island of Björkö) began to expand at the expense of the Helgö settlement, and at the end of the tenth century Sigtuna took over from Birka. Birka, like Hedeby, was fortified by a bank in the tenth century, but in this case the enclosed area was smaller and only a minor part has so far been excavated. The dead were, however, buried outside the fortification, some of them in wooden chamber-tombs

18,19

20

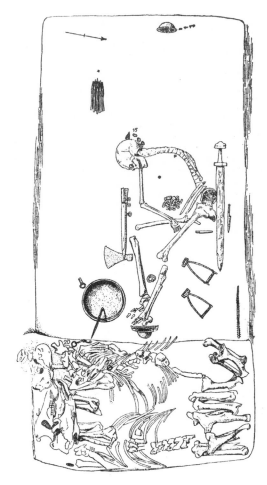

Grave of a rich man at Birka. He was buried with his weapons, stirrups and other personal belongings such as bowl and comb, and with his horse at his feet. (6)

with or without a mound, and many were richly furnished with valuable possessions which demonstrate trading connections with western Europe, the British Isles, Russia, Byzantium and the Arabic countries of western Asia as well as other parts of Scandinavia. Here we find evidence of a kaleidoscopic and cosmopolitan world, in which the women were adorned with magnificent jewels and trinkets from the four corners of the world, of a variety and splendour unmatched until the present day. We may assume that numerous languages could be heard in Birka, and that it would have been possible to eat there in the Swedish, French or Russian style. A multitude of gods were worshipped: not merely Odin, Thor, Frey and other members of the Nordic pantheon, but also Allah and Christ, as well as Slav, Finnish and Lappish gods. After a mission led by a German cleric named Ansgar, there was even a Christian church in Birka for a short time during the ninth century.

6

The earliest Norwegian towns, such as Oslo, Tønsberg and Trondheim, seem to have originated no earlier than the eleventh century, or perhaps as early as 1000, when many new towns were founded also in Sweden and Denmark: towns like Skara, Sigtuna, Lund, Roskilde, Odense, Ålborg and Schleswig, all of which still exist today. Viborg was already expanding by this time, and Århus, within its encircling wall, dates back to about 900. On the south coast of Norway, however, an international trading centre was established about 800 at Kaupang which was to operate for a hundred and fifty years. Ottar from Hålogaland in north Norway put in here on his long voyage to Hedeby and one must assume that Kaupang functioned as one of the ports for the export of such goods as iron tools, whetstones, and the fireproof soapstone cooking-pots which could be cut directly out of the living rock and were extremely popular in Denmark (they are found in great quantities at Hedeby, for example). Trade in the Viking Age was not confined to luxuries: as industry generally became more specialized, so more everyday items became objects of trade. Kaupang also had connections with western Europe – with both the Continent and the British Isles – and as scholars have gradually modified their impression of the Scandinavians in the Viking Age, it seems likely that some of the cheap metal jewellery or mounts reworked as jewellery are less likely to be loot from the monasteries of western Europe than trade goods, souvenirs and gifts.

Money and ships

Silver was the most common means of payment, whether in the form of coins, ingots or jewellery. Value was calculated by weight, so any jewellery might have to be cut into pieces of convenient size if used in payment; and so merchants would carry a box containing a set of folding scales and a series of weights to weigh the bullion. Silver came to Scandinavia in great quantities and, while some of it remained in its original form, much silver was remade into jewellery of considerable artistic quality. Apart from silver jewellery, recorded hoards of Viking Age date contain over 84,000 Arabic and 42,000 English coins, along with coins from other areas. Much silver was acquired by trade, but large quantities arrived in Scandinavia by other means, as for instance by the payment of Danegeld in England in the period about 1000. This tax benefited not only the Danes, but the Norwegians and Swedes as well. A runic inscription in Yttergärde, Uppland, on a stone raised to the memory of a certain Ulf concludes: 'and Ulf had in England taken three gelds. That was the first which Tosti paid. Then Thorkild paid. Then Knut paid.' The two last mentioned were Torkild Høje, a Danish chieftain whose men operated more or less independently in England for several years, and Knut, king of Denmark and England. Other rune-stones tell similar stories.

p.179(8)

Coins were first minted in Scandinavia as early as the ninth century, but it was not until a century later, after production had temporarily ceased, that minting began to expand. In the eleventh century, however, the growing central power provided impetus for more rapid developments, and for the first time payment began to be made according to the face value of the coins rather than to their weight and standard. Issuing coins was a lucrative business, for (following western European example) the moneyers, and the authorities who controlled them, often allowed the nominal value to exceed the value of the silver and pocketed the difference.

Silver was good, but gold was better. Those who were generous with their gold were celebrated in song by the scalds, one of whom spoke for many with the lines, 'life seems brighter to me / when seen through a gold ring'. Gold was often elaborately worked, as on the famous jewels found on the island of Hiddensee in the country of the Slavs, which are decorated with filigree birds' heads. But at other times it is the sheer size of the jewellery that is impressive, as is the case with a great gold neck ring found in Denmark in 1977, which has a diameter of about 30 centimetres and weighs just under two kilos. Its owner, whether male or female, must have been uncommonly rich and must have had a splendidly broad chest.

p.189(11)

The range of trading and other activities in the Viking Age depended on efficient sailing ships, which are well known from many finds. The best preserved and most famous of these were found at Oseberg and at Gokstad in Norway. Members of the Vestfold royal family were buried in the ships – a woman in one and a man in the other – together with many grave-goods and covered by large burial mounds. Due to special soil conditions most of the wood has been preserved, and the enormous high-prowed ships in the Bygdøy museum in Oslo are composed almost entirely of their original timbers. These are typical Viking ships: in favourable winds their sails would be raised, but they could be rowed if necessary. The keel was of a modest dimension, and the draught was slight enough to allow the ship to sail in very shallow water and run straight up onto the shore. By lashing the ribs to reserved cleats on the planks, rather than using nails, the hull was given an added elasticity and strength which made the vessel more seaworthy. The scantling of the timbers was as small as possible, so the ship was light and the sail and oars could be used with maximum efficiency. It was rigged with a square sail, and fitted with a large steering oar at the stern on the side we still know as starboard (from Old English: *stéorbord*, steering side). The Oseberg ship is the earliest of the two great Norwegian finds, dating from *c.* 800; the hull is about 22 metres long and her design would suggest that she was best suited for use in sheltered waters. She was indeed fit for

25–31

29 a queen to travel in, being richly carved at stem and stern. The Gokstad ship, which is half a century later in date, was however a seagoing vessel. The mast is firmly seated, and the high sides, measuring 1.95 metres between keel and gunwale, were designed to prevent the seas washing over the side in bad weather. For the same reason the sixteen oar-holes on each side could be closed by internal shutters: the number of oar-holes suggests that the 24-metre-long vessel could be rowed by thirty-two men. A copy of the Gokstad ship was sailed across the Atlantic from Norway to America in 1893, and was much praised for its excellent handling. Such ships carried the Vikings overseas.

Five ships from Skuldelev in Denmark bear witness to the range of ship-building techniques in the late Viking Age. The ships were built about 1000 and scuttled in Roskilde fjord in the eleventh century in an attempt to block the best sailing channel leading to the important town of Roskilde. When the remains of these ships were raised they were found to represent a number of specialized types: a seagoing cargo vessel 16.3 metres long; a smaller cargo vessel intended for coastal traffic 13.8 metres long; two war ships 17.4 metres and about 29 metres long; and a boat 11.6 metres long, which was presumably a ferry or fishing boat.

7
32–34
The rich and ample appointments of the Oseberg queen's grave reveal many aspects of the daily life of a royal household. The elaborately carved cart is the only complete example remaining from the Viking Age, although various bits and pieces found elsewhere demonstrate that carts of this type were not uncommon. The sleighs are also unique: three are highly decorated and presumably intended for special occasions, whereas a fourth is strictly functional. The furniture consists of a chair and several beds, together with chests – standard furniture for larger houses for many hundreds of years. In addition, the grave contained oil lamps, kitchen ware, tools and equipment for weaving and spinning, and much else besides.

Art of the Vikings

Ornamental and representational art, so well exemplified in this find, stood at a high level of technical and artistic excellence throughout the Viking Age. Like scaldic poetry it had its own unique style and development. It derived from the animal ornament of the Germanic Iron Age, and all manner of animals – joyously acrobatic animals, thin ribbon-like animals, large aggressive animals, prancing animals, running animals and slim phlegmatic animals – remained the most important element of the art. Contemporary European ornament inspired the incorporation of plant motifs into the art; and, later on, Christian motifs were also introduced. In the course of the eleventh and twelfth centuries Nordic animals were replaced by the ornament of Romanesque Europe.

Scandinavian art is in broad terms divided into a number of consecutive styles: Styles I, II and III belong to the Germanic Iron Age (although Style III continues into the Viking Age, to be splendidly represented on wood-carvings in the Oseberg find, for instance). Style III was succeeded by the Borre Style (named after the ornament on a group of gilt-bronze objects in a Norwegian grave) and by the Jellinge Style, named after the ornament on a small silver cup found in a royal 40 grave at Jelling in Denmark. These styles were followed by the Mammen Style, exemplified by the 41 animal ornament inlaid in silver on an axe from Mammen in Denmark, which grew into the Ringerike 42 Style (named after the ornament which appears on a group of stones in the Ringerike area of Norway). The final art style of the Viking Age, the Urnes Style, takes its name from the elegant ornament carved on the timbers of a small church at Urnes in west Norway. 43 Traces of colour survive on some objects: on the stone, for example, dating from the time of Knut and decorated in the Scandinavian style, found in St Paul's p.165(12 churchyard in London. These finds demonstrate that Viking Age ornament on wood and stone was often embellished with strong colours, as with the earlier

The Oseberg cart, a unique survival from the Viking Age. Fragments from other sites prove that such carts were not uncommon, though this one was unusually richly decorated. A detail is shown on p. 142. (7)

33
22
picture stones of Gotland; the austerity of the natural colours of the Oseberg carvings and the large Jelling stone, for example, are attractive to modern taste, but hardly reflect the striking and colourful aspect these objects originally offered.

Such objects reflect the culture and taste of the upper classes; these were the works which were made for kings, courtiers, large landowners and merchants. Such people set the fashion, and in them the craftsmen had customers with eclectic tastes and extensive purchasing power. Fashions in decoration spread from towns to villages and farms through the medium of mass-produced articles, such as jewellery, and by means of itinerant craftsmen. The same art styles occur, therefore, on such articles as on the property of the wealthy; only the medium and the quality of the execution distinguish the two.

Farmers and kings

The farms were the backbone of society: most of the population lived on the land and surplus agricultural produce aided the economic system by being sold to town-dwellers or exported abroad. Slaves apparently played an important role as farm labourers: it is likely that both warfare and special expeditions provided an ample supply of slaves in the Viking Age, and it was perhaps this labour which contributed to the great increase in the amount of land under cultivation and made possible such ambitious projects as the building of forts, walls, bridges, canals and royal memorials. At
17 Lejre and Stengade in Denmark we find macabre evidence of what slavery could mean: the bodies of slaves sacrificed in their masters' graves.

Peasant dwellings, farms and villages are best known from Denmark. As in the Migration Period, houses were built of wood or wattle-and-daub, and the roof was usually supported by two rows of posts. But the long walls were now often curved and the roof arched in a shape which was imitated on Viking 'hog-back' gravestones like those at Brompton in Yorkshire, and in the shape of the large Cammin casket. These houses could be more than forty metres in length, the dwelling area being divided into different rooms. In only one case has it been possible to establish traces of a byre at one end of a house and to identify a group of houses as belonging to a single farm, defined by the remains of a fence. This occurred at Vorbasse, where traces of an enclosed farm were found in 1978 near the Migration Period houses. The farm consisted of a main building, over 30 metres long, with stabling for twenty cattle at the east end and several smaller outbuildings, one of them a smithy. It is evident that the layout of Danish farms had not greatly altered since the Migration Period. This apparently also applies to villages. At Sædding, in south-west Jutland, large parts of a village from the Viking period have recently been excavated,

although individual farms cannot as yet be distinguished among the numerous houses. It is, however, interesting to observe that the houses are grouped around a large open common, like the houses at the Migration Period village of Vorbasse.

From the tenth century onwards Denmark at last emerges as a single kingdom under one king. The present Queen of Denmark can trace her family back generation by generation to the king who was one of the most powerful Viking rulers, Harald Bluetooth (who died a Christian in about 986), and to his pagan parents King Gorm and Queen Thyre, who died forty or fifty years previously. Harald Bluetooth created a unique monument to himself and his parents at Jelling, of which a central element is the vast rune-stone, the largest and most impressive in the world. The 22 inscription reads: 'King Harald ordered these monuments to be made in memory of his father Gorm and his mother Thyre: that Harald who won the whole of Denmark and Norway for himself and who made the Danes Christian.' These proud words are dramatically confirmed by the mighty building projects which were carried out in Denmark.

Some of Harald's monuments may still be seen at Jelling. When his parents died he buried them, along with numerous grave-goods, in the pagan fashion, in a wooden chamber covered by a large mound, which today is 8.5 metres high and 65 metres in diameter. Some standing stones set in the outline of a ship were 21 presumably associated with this mound, but today only the southernmost part of this stone setting exists, because most of it was covered in antiquity by another, larger mound – the largest in the country. This mound (which today is 11 metres high and 77 metres in diameter) is, like the first, carefully built of turf but contains no grave and may have been intended as a cenotaph. The burial chamber of King Gorm and Queen Thyre has been many times excavated, and the small silver cup, from which the Jellinge Style has taken its name, was among the few objects to be found there. It is clear that the chamber was opened long ago and (as 40 yet unfinished) excavations inside and outside the church, which is situated between the two mounds, have thrown new light upon the opening of the mound and on Harald's conversion to Christianity, which written sources tell us took place about 960.

The new faith

Beneath the present stone church, which was built about 1100, traces of three earlier wooden churches of remarkable size have been found, as well as a large centrally placed grave of the same date as the earliest of these churches. This grave contained the disjointed skeletons of a man and a woman, evidently moved from elsewhere; also found were numerous fragments of gold thread from valuable textiles, and a silver mount of an unusually high quality with an animal head, the style of which completely accords with the objects found in the burial chamber in the mound. There can be no doubt that Harald wished to mark both his conversion and the conversion of his people to Christianity by reburying his parents in a Christian manner. Their bodies were taken from the pagan burial mound and interred in a prominent place in the large new church, outside which (exactly equidistant from the centre of the two burial mounds) he raised the great three-sided rune-stone, specially made for the occasion, its one face bearing the figure of Christ, the second an arrogant animal and the third the long inscription. We can only guess at the splendour of the ceremonies which accompanied this action.

23   Harald consolidated his rule throughout Denmark by the construction of large fortresses which were probably used for both civil and military purposes. These were Trelleborg on Sjælland, Fyrkat in north-east Jutland, Aggersborg on the Limfjord and probably also a fortress on the island of Fyn. These fortresses varied in size, but were all built to the same strict design: a truly circular wall, with gates facing the four points of the compass, enclosed an area divided into quarters, in each of which elegant houses formed rectangular court-yards. It seems likely that Harald also initiated large-scale extensions of the Danevirke (which twice saw great battles between Harald and the German imperial forces) and that he also built the bridge over the marshy river valley at Ravning Enge, near Jelling, which is about half a mile long. Furthermore it was possibly under his orders that a canal, over half a mile long, was built across the island of Samsø. But the fortresses, bridge and canal were not long in use; it is possible that they were all abandoned when Sven Forkbeard became king in 986 after staging a successful coup against his ageing father, who had in fact been too ambitious in his building projects. For several generations after this the Danish kings were mainly preoccupied with Viking raids, foreign policy and the crown of England, which Harald's grandson Knut acquired in 1016.

p.167(18)   In the course of the tenth and early eleventh centuries, Norway also was centralized under a single king, following events which started with the unification of the coastal areas by the Vestfold king Harald Finehair about the year 900, after the battle of Hafrsfjord. It is likely that the unification of Sweden took place at the beginning of the eleventh century; Olaf Skötkonung, who died in about 1020, is the first king who is recorded to have ruled over both the Svear in the east and the Goths in the south-west. The achievement of centralized power was everywhere accompanied by the establishment of Christianity, which was invariably supported by the kings. It was greatly to the king's advantage to deal with a literate

p.214(12) placed to the left: see below

clergy who were centrally organized and who recognized the importance of authority, while at the same time retaining close contacts with the people. But the Christian faith gained ground only slowly. In Sweden and Norway some independently minded chieftains led movements of pagan reaction. In Norway, indeed, Christianity had to be introduced by force, and was only finally accepted under King Olaf, the least saintly of men, who became the first royal saint of Scandinavia after his death at the battle of Stiklestad in 1030.

In Sweden the conversion took even longer, but, in the course of the eleventh century German missionaries worked their way steadily northwards from the south-east. One such missionary was the extremely devout Adalward, bishop of Skara, whose grave in Skara Cathedral contained a small silver chalice bearing the moving inscription 'Adalvvardus Peccator' (Adalward the sinner). When Master Adam of Bremen wrote his description of the Nordic countries in 1070, paganism was still flourishing in the land of the Svear. Adam describes a large pagan temple at Gamla Uppsala with idols of Odin, Thor and Frey, and recounts some of the horrendous pagan rites performed there. It has been claimed that faint traces of this temple have been discovered underneath the church, which is situated near the old royal burial mounds, which date from the Migration Period: but the claim is unconvincing.

A few decades later the Svear had finally accepted Christianity and, by about 1100, the Scandinavian countries were on the way to becoming integrated into the common European culture. The English crown was lost when Knut's son died 'standing at his drink' at a wedding in 1042 and, despite various abortive attempts by Norwegians and Danes to recreate Knut's empire, such dreams were finally abandoned in the second half of the eleventh century. The restless centuries of the Viking Age were followed by a period characterized by the consolidation of what had been achieved in that turbulent period. Harmonious cooperation was established between King and Church, with the aim of placing their power on a firm basis and hold at bay their enemies, both fellow Scandinavians and the newly restless Slav tribes to the south of the Baltic. But the achievements of their great forefathers were not forgotten. In the centuries which followed, and up until modern times, the people of the Viking Age have inspired literature, the visual arts, political events and general nostalgia both in Scandinavia and in Europe, where the Nordic legacy included such everyday matters as place-names and loan words. English speakers can neither thrive, be ill and die, nor eat eggs and bread, without using Scandinavian words. Indeed, in various parts of the western world – on the Isle of Man, for example – it has become a matter of pride, worthy of much celebration, to be seen as the descendant of the once feared Vikings.

6
THE
VIKING
ADVENTURE

DAVID M. WILSON

'They put to sea as soon as they were ready
and sailed for three days until land was lost to sight below the
horizon. Then the fair wind failed and northerly
winds and fog set in, and for many days they had no idea what their
course was. After that they saw the sun again and were
able to get their bearings; they hoisted sail and
after a day's sailing they sighted land.
They discussed among themselves
what country this might be.'

The Greenlanders' Saga

Before the thirteenth century

Strangest of all stories of early medieval Europe is the story of the Norse people. At a time when most of the Germanic tribes were beginning to establish nations in new homelands, the Scandinavians began a series of journeys that took them farther than any of the others – west to Scotland and England, to Ireland, to the distant shores of Iceland, Greenland and America; south to Normandy; east to the Baltic and Russia. They came first as raiders and pirates, but stayed as colonists and farmers, often adopting the culture of the host country and even losing their own language. Later, in the eleventh century, the Gallicized Norsemen began a new series of adventures – military conquest this time rather than simple piracy – that gave them kingdoms in England and Sicily. On these last expeditions we shall not follow them.

Unlike the peoples featured in other chapters of this book, the story of the Norsemen overseas is better chronicled in written sources than in archaeology. By the time they made their impact, fairly detailed histories were being written. To such annalistic record can be added the tangled skein of the medieval historical and semi-historical Icelandic sagas, which portray the life of the Norsemen in a way that is never encountered in relation to Saxons, Franks, Slavs or Celts. Material remains, on the other hand, tend to be disappointing, though recent archaeological discoveries in Orkney, Shetland, Dublin and York may add to the story.

The Gosforth Cross (*opposite*) was set up in the early tenth century within a generation or two of the Scandinavian settlements of north-west England. The settlers were now Christian and had adopted the stone cross from monuments common in Britain during this period. On the shaft is a strange iconography, which has been interpreted as a mixture of pagan Norse and Christian motifs. The scenes are difficult to identify, and the way they are placed is confusing. On one side is the crucifixion, on this side are scenes of pagan origin. Together they may be taken to represent the triumph of the Church, through Christ's death, over the pagan world. (1)

On previous page : rune-stone from
Gripsholm, Sweden. The inscription tells of
the journey of Harald a Swede who died
in the Saracens' land. (1)

The Vikings in Britain

Greensted church, in Essex, is unique in England in having walls of tree-trunks split in two and placed with the curved side outward. The technique is paralleled in eleventh-century Denmark. (2)

York was for a period an important Viking merchant centre. Buried under the present great cathedral were gravestones (*above*) carved in an Anglo-Scandinavian style. Excavations in recent years have revealed the wooden remains of houses of the craftsmen of the Viking period. (4)

Orkney in the eleventh century was an earldom rivalling in power the kingdoms of Scandinavia. Remains on Birsay (*above*) show the cathedral of the Viking Age; the houses on the slope and the cliffs in the foreground are perhaps the remains of a Norse aristocratic settlement. *Right*: Viking settler's grave at Westness, Rousay, Orkney. (3,5)

It was as raiders that the Vikings first came to the British Isles. The first attack came in 793 when the abbey of Lindisfarne was sacked and destroyed. This memorial stone was perhaps set up to record the event, showing on one side warriors brandishing swords and axes. (6)

Jarlshof in the Shetlands (*below*), originally a Pictish settlement, was taken over by Vikings in the ninth century, when the first house was built. Further houses were built on the site and adapted to various uses throughout the Viking Age; it was still occupied in the seventeenth century. A reconstruction (*inset*) shows the tenth- or eleventh-century settlement surrounded by its barns and cowsheds. (7,8)

To the ends of the known world

Into Scandinavia flowed a stream of treasures from abroad, either plundered or purchased; some few objects certainly came from churches and may have been stolen or may represent missionary activity. *Left*: the head of a crozier from Ireland, found at Helgö, near Stockholm, Sweden. *Below left*: bronze-gilt mount of Northumbrian workmanship, imported into Norway. Another import from Scotland or Ireland is shown on p. 107 (pl. 29), part of a bronze vessel found at Myklebostad in Norway. (9,10)

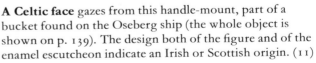

A Celtic face gazes from this handle-mount, part of a bucket found on the Oseberg ship (the whole object is shown on p. 139). The design both of the figure and of the enamel escutcheon indicate an Irish or Scottish origin. (11)

Two Norsemen died at opposite ends of Europe, leaving their memorials in stone. *Above*: tombstone erected by Ginne and Toke in St Paul's churchyard, London, in the early eleventh century. Carved in a superbly vigorous style with a design related to that of the stone raised by King Harald at Jelling, Denmark (p. 136), it seems to represent a fight between a snake and a lion, both creatures being conceived in terms of swirling and spiralling lines. Here the original colours have been restored. (12)

To the Black Sea and thence to Byzantium, the Vikings came by way of the Dnjeper. Trading stations were established along the route, where Norse merchants might live for considerable portions of their lives. *Left*: tombstone with runic inscription found near Odessa. (13)

Viking multinational

Through their journeys, their conquests, their colonization and their opening up of trade routes, the Vikings more than any other people contrived to break down cultural barriers. These pages illustrate the two-way traffic in ideas.

The crozier made for a twelfth-century bishop of Clonmacnoise (*left*) is decorated with Scandinavian ornament, interlaced snakes and stylized head. **Iceland**: a carved board (*above*) combining Ringerike ornament and haloed saints was made in the eleventh century soon after the introduction of Christianity. **Normandy** (*below left*): oval brooch, from a woman's grave at Pitres. **Germany** (*below*): among the most satisfying works of Viking art is a solid casket of gilt bronze and walrus ivory, carved in an early eleventh-century style. (14–17)

From Ireland or Scotland came a small reliquary found in northern Norway (*top*). **From the Muslim east** came many of the coins found in a hoard at Birka (*centre*); the other objects seem to be included as silver bullion. **From northern India**, most amazingly of all, came a bronze Buddha, with eyes inlaid with silver; found at Helgö, Sweden. (20,21,22)

The struggle for England spread over hundreds of years. In 1017 Knut the Dane was proclaimed king of Denmark and England. *Above*: page from the *Liber Vitae* of New Minster, Winchester, showing Knut and his wife Emma giving a cross to the high altar. *Left*: coin of Sihtric III Silkbeard of Dublin *c*.1015. (18,19)

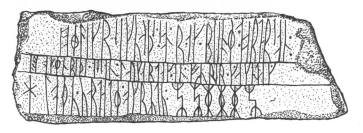

Runic inscription (10cm long) found on the west coast of Greenland, recording the visit of three Norsemen in 1333. It is the most northerly object of the medieval period found in Greenland (72°–73°N). (2)

THE VIKING ADVENTURE

'THE BRITISH OCEAN', wrote Master Adam of Bremen in the middle of the eleventh century, 'is of immense breadth, terrible and dangerous, and on the west encompasses Britannia to which is now given the name of England. On the south it touches the Frisians and the part of Saxony that belongs to our diocese of Hamburg. On the east are the Danes and the mouth of the Baltic Sea, and the Norwegians who live beyond Denmark. On the north that ocean flows by the Orkney Islands and then encircles the earth in boundless expanses. On the left there is Hibernia . . . now called Ireland. On the right are the crags of Norway, and farther on the islands of Iceland and Greenland.'

The people who had made this terrible ocean their own by means of seamanship and in search of wealth were the Vikings, who in Adam's time had begun to settle into the general structure of European Christendom. But not only did the Scandinavians of the Viking Age feel masters of the western seas; they also at various times controlled the Baltic and the great rivers of the Slavs through Russia and Poland; they attacked France and Germany; fought for the Byzantine Empire and in the Caspian Sea; reached out into Arabia and the Mediterranean and raided in Spain.

From the late eighth century until the middle of the eleventh century the Scandinavians were a force to be reckoned with in Europe – a maverick force perhaps, representative of nations little understood by contemporaries who considered themselves more civilized. History portrays the Vikings with many faces – as raiders, pirates, merchants, colonists, politicians, poets, seamen and mercenaries – but it is their reputation for brutality which stands out in the popular imagination. Brutality of a romantic cut perhaps, but the view we are presented with is of a cruel and terrible people who had valour, but played no game but their own.

The history of the Vikings does not reveal a unity of organization or achievement. In different areas and in different ages the aims and activities of the Vikings varied. In the early ninth century, for example, Scandinavians were raiding England, settling in the Hebrides, developing trade along the Russian rivers and supporting campaigns in north Germany against the Frankish emperor. In the early years of the eleventh century they were trading in the Irish Sea, colonizing certain areas of Greenland, adventuring on the North American coast, building a Danish kingdom in England and fighting for the Byzantine emperor as mercenaries. People from widely different areas of Scandinavia took part in these activities: people from Danish farmlands, from Baltic islands and from the deep fjords of western Norway; colonists from Iceland and Orkney, England and Normandy; merchants from Dublin, Novgorod and Pomerania. The story to be told is complicated and repetitive.

Our knowledge of the Vikings is (until the eleventh century at least) one sided, as until then all written accounts of their activities were produced by historians and polemicists outside Scandinavia. The Vikings, into the last half of the tenth century at least, were pagan people: literacy was rare until the Church brought

◁ **Even the wastes of Greenland** did not discourage the Viking settlers, and the southern tip at least was hospitable enough to make colonization viable. According to the early sources, the farm of their leader, Eirik the Red, was at a place called Brattahlid. This has been identified and excavated (*opposite*), revealing the remains of farm buildings, as well as the church built by his wife Thjodhild. It was from Greenland that the Norsemen set out yet again for the west and made landfall at Newfoundland, the first Europeans to set foot in the New World. On Greenland they stayed for five hundred years. Gradually the colony dwindled. Finally, in the early fifteenth century, they are heard of no more. Did they return to Iceland, were they wiped out by plague or Eskimos, did they perish in some natural disaster? We may never know. (23)

books into the north. The great corpus of Scandinavian saga literature, some of which purports to be history, was mostly written down in the Christian high Middle Ages (see Chapter 1) and preserves only a traditional and stylized history of the Vikings' activities. It is a corpus to be used with care by the historian (especially for the early Viking Age), but the vivid pages of the histories and family sagas reveal a view – at once shadowy and substantial – of the personalities involved. For the rest we rely on the rather patchy archaeological record.

Raiders from the north

In the early 790s Norwegian and Danish raiders appeared in the western seas. Historians tell of them as despoilers of monasteries, who raided, stole, killed and ravaged, disappearing quickly from the scene to raid elsewhere. The most famous such attack was that which

6 took place in 793 on the monastery of Lindisfarne, one of the richest and most prestigious in England, the repository of the relics of St Cuthbert. Alcuin, an Englishman, safely ensconced at the court of the Frankish king Charlemagne, could write in hyperbole of this attack of the pagan peoples who had 'desecrated the sanctuaries of God, laid waste the house of our hope, trampled on the bodies of our saints in the temple of God like dung in the street. . . . What assurance is there for the churches of Britain if St Cuthbert, with so great a number of saints, does not defend his own?' The

7 attack on Lindisfarne was the precursor of many – Iona, the sacred home of St Columba, burned in 802; Inismurray in Ireland, attacked in 807; Noirmoutier, south of the mouth of the Loire, frequently raided between 814 and 819. The accounts of such attacks, while written by the sufferers, are probably reasonably accurate. But they are also incomplete. It is unlikely in this early stage of their activities that Scandinavians confined their attention to monasteries. There must have been some general plundering of the type recorded laconically in the Anglo-Saxon Chronicle in 833: 'in this year heathen men ravaged Sheppey'. But contemporary accounts would suggest that such attacks (during the first fifty or sixty years of the Viking Age) were uncoordinated. Only in north Germany was the Danish king Godfred engaged in regular and continuous warfare with the Frankish emperor.

It is reasonably clear, however, that soon after the first raids in northern Britain Scandinavians were settling to farm in Orkney, Shetland, on the north coast of Scotland and (perhaps somewhat later) in the Hebrides and Faroes. The classic settler's farm is the

7,8 rich site of Jarlshof (so named by Sir Walter Scott) on the southern tip of Shetland, where excavation has revealed continuous settlement from prehistoric times to the seventeenth century. Early in the ninth century Norse settlers took over from the native Picts a substantial farm complex and built a two-roomed stone house some 32 metres long. One room was a kitchen with oven and fireplace; the other was the main living room of the house with a central fireplace. With little change – save for the addition of outhouses – this building remained in use until the eleventh century, when it was replaced by a very similar structure. Here, as elsewhere in Scotland, the houses were rebuilt from time to time until the Norse culture collapsed in this area in the late Middle Ages.

In England, however, settlement was to come later. The character of the raids – which initially seem to have been somewhat spasmodic – changed in the middle years of the ninth century and professional armies were mustered which could challenge the might of the English kings. As the English became exhausted, treaties were arranged. Thus in 876 a group of Scandinavians under Halfdan started to settle in Yorkshire, while in 881 (after treating with Alfred the Great) Guthrum and his followers settled in East Anglia.

The driving force behind the initial raids had been the acquisition of wealth: wealth in a portable form – raw material of gold and silver obtained from broken-up jewellery and church treasure. The extent of the robbery is exemplified by the fact that after the attack on St Bavon in Ghent seven-eighths of the monastery's treasure had been stolen. Such portable wealth – bullion – was important to the Vikings, for Scandinavia had not yet established a monetary economy. Other wealth came to them in the form of captives, for whom there was a ready sale in the slave markets of Gaul and of Scandinavia. Permanent wealth within Scandinavia resided in land and goods and the raids themselves presumably contributed only marginally to the national wealth of the homelands. The individual, however, benefited by the raids and was thus able to improve his standing at home, either by the purchase or enlargement of his farm or by buying new stock. Soon the Scandinavians found that the practice of raiding monasteries was subject to the law of diminishing returns and started to levy tribute – blackmail – on the people of the lands which they attacked. As early as 819 they had levied tribute in Frisia and from 845 until 926 the western Franks were paying regular ransom to the leaders of the Scandinavian raiders. Kent paid its first tribute in 865: but it was not until more than a century later (in 991) that the Danegeld proper was instituted in England.

The interest in wealth, seen in loot, tribute and the acquisition of land, also expressed itself in trade. At all periods a raider could turn at will to become a trader – there was indeed little difference – and this is seen in Scandinavian activity in towns. Towns were being developed in Scandinavia in the course of the ninth century as both administrative and mercantile centres.

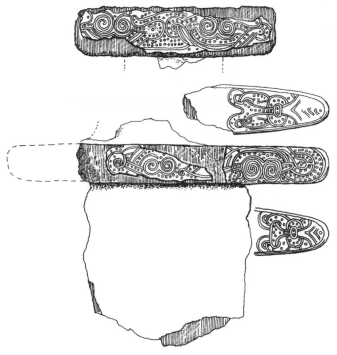

Fragments of a Viking sword found on the Ile de Groix, Brittany. The two ornamented bands formed the hilt with a hand-grip (missing) in between. The lower band is shown with its upper- and under-sides included above and below it. (3)

In Frisia the Scandinavians had for a short time attempted to take over some of the major trading centres. In 850 the Danish chieftain Rorik received Dorestad and its province. Dorestad was a major trading station on the Rhine and had been the subject of a number of Viking raids, but any attempt to keep this as a Scandinavian market came to an end when Rorik left Dorestad in 857 (the town being sacked in 858). It was, however, York which became the first major trading station in western Europe outside Scandinavia to be taken and controlled by the Vikings. In 867 it fell to the Danes and remained in their hands as a major mercantile centre until 954.

The route to Byzantium

The idea of using foreign trading stations was already familiar to the Scandinavians in the east. Even before the eighth century the Swedes had been founding settlements, presumably trading centres, on the southern and eastern coasts of the Baltic, and had also established a presence on Lake Ladoga in northern Russia at the town now known as Staraja Ladoga. Excavations at Grobin, Latvia, have shown the presence of some sort of Swedish colony before 800. The excavations at Staraja Ladoga are not so easily interpreted but the material culture in at least one of the layers has a strong Swedish taste, while there is

considerable evidence of a Scandinavian or a Scandinavian-influenced population in the burial mounds of the Ladoga region, where the grave-goods show specific Swedish characteristics.

The historical record of the events in the middle of the ninth century in northern Russia is both clear and controversial. The so-called Primary Russian Chronicle, in its oldest extant form compiled and written between 1111 and 1113 in the Cave Monastery outside Kiev, records that in 859 the Varangians:

from across the sea took tribute from the Cuds and from the Slovenes, from the Merians and from the Ves' and Krivicians ... In the year 862 they drove the Varangians over the sea and they gave no tribute, and they began to rule themselves; and there was no law among them, and kin rose against kin ... and they began to fight among themselves. . . . And they crossed the sea to the Varangians, to Rus' ... And to the Rus' said the Cuds, Slovenes, Krivicians and Ves', 'Our land is rich and large, but there is no order in it. So come and be king and rule over us.'

And three brothers with their kinsfolk were chosen; they took all the Rus' with them and came here: the eldest, Rurik, settled in Novgorod, the second, Sineus in Beloezero and the third, Truvor, in Izborsk.

The story told in this version of the Chronicle, and supported by a number of other sources, is usually considered to be a legendary, rationalized account of the foundation of Novgorod by Swedish adventurers. The Rus' appear in various sources in both east and west and are usually agreed to be Scandinavians. The term Varangians is to be understood as a generic term for the Scandinavians. The tradition of the foundation of Novgorod by Scandinavians has been the subject of discussion and controversy over more than two hundred years. For, if this Chronicle entry is true, the earliest recorded rulers – perhaps the founders – of the Russian state are not Slavs but Swedes. Many Russian scholars have been unable to support this theory and a controversy – virulent at times – has grown up in which the main protagonists are the northern European scholars (who emphasize the Scandinavian element in Russian sources and are thus known as Normanists) and certain Russian scholars (who reject practically all Scandinavian influences in Russia and are distinguished as the anti-Normanists).

It is now difficult to write the story of the Scandinavians in Russia without qualifications of such an intensity that they obfuscate the whole story. One interpretation will be found in Professor Herrmann's chapter. That presented here is slightly different. There can be little doubt on archaeological grounds that the Scandinavians were burying their dead in a Scandinavian fashion along the Russian rivers from the middle of the ninth century onwards. There is also a considerable body of archaeological material in

Two Viking objects found in Russia: (top) part of a scabbard from Danilovka, in the province of Saratov, and (below) a large silver brooch found near the River Don. (4,5)

p. 167(21)

p. 144(44)

Sweden, particularly in the graves of the major market town of Birka (which was already flourishing in the first quarter of the ninth century) and of the island of Gotland, to show a contact with Russia and the lands of Byzantium and the Middle East. From the beginning of the tenth century a large number of Arabic coins (the latest estimate for Sweden is 80,000) appeared in Scandinavia; at an earlier period Arabic coins had appeared in the Baltic lands, but rarely in Sweden.

External sources, Arab travellers and Byzantine documents, confirm the presence of Scandinavians in Russia. Place-names and the personal names of some of the leaders of the Rus' show that this presence, testified in the archaeological record, was real. The intensity of their presence, the length of its effectiveness and the strength of its influence are difficult to determine. At certain times Kiev, the kernel of the ancient Russian state, was under the control of Scandinavians: a chronicle reference to the leaders of the town, for example, includes Scandinavian names such as Karl, Ingeld, and Farolf. Kiev itself was one of the great trading centres of Europe. Here met the main west-east European route from the Rhine at Mainz to the Caspian at Itil, together with one of the main north-south routes from the Baltic to the Black Sea by way of the Dnjeper.

Evidence for rural settlement by Scandinavians in Kievan Russia is exiguous. Most of the archaeological material of Scandinavian origin is found either in the 4,5 towns or in graves. The graves include the bodies of women – Scandinavian women adorned after death with Scandinavian jewellery – showing that the settlers here were not simply male warriors or merchants, but settled family men. Such finds indicate a fairly settled community. These people apparently lived at peace with their Slav neighbours, perhaps because they had different economic interests or perhaps because there was room for both Slav and Scandinavian within the existing economic system. Whether the Scandinavians ever farmed any major proportion of the Russian land is unknown – little excavation has been directed to this question – but the distribution of their burials, particularly those in the great linear barrow cemetery of Gnezdovo, near Smolensk, and along the shores of Lake Ladoga, might suggest – as in later Ireland – that there were a few rural settlements of Scandinavian character along the trade routes or in the neighbourhood of towns.

The main interest of the Scandinavians in this part of the world must, however, have been trade. From Lake Ladoga (easily reached from the Baltic), through the Gulf of Finland, it was a short distance by river to where Novgorod stood on the Volchov to the north of the Ilmen; and by way of the Lovat, Usviat and Kasplja it was possible by means of a short portage to reach the headwaters of the Dnjeper. Thence the river led to Smolensk, Kiev, Katerinaslav, and the Dnjeper rapids (some of which still bear Scandinavian names), and so to the Black Sea. Thus, not without a certain hardship and some danger, the passage from the Baltic to the Black Sea and thence to Constantinople could be accomplished by traders and adventurers. The six-week-passage of the Rus' from Kiev to the sea was described in the tenth century by the Byzantine emperor Constantine Porphyrogenitus; it is a story of danger both from the river and from hostile people, involving portages and off-loading of ships. This was the main route of the Scandinavians.

But these same people are also to be traced as merchants along other north-south routes in the east. From the headwaters of the Dnjeper it was possible after a portage to reach the Dvina which empties directly into the Baltic. The Caspian could be reached by way of the Volga and by this route the Scandinavians could stretch out towards the 5000-mile silk route to China. Graves illuminate this route in the provinces of

Tjemchai and Bjelimer and we have records of sizeable Scandinavian fleets fighting in the Caspian in the tenth century. Another route traversed Poland along the Vistula to the Dnjester and the Black Sea. Along the southern coast of the Baltic archaeological excavators are picking up finds which reflect the presence of Scandinavians in the ninth and tenth centuries – on the island of Rügen, on the River Peene and at a dozen sites in north Germany and Poland.

The Scandinavians continued to use the eastern rivers as merchant routes until well into the eleventh century. Inscriptions in runic characters on memorial stones in Sweden tell of their adventures. From these stones we learn the Swedish names for parts of these distant eastern lands: Grikkland for Greece or Byzantium; Gardaríki for Russia; Aldeijuborg for Ladoga; Micklegard for Byzantium; Holmgard for Novgorod, and so on. Some inscriptions are terse, but others tell of important people and exciting adventures. p.10(4) A huge boulder at Ed, north of Stockholm, tells of a woman:

> Ragnvald had the runes cut in memory of Fastvi his mother, Onam's daughter. She died in Ed. God rest her soul. Ragnvald had the runes cut. He was in Greece, he was the leader of the host.

Ragnvald was apparently then the commander of the Varangian Guard of the Byzantine emperors in Constantinople – a great man indeed. Another stone *1* from Gripsholm tells of Harald, brother of Ingvar the Far-travelled; it ends with a verse which tells of Serkland – the land of the Saracens – and the reason for their journey.

> *They fared like men*
> *far after gold*
> *and in the east*
> *gave the eagle food.*
> *They died southwards*
> *in Serkland.*

The rune-stones of Sweden tell of individual enterprise and are a constant and personal reminder of the far-flung contacts of the Swedish Vikings. More *13* immediate perhaps is the presence of a Swedish stone in the island of Berezanj in the Black Sea where Grane buried his comrade Karl who had died far from home in a sea bigger than the Baltic. But more dramatic by far is the magnificent marble representation of a lion, in Venice since 1687, which had once kept guard in the Piraeus, the port of Athens. On the flanks of this lion a Swedish Viking has cut a runic inscription – now almost illegible – but witnessing still to the wide-flung contacts of the eleventh-century Swedes. Other runes appear cut on the surface of a balustrade in St Sophia in Istanbul, carved perhaps by a member of the guard of the Byzantine emperor in a moment of bored vandalism.

Our record of the Scandinavians in the east depends largely on the literary record. Archaeological investigations have been sporadic and the size of the area to be investigated makes for difficulties in constructing a complete picture. The historical record is also one-sided: only the rune-stones tell an unvarnished story, the Slavonic and Byzantine sources are biased or recount second-hand information. Arab sources are colourful, but the travellers and merchants who tell of the people whom they met on their travels may not have been able to distinguish between Swede and Slav, Khazar or Finn. It is perhaps better to understand them through western adventures which are chronicled in both history and archaeology.

The settlement of England

If there is doubt about the function of Novgorod under the Vikings, there is much less to question concerning the function of York and later of Dublin. The capture of York in 867 has already been mentioned. Around York Scandinavian warriors had settled, taking over land already farmed by Englishmen, often as tenants of monastic houses. New capital was injected into these farms by Scandinavian warriors who had had successful seasons of raiding. As well as portable wealth the new settlers probably had slaves who could be put to work so that the land might be more efficiently cultivated; surplus produce could be sold at local markets. Some of these markets grew into important towns: York, for example. As the head of a kingdom, it received through the king an access of money in the form of taxes. Its administrators needed feeding, and beasts and farm produce would be brought to the town to provide for the non-agricultural population. The farmers would have surplus money and would buy at the market articles which they could not themselves make – combs, brooches, buckles, even shoes, made by craftsmen who had settled near the market – and of course exotic luxuries provided by merchants who had travelled from abroad. As the power of the king was established the merchants came under his protection, for a consideration. Tolls were levied and coins were struck (some of the first coins to be struck by Scandinavians). A full-blown town economy was soon flourishing in the ancient town of York, based on a commercial centre outside the walls of the Roman fortress on the banks of the broad River Ouse. The Vikings of York and the surrounding district became Christian and buried *4* their dead in Christian fashion, but under stones decorated with motifs in their own taste.

York was not alone in England as a town under the control of the Vikings. Half the country was under the control of the incomers and at centres like Stamford, Lincoln, Derby, Leicester and Nottingham (known collectively as the Five Boroughs) markets were established and fortifications built. Other towns too were, at least for a short time, controlled by Scandinavians – Chester and Thetford for example. But gradually the Danelaw (as the Scandinavian areas were called) was reconquered by the English and the settlers' descendants, probably too numerous to be dispossessed of their lands, were absorbed into the normal Anglo-Saxon population. By 954 the whole of England was temporarily free of the attention of the Scandinavians.

The Celtic west

Meanwhile in north-west Britain Scandinavian settlements had flourished. Orkney grew in power and had become an earldom as important as any of the main kingdoms of Scandinavia. *Orkneyinga saga* gives a rather glossy account of this important earldom, but, behind the political bias of the writer, an outline at least of its history can be discerned. The first recognizable ruler (towards the end of the ninth century) was Sigurd, a member of a royal Norwegian family. At its greatest extent, under Thorfinn the Mighty in the mid-eleventh 3,5 century, the earldom controlled Orkney and possibly Shetland and much of Caithness, Sutherland and Ross and Cromarty – sometimes pushing southwards to the Moray Firth. But by 1468, when they were pledged to Scotland, Shetland and Orkney were all that was left of a once mighty earldom. Much remains in these lands of the Viking period, particularly place-names, but here perhaps more than anywhere else in the Atlantic area can be seen the remains of the daily life of the Scandinavian settlers, as farmsteads are excavated and graves uncovered.

Farm sites and graves, together with place-names, record the spread of permanent settlement by way of the Hebrides to the Isle of Man and the Irish Sea. Even on the isolated island of St Kilda a woman's brooch tells of a Viking family living there – farmers presumably; but possibly also pirates, plundering the people who reached south from the North Atlantic to Ireland and England and the mercantile, piratical and political possibilities of that rich area. A string of tenth-century hoards of silver bullion and coins found buried in the Isle of Man, the Hebrides, Orkney and Shetland spell out the booty and wealth available to settlers in this area. At first they buried their dead in the pagan manner, sometimes (as at Ballateare in the Isle of Man) with human sacrifice; but soon they were to become Christian. Memorial stones displaying sculptured 6 Christian crosses appear in the Isle of Man in the tenth century, with runic inscriptions which tell of the newly Christianized settlers' descendants, still bearing Scandinavian names and speaking a Scandinavian language. At some time the kingdom of Man and the Isles (i.e. the Hebrides) came into being and, to reflect the political power, a new bishopric was founded to balance that in Orkney: a bishopric which survives to this day as the see of Sodor and Man – the 'Sodor'

element referring to the southern isles – 'southern' when seen from Norway.

The Irish Sea had become a Scandinavian sea by the middle of the tenth century. Although English kings and Welsh princes officially controlled the eastern shores, it was Scandinavian traders and chieftains who controlled it in commercial terms. By the end of the century Dublin had become one of the most important commercial assets of the Scandinavian people.

Until the advent of the Scandinavians, Ireland had looked in on itself. The monasteries and family organizations of the native Irish were not greatly interested in overseas ventures. It was the Norsemen who brought them face to face with the outside world; raiding first, then founding small encampments around the coast; venturing into the interior only to raid and trade. At first these encampments can hardly have been very large but the cemetery at Kilmainham, just outside Dublin, reveals a substantial, warlike, pagan society in the furnishing of its graves. The first bases of the Scandinavians in Ireland were founded round the coast – at Dublin, Linn Duachaill (probably Annagassan in Co. Louth), Lough Ree (in the middle of the Shannon) and in Strangford Lough. But these have rightly been described as lairs. Dublin, Waterford, Wexford, Cork and Limerick were to become the true bases – and trading centres – of the Scandinavians, but these only emerged during the early years of the tenth century at a period when there was no strong High-kingship in the south of Ireland.

The towns thus founded became independent, if minor, elements in the political structure of Ireland; their inhabitants became Christian and retained some measure of ethnic and economic independence. Dublin 19 was by far the most important. On the banks of the Liffey grew up one of the great trading towns of western Europe – its commercial importance symbolized in the late 990s by the striking of the first coins to be minted in Ireland. The towns were not, however, as in England, backed by a rural Norse settlement of any size or permanence. The Norse at various times did occupy a considerable territory in the hinterland of Dublin, reaching to Wicklow in the south; elsewhere there were smaller scattered settlements dependent on other towns. But, like the towns, these lands became subject to the Irish, and it was as merchants and traders that the Scandinavians of Ireland – and particularly those in Dublin – survived and made their greatest impact. The wiser Irish kings saw the potential of these towns and their inhabitants and ruled the foreigners with a light rein, appreciating their commercial acumen, economic strength and foreign contacts.

Excavations in Dublin since the early 1960s have revealed much of the Viking town. Traces of ninth-century material are rare, but in the later levels of the excavations more and more finds are revealed, showing

Dublin as a rich manufacturing and merchant community with wooden houses (some of which are of Scandinavian form), wooden paved streets, craftsmen's yards and workshops and the detritus of a dozen trades. Particularly interesting are a large number of pieces of bone on which metalworkers have drawn out their patterns before transferring them into bronze. Many of the patterns are influenced by Scandinavian taste and some are clear representations of motifs drawn in Scandinavian style. One piece of bone, for example, bears a craftsman's accurate working pattern of an animal design almost exactly paralleled on the side of a major piece of Irish metalwork, the shrine of the Cathach of St Columba. It is clear that Scandinavian craftsmanship was held in high regard by the Irish themselves as some of the most splendid pieces of Irish ecclesiastical metalwork of the early eleventh century – the Shrine of the Bell of St Patrick's Will, St Manchan's Shrine and the Cross of Cong with its royal dedicatory inscription – are executed in Scandinavian styles. Similarly stone sculpture in the deeply Irish areas (County Clare, for example) is decorated in a style much influenced by Scandinavian masters.

The Scandinavian settlers of Ireland in the eleventh and twelfth centuries not only influenced the art of the whole of Ireland, they also influenced its economy. The vast number of hoards of silver (and even of gold) of Viking Age date and Scandinavian type found in Ireland show the strength and wealth of this influence. About 110 hoards and more than 150 single finds of silver and gold objects have been recorded by archaeologists. (Comparison with Scotland, where only 31 hoards and single finds have been recovered, points to the great commercial prosperity of Ireland at this period.) The international merchant had a great effect on Ireland. Little material has been found in Dublin which actually came from Scandinavia (although the ninth- and early tenth-century cemetery outside the city walls at Kilmainham has produced many Scandinavian objects), but fragments of bowls made of soapstone (imported from Norway or Shetland) have been found among the excavated material within the town as were three objects inscribed with legends in the Scandinavian runic alphabet. These and other objects show the Scandinavian contacts of the people who lived in Dublin in the eleventh and twelfth centuries. Pottery from France is quite common in the eleventh-century levels and indicates the direction of some of the trading interests of the Dubliners. Contact with England is indicated by the presence of pottery made in Stamford and Thetford, by coins of Æthelred and Knut the Great and by a leather scabbard made by an Englishman called Edric.

The evidence found in the Dublin excavations, then, reveals considerable trading contact out of Ireland with the Scandinavian north, with France and with England.

'Gaut made this and all in Man', says the inscription on this stone from Kirk Michael, Isle of Man. It was raised in the tenth century to commemorate a Viking colonist. (6)

We have seen that, by the end of the tenth century, the Scandinavians of Dublin were striking coins: the earliest, significantly, copy those of the English king Æthelred II, some of them substituting his name for that of a Norse king, Sihtric or Anlaf. The place-names of Wales reveal the main route into England, for all along the coast of south Wales into the Bristol Channel are Scandinavian place-names. Most of the names of the sea-markers of the northern side of the Bristol Channel were given by Scandinavian traders from Dublin making for the River Severn to bring their wares into the heart of England. Skokholm, Worm's Head, Rothers Sker, Tusker Rock, Flatholm and Steepholm are among the names, still with a Scandinavian tang, which record this passage. A northern route into Chester was probably earlier, producing only early tenth-century finds and a handful of place-names, although there were certainly Scandinavians in Chester in the eleventh century.

For more than a century and a half Scandinavian merchants dominated the Irish Sea. Often their political

base was slender, as Dublin was controlled by Irish kings. But, as the Irish were not interested in international trade, the Scandinavians adapted the tactics of their distant cousins in Russia, trimming to the political climate but controlling the economic means. What then did they trade? From Ireland and the lands around the Irish Sea, from piracy, wars and raiding, came slaves. This trade, roundly condemned by the Church, nonetheless flourished in western Europe, and Dublin was one of its centres. There was a ready market for slaves throughout Europe well into the twelfth century. But other goods were traded. The French pottery in Dublin is a fossil of a flourishing wine trade; the fragments of soapstone indicate trade from Norway (perhaps there was already trade in timber), while the presence of walrus ivory objects in many of the treasuries of the European Church in the pre-Romanesque and Romanesque periods indicates a trade from the far north from Iceland and Greenland. But most of the objects of trade may have been perishable, like wine and slaves, unlikely to leave any real trace in the archaeological record. Scandinavia and Greenland, for example, were areas of enormous importance to the European fur trade. There is early documentary evidence of trade in ivory and fur in the works of King Alfred, who wrote an account of the voyage of a Norwegian trader, Ohthere, round the North Cape:

Chiefly he went there, as well as to see that land, to get walruses, for they have a noble bone in their tusks . . . and their hide is very good for ships' ropes.

With the exception of salt the Scandinavians at home had a reasonable abundance of food and clothing, although in Iceland the type of food available was rather limited and meal and malt would have been imported. Thus it is likely that the chief imports, other than slaves, would have been luxury goods. Many of these may have been imported by way of Dublin; particularly wine, spices, weapons, semi-precious stones and possibly fine woollen cloth. Silks, furs and spices would have been imported by the eastern route. And always silver: silver as bullion, silver for coins, silver for ornaments, silver for general exchange. There was an insatiable demand for silver in Scandinavia. In Sweden, for example, in the coin hoards remaining to this day have been found (as has been shown) 80,000 Arabic coins, but also 33,700 Anglo-Saxon coins and 154,776 Frankish and German coins, mostly of the tenth and eleventh centuries. The figures for Norway and Denmark (possibly for internal political reasons) are very much less, but the figures are an indicator at once of the importance of silver in the Scandinavian economy and of the wealth of the Scandinavians at the end of the Viking Age.

The Irish Sea and the Russian rivers provided a route for the passage of this wealth. In the east the trade

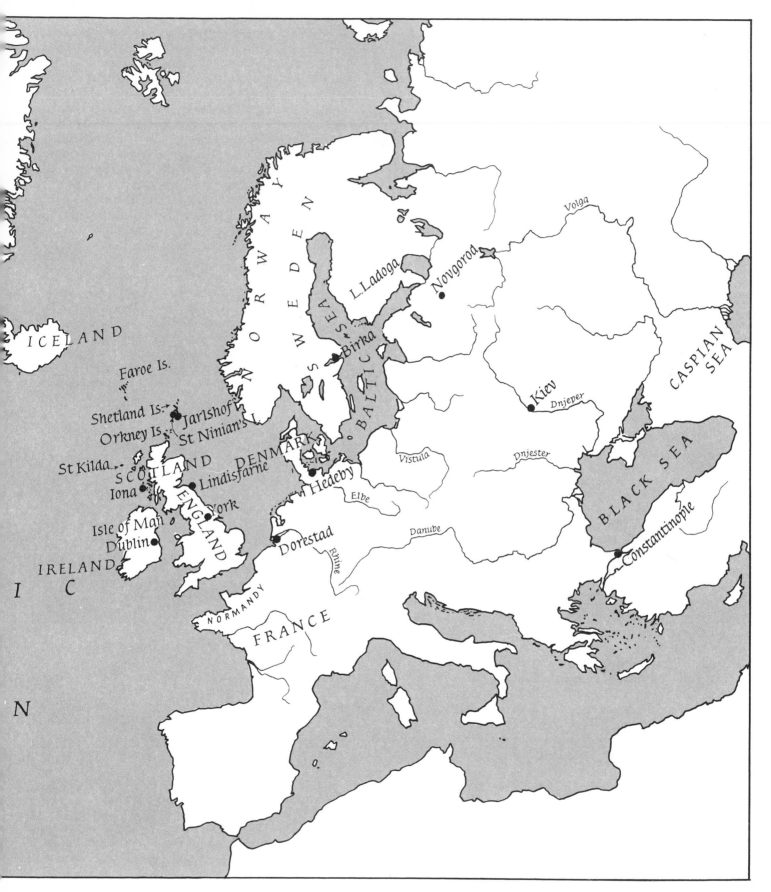

ICELAND

Faroe Is.

Shetland Is. — Jarlshof
Orkney Is. — St Ninian's

St Kilda

SCOTLAND
Iona — Lindisfarne
ENGLAND
York

Isle of Man
Dublin

IRELAND

NORWAY

SWEDEN

BALTIC SEA

L.Ladoga

Birka

Novgorod

Volga

Kiev
Dnjeper

CASPIAN SEA

DENMARK
Hedeby

Elbe

Vistula

Dnjester

BLACK SEA

Danube

Constantinople

NORMANDY

Dorestad

Rhine

FRANCE

I C

N

gradually passed into the hands of the Slavs and ultimately the Hanseatic League; in the west a single political event – the Norman Conquest of Ireland in 1169 – drastically reduced the Scandinavian merchant's control of his own economic destiny. Dublin was no longer an open port to him, his influence was destroyed and his power in the west was confined to those few islands in Scotland and the Irish Sea which remained nominally under his control until the Battle of Largs in 1226. The Norse influence has never entirely passed from these areas. The town of Dublin stands as a permanent reminder of the Norsemen, as do many Irish seafaring terms (*ancaire*, anchor; *bád*, boat; *tochta*, thwart; and so on). In the place-names of the Isle of Man and its present-day parliament (Tynwald); in the personal names of Lewis, Harris and Skye – MacAulay (Olafsson), MacNicol (Nicolson), MacRailt (Haraldsson); and in the ancient language of Orkney (*norn*), dead for two centuries, can be seen the ancient Viking lineage.

Knut the Great, king of Denmark and England

One British element has so far been omitted from this story: the situation in England in the late tenth and eleventh centuries. York had fallen in 954 and an English kingdom had been tactfully constructed; a kingdom accepted in the north where the Scandinavian settlers were losing their original language and had in effect become English.

In the quarter of a century after 954 England grew to nationhood. Church and state were welded together through the genius of King Edgar and his advisers and the country itself was brought under one strong hand. England prospered and for the first time for many years the country was at peace. The break-up and re-organization of the old monastic estates in the period of Viking settlement had resulted in a more economic use of the countryside and the production of more land and more capital. England grew rich. Unfortunately Edgar, a young man in his early thirties, died in 975 and, in sad and even suspicious circumstances, Æthelred came to the throne. Peace was shattered and the next thirty-five years encompassed the bitterest and most difficult period of Anglo-Scandinavian relationships. From 980 onwards England was visited by a series of attacks. No part of the kingdom was safe: Thanet, Cheshire, Devon, Dorset, London, were all attacked in a series of bloody and deliberate campaigns. The campaigns came to a climax in 991 when the Anglo-Saxon Chronicle records:

And in that year it was determined that tribute should first be paid to the Danish men because of the great terror they were causing along the coast. The first payment was 10,000 pounds. Archbishop Sigeric first advised that course.

The Danegeld once paid encouraged the adventurers

to ask for more. In 994 the sum paid out was £16,000, and there was peace for a year or two. But from 997, despite various attempts to fight back by raiding bases and retaliation, the Chronicle records a continuous series of raids. In 1002 the Danegeld was £24,000, but peace was not bought so easily and the attacks continued; four years later a new geld (£36,000 this time) was paid. In 1012 everything went wrong for the English: the Archbishop of Canterbury was captured and murdered at a drunken feast, £48,000 was paid out and a 'protecting' force of forty-two ships was left behind when the Danes returned home. In a series of campaigns over the next few years the Danish leaders, Sven and Knut, brought England to its knees. In 1016 Æthelred died and at the end of the year his successor, Edmund Ironside, followed him to the grave and Knut had himself elected king at London.

Knut was now king of Denmark and England, powerful, rich (he made levied gelds of £83,500 in the year after his accession) and married to Æthelred's widow, Emma, to give some legitimacy to his claim. By careful control, mixed with flattery, he built a stable state in England with only a few hatchet men to see to the collection of taxes and to pamper the Church. He

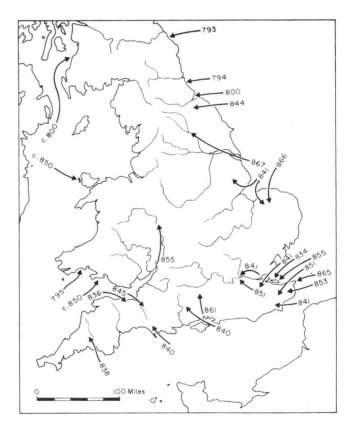

Map showing the main Viking attacks on England between 793 (the first raid on Lindisfarne) and 867, when York became the capital of an established Viking kingdom. (7)

died at Shaftesbury in 1035 and was buried at Winchester in a peaceful kingdom. For seven years there was some uncertainty about the strength of his successors, but when in 1042 'Harthacnut, king of the English' died as he was drinking at a wedding party, the last Danish king to reign in England was succeeded by the pious Edward, known as the Confessor.

8 The Scandinavians received considerable wealth from England. Rune-stones at home and chronicles in England dramatize this aspect of their final adventure, but for a few more years only was Scandinavian power a threat to England. (Harold of England beat an invading Norwegian army at Stamford Bridge only days before the Battle of Hastings.) Never again did the military might of the north have any real effect on England. Scandinavian merchants, however, still worked out of London and York and met with their cousins from Dublin who entered England by way of the Bristol Channel.

Lands of mists and monsters

The North Atlantic, since it was first described by classical writers, had been an area of mist and monsters. An Irish monk, Dicuil, one of the learned men at the court of Charlemagne at the beginning of the Viking Age, has left a treatise entitled *On the measurement of the Earth*. He writes with more knowledge than most, as he had obviously visited the Hebrides and even the northern Isles. He tells of Irish monks living on an island, Thule, a land where the sun shines at midnight, and perhaps describes the Faroe Islands for the first time:

There is another set of small islands, nearly all separated by narrow stretches of water; in these for nearly a hundred years hermits sailing from our country, *Scottia*, have lived. But just as they were always deserted from the beginning of the world, so now because of the Scandinavian pirates they are emptied of anchorites, and filled with countless sheep and very many diverse kinds of sea birds.

Evidence of an Irish presence in the North Atlantic before the Viking Age is thin indeed: Dicuil is the only major author to give a reasonably circumstantial account of the activities of the Irish hermits there.

The Scandinavians, however, were, as Dicuil states, active in the northern islands from the beginning of the Viking Age. Settlement of the Faroes and Iceland would follow naturally from the settlement of Orkney and Shetland. The first Norwegian visitors to Iceland are reputed to have been blown there by accident while sailing from Norway to the Faroes (where traces of early Scandinavian settlement have been revealed archaeologically). The first sightings and visits in the mid-ninth century were quickly followed by wholesale colonization of Iceland between *c.* 870 and 930.

The settlers came mainly from the west coast of

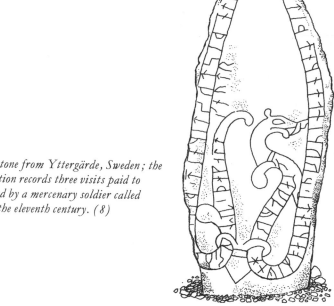

Rune-stone from Yttergärde, Sweden; the inscription records three visits paid to England by a mercenary soldier called Ulf in the eleventh century. (8)

Norway, but a few may well have come by way of the British Isles. Iceland was seen by these first, semi-aristocratic settlers as a country where the grass dripped with butter. It provided rich grazing for the settlers (initially probably about 20,000 of them) who came from politically-disturbed Norway. They created single, large farms out of the uninhabited landscape, *9* bringing in stock and seed from their old homelands. They organized local assemblies (*things*) as well as a national assembly (the *Althingi*) which met for a p.209(1) fortnight each summer. In this island there was no king or earl – a man's authority lay in the number of his followers – the great chieftains (ultimately forty-eight of them) wielded power and justice locally and centrally. It would be wrong to describe Iceland of the settlement period as a democracy, but in a system which tended to preserve the individual from interference, with a constitution, which divided the country into stable units and provided a reasonably equitable society, it may not have been far from this ideal.

Iceland became Christian by agreement of the *15* *Althingi* in 1000, perhaps the nearest event approaching a constitutional crisis to face Iceland in the Viking Age. Churches were set up and bishops visited the island to preach. In 1056 the first native bishop, Ísleif, was consecrated. For two centuries the bishop was the most powerful, and sometimes the most important, man in the country. But feuding, quarrels between Church and state and lack of moderation by the bishop and others led the Icelanders unwillingly into submission to the Norwegian crown between 1262 and 1264.

Excavated plan of an early eleventh-century farmhouse at Gjáskógar, Iceland. The main hall (A) was fifteen metres long and had a fireplace in the centre. Opening from it was a living room with benches (B) and a dairy (C), with a large vessel sunk into the floor. Right: reconstruction of Thjodhild's church at Brattahlid, Greenland. Only two metres broad, it was built of turf with a wooden roof and interior walls. (9,10)

From Iceland to Greenland was no great distance. The man who discovered it was Gunnbjorn Ulf-Krakason, but the man who first settled there was Eirik the Red about 985 after a preliminary survey lasting three years. Eirik was a man born to trouble, but Greenland tamed him and, to some extent, he tamed Greenland. Settlements were founded round the areas now known as Julianehaab and Godthaab, the only farming areas of the new, unfriendly, and to all intents uninhabited, land.

At first settlement flourished. Farms were built, land was divided out, newcomers came to join the earliest settlers of this fabled country. Early sources, some as early as the early twelfth century, tell the story of the settlement in some detail, while almost continuous archaeological work by Danish scholars over the last fifty years has revealed the physical remains of the settlers and of their descendants. The site of Brattahlid (now known as Qagssiarssuk), Eirik the Red's farm, has received much attention and the church built by Eirik's wife, Thjodhild, one of the earliest Christians in the new country, is one of the more remarkable relics of the Norse settlement. The skeletons found in and around the church may well be the physical remains of Eirik the Red and his close family.

Other sites investigated include the episcopal site of Gardar (Igaliko) with its great bishop's residence and its small cathedral (only 27 metres long) built on a site chosen by Arnald, the first bishop of Greenland, at the time of his arrival in Iceland in 1126. Ruined farms and churches tell of the Norse settlement and the fact that they remain deserted as heaps of rubble tells of the uncertain quality of life in Greenland. The scattered nature of the settlement, the climate and the length of both internal and external communications were all contributory factors to the gradual extinction of the colony. For five hundred years the Scandinavians remained in Greenland. The last mention of their presence is recorded in the medieval Icelandic annals. As late as 1408 there was a wedding in Hvalsey church, at which many people were present. No further written evidence survives, finds from Herjolfsnes suggest that a Scandinavian population survived well into the fifteenth century. But the nature and economy of that settlement is not known: the population disappeared. The farms were deserted and the churches disroofed. Nobody knows how or why. Many theories have been erected: that the Norsemen were exterminated by the Eskimos; that they were wiped out by plague or by a deterioration of climate; that the population became degenerate and could not produce children; that they emigrated to America; that they died in a storm as they tried to evacuate Greenland. We do not now know and only archaeology can provide the answer.

Vinland the Good

There is no doubt that the Vikings reached America. The literary sources are explicit, if late, and sufficient is known to allow us to reconstruct some small part of the story. About 986 Bjarni Herjolfsson was driven by adverse winds to within sight of the North American shore. Prudent perhaps, and with set intention, he sailed for three days along the inhospitable coast before returning to Greenland. But it was Leif, the son of Eirik the Red, who sailed in Bjarni's own boat to America and made landfall in Baffin Island (named Helluland by Bjarni), Labrador (Markland) and a land he called Vinland, which was probably Newfoundland. Leif landed on American soil and returned home, to be followed by his brother Thorvald, who made a more thorough exploration. Thorvald was killed there by natives, who were named *Skrælings* by the Norsemen.

In the early years of the eleventh century – according to Eirik the Red's saga – Thorfinn Karlsefni with a hundred and sixty men (some accompanied by their wives) sailed westward in three ships. They took with them livestock of various kinds and attempted to settle permanently, probably in Newfoundland. It was, by their standards, a rich land: there were fish in the rivers, good soil and fine grazing. Accounts of this major enterprise vary; but it ended after three years in quarrels and fear caused partly by the presence of the European women, partly by the local inhabitants, and almost certainly in part by the long and tenuous line of communication with the rest of the Norse world. After the early years of the eleventh century we have casual references of visitors to Vinland, including the excursion of an Icelandic bishop between 1110 and 1121.

Dramatic confirmation of the Viking presence in America was provided by the discovery in 1960 by a Norwegian journalist, Helge Ingstad, and his archaeologist wife of what is almost certainly a Norse settlement at L'Anse aux Meadows on the northern tip of Newfoundland (51°36′N, 55°32′W). The settlement lay on a terrace above a wide curved bay. The foundations of various buildings of a semi-industrial and domestic nature were discovered. Bones of domestic animals were found, as was a certain amount of industrial waste. The find of a ring-headed pin of European Viking Age type together with the dates provided by the radio-carbon method clinch a date in the Viking period.

No other finds in America give any evidence of the Viking presence. A runic stone from Kensington, Minnesota is a fake; a tower at Newport, Rhode Island is a seventeenth-century windmill; the Beardmore find from Canada was certainly salted. Even the famous Vinland Map, an expensively purchased and lavishly published treasure of Yale University, has been proved to be false. The industry of providing America with its Scandinavian antiquities has boomed in this century and only in the last few years has scepticism swept all but L'Anse aux Meadows into oblivion.

There were Vikings in America; they lived there from time to time, but they have left little memorial of this, one of their most exciting adventures.

The Viking heritage

The Scandinavian attacks on Europe were not easily forgotten. Their settlements remained and Danes and Norwegians became, for example, Yorkshiremen or Icelanders; but their initial raids and their terrible plunderings were never forgotten by historians. They were not glamorized, made respectable, until the

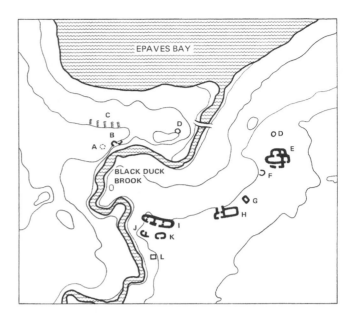

The only certain site of Viking occupation in America so far known is at L'Anse aux Meadows, Newfoundland. Here the following remains have been excavated and convincingly identified: A, charcoal kiln; B, forge; C, boat sheds on the old shore line; D, cooking pits; E, large house; F, sauna; G, workshed; H, I, J, K, houses; L, natural deposit of bog iron-ore. (11)

nineteenth century. In the Middle Ages they received little notice, but early Saxonists like the Elizabethan William Lambarde (who published his *Perambulation of Kent* in 1576) were interested in the Danish raids and discussed them at some length. R. Verstigan, writing in 1605, even went so far as to say that Knut, 'was the greatest King . . . that ever England had'. But it was not until the late eighteenth century that they were properly and seriously discussed outside Scandinavia. Edward Gibbon, while acknowledging that their 'name was already odious and formidable in France', talks of the Scandinavians in Russia in glowing terms:

The vast, and, as it is said, the populous regions of Denmark, Sweden and Norway were crowded with independent chieftains and desperate adventurers, who sighed in the laziness of peace, and smiled in the agonies of death. Piracy was the exercise, the trade, the glory, and the virtue of Scandinavian youth. Impatient of a bleak climate and narrow limits, they started from the banquet, grasped their arms, sounded their horn, ascended their vessels and explored every coast that promised either spoil or settlement.

There was a glorious quality about the Scandinavians, which carried with it none of the horror or odium associated with the Huns and the Goths. Their courage was lauded and they were portrayed as heroic men who faced the elements and death with courage and cheerfulness. In a period when Alfred the Great became a symbol of nationalistic and religious feeling, the Danes were more and more portrayed as worthy – if brutal – antagonists of clean-limbed Anglo-Saxons.

By the end of the nineteenth century they had become in the popular imagination almost benefactors of the people they raided. They were seen as the founders in many places of democracy and the most respectable exponents of nationalism. Thus William Morris:

It would seem fitting for a Northern folk, deriving the greater and better part of their speech, laws and customs from a Northern root, that the North should be to them, if not a holy land, yet at least a place more to be regarded than any part of the world beside, that howsoever their knowledge widened of other men, the faith and deeds of their forefathers would never lack interest for them, but would always be kept in remembrance.

In some parts their presence was never forgotten: Iceland remains a Viking land; the sagas and other literature of Iceland kept some knowledge of Viking history alive throughout the Middle Ages. The Faroes and Shetland – together with Orkney – built a nationalism on their Norse foundations which manifests itself today: in a certain lack of respect, for example, of the governing Danes in the case of the Faroes, and in such extraordinary celebrations as *Up-Helly-Aa* in Shetland (originally a Scottish folk festival in which nowadays a Viking boat is burned annually on Twelfth Night). In the Isle of Man the Viking presence is nowhere more remembered than in the open-air Tynwald ceremony.

Other countries are less eager to recognize their Scandinavian heritage: the example of Russia has been discussed above. Normandy became French almost as soon as it had been settled. Apart from dialectologists, few people in England were until the late nineteenth century particularly romantic regarding their Viking heritage, although the present excavations in York have led to a reawakening of interest in the Viking century in the north of England.

The extraordinary phenomenon of Viking America is, however, of some interest. For hundreds of years the fact that the Scandinavians had discovered America was forgotten, or known only to a few scholars. With the great immigration of Scandinavians into the upper Midwest in the late nineteenth century, the need to establish an identity in a foreign land led to a rediscovery of this fact. This at times led to ludicrous studies: Reider T. Sherman, for example, attempted in five volumes of vocabulary to isolate Scandinavian elements in the language of the North American Indians (there are, of course, none)! But specious scholarship with regard to the Scandinavian presence is nowhere more virulently seen than in the vast literature which surrounds the completely false Kensington stone, which is now at Alexandria, Minneapolis.

The stone was allegedly found by a Swedish immigrant farmer, Olof Ohman, in 1898. It bears a runic inscription which allegedly dates it to 1362. It has been shown beyond doubt (the evidence includes a confession by one of the forgers) that it is a fake. But the persistence of the belief that it is genuine is difficult to understand, save in terms of romantic nationalism reflecting the experiences of Scandinavian pioneers in North America at two periods. Other American finds and monuments – until L'Anse aux Meadows – proved to be equally spurious.

In many areas a Scandinavian heritage seems respectable, even desirable. At periods of high romanticism the Vikings have lent themselves to adulation. Their activities were interpreted as highly romantic, the barbarians of the north were more acceptable than the barbarians of the east, who were certainly a more real menace to Europe and were continually shown to be so.

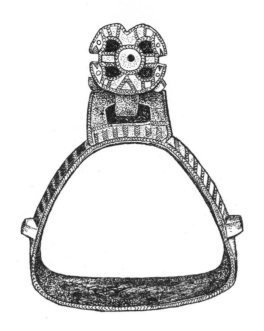

7
THE NORTHERN SLAVS

JOACHIM HERRMANN

'In the temple stood a huge image,
far overtopping all human stature, marvellous for its four heads and four necks,
two facing the breast and two the back. Moreover, of those in front
as well as of those behind, one looked leftwards and the other
rightwards. In the right hand it held a horn wrought of divers
metals, which the priest who was versed in its rites
used to fill every year with new wine,
in order to foresee the crops of the next season
from the disposition of the liquor.'

Saxo Grammaticus
Gesta Danorum

description of the god Svantevit at Arkona

About 1200

More unanswered questions hang over the Slavs than over any of the other peoples covered by this book. Their material culture overlaps at so many points with that of their neighbours that it is sometimes difficult to assert categorically that an object is indubitably and exclusively Slav. Their place of origin may be located between the rivers Vistula and Dnjeper, their migration routes were varied and the area they came to occupy extended from Greece in the south to the Baltic in the north and to the River Main in the west. Nor did they at any time enjoy political or social unity. The best criterion would be linguistic, since there is certainly a language, or group of languages, that can be called Slav; but it was not written down until the ninth century, and even after that, documents are meagre.

Yet the vital importance of the Slavs in the formation of eastern Europe has never been disputed. Moving in from the great plains at the end of the Bronze Age, they divided into groups that the linguists define as: the eastern Slavs, who became the ancestors of the Russians, Belorussians and Ukrainians; the western Slavs, from whom spring the Czechs, Moravians, Slovaks and Poles; and the southern Slavs, the Serbs, Croats and Bulgarians. The northern Slavs, with whom this chapter is concerned, belong mainly to the western branch. Each of these groups, however, retained much that was common to them all. And as the medium of contact between many disparate cultures – Germanic, Norse, Illyrian, Iranian, Byzantine – they were collectively the most important, if the most mysterious, of the groups determining the make-up of the post-Roman world.

The island of Rügen lies off the southern Baltic coast, due north of Berlin. Its many peninsulas and inlets make it ideal as a trading station. For the Slavs it was the gate to Scandinavia, for the western Scandinavians one stage of the route that could take them to Byzantium. Here have been found, at Hiddensee, one of the richest of Scandinavian treasures (pl. 11); at Altenkirchen, carved stones representing Slav gods (pl. 15); at Ralswiek, the remains of jetties and boats (pl. 7); and at Arkona, a promontory on the extreme north side, was once the most famous of Slav temples. The description by Saxo Grammaticus, quoted at the top of this page, belongs to the early thirteenth century, but the temple had been destroyed by the Danish king Waldemar nearly a century before.

Arkona today (*opposite*) is a place of slightly sinister beauty. The great rampart built by the Slavs to defend their citadel is still easily recognizable. Behind it, now destroyed by the sea, was the site of the temple of the god Svantevit. His huge idol occupied an inner room hung with purple rugs. (1)

On previous page: richly decorated stirrup of iron, with silver and gold inlay, found in the River Havel at Pritzerbe, near Brandenburg. The Slavs seem to have adopted the improved straight-bottomed stirrup from the Prussians east of the Vistula estuary. (1)

Trade and war

As society stabilized the old 'military democracy' that seems to have characterized the early Slavs was replaced by a class system headed by an aristocracy. About 1150, the area round Berlin was ruled by a feudal prince called Jacza of Köpenick, some of whose coins (*left*) survive. *Below*: the lower layers of a wooden block house at Danzig; internal features, including a hearth, have been left untouched on artificial 'plinths' by the excavators. (2,3)

The rich town of Hedeby, one of the centres of Scandinavian trade, lay across the isthmus of Schleswig from the Slavs. At the end of the tenth century a Slav army (of Obodrites) marched into Hedeby and destroyed it. *Below*: the extensive remains of the town as excavated. About 1050, it seems to have been abandoned for good and refounded at modern Schleswig. (4)

'A land of forts' was how the Scandinavians described the territory of the Slavs. Traces of two thousand of them survive, often circular in shape and highly sophisticated in their defensive techniques. *Right*: reconstruction of the fort of Tornow, showing the round fort containing houses, surrounded by a moat, ditch and rows of stakes. Entrance was via a bridge, which became a tunnel underneath the main wall. (6)

Remains of the rampart, stakes, piles and entrance passage have been exposed at Behren-Lubchin (*above*), which in the eleventh and twelfth centuries stood in the middle of a marsh or lake. (5)

Frankish swords were in high demand all over the Slav and Scandinavian world. Of these two (*above*), found in northern Poland, one, on the left, bears the name Ulfberht inscribed on the blade. Slav swordsmiths imitated them, even copying the names of Rhenish craftsmen. (8)

Sea-going ships have been unearthed at Ralswiek on the island of Rügen. They date from between 900 and 1100 and the best-preserved is fourteen metres long. Ralswiek was a busy port, with jetties and berths for ships built out into the water on piles. Here merchants from Scandinavia could meet traders from the south. (7)

'Gold, silver and rich booty'

Through trade or through war the Slav ruling class accumulated considerable treasure, and some spectacular discoveries have been made by archaeologists. Sometimes the workmanship proclaims a Scandinavian origin; sometimes they come from outside Europe altogether. The small figure of a man (*left*) from Schwedt was probably made in the Baltic area in the eleventh or twelfth century. (9)

At Hiddensee, off the island of Rügen, a splendid collection of Scandinavian silver (*opposite*) was discovered: five pendants and a circular brooch, all of the highest quality. (11)

The silver hoard found at Borucin, in Poland (*below*), was assembled from over a wide area. The chain terminating in animal heads is Scandinavian; some of the beads are Russian; and the small casket in the foreground is local or Eastern. (10)

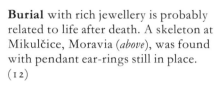

The after-life

Pagan beliefs persisted among the Slavs well into the twelfth century, long after the rest of Europe had become Christian. Their gods had little in common with Germanic religion (though one remembers the quadruple heads on the Sutton Hoo sceptre), but seem to go back to a distant Indo-European past.

Burial with rich jewellery is probably related to life after death. A skeleton at Mikulčice, Moravia (*above*), was found with pendant ear-rings still in place. (12)

Filigree decoration reaches a high point of elaboration in this basket ear-ring from Niederlandin (*left*), locally made but copied from foreign prototypes. (13)

The god Svantevit in the temple at Arkona, says Saxo, held a drinking horn as the symbol of fertility in his right hand. A carved stone from Altenkirchen (*right*), close by on the same island of Rügen, is plausibly interpreted as the funerary monument of a priest or ruler with the horn of fertility. (15)

A wooden temple, dating from the ninth century and excavated at Gross Raden, near Schwerin, gives us our most complete picture of a Slav religious building (*right*). The ends of the planks of the façade (*above*) were carved into symbolic male and female heads. (14,16)

Many-headed gods were characteristic of the Slavs. Svantevit sometimes had four heads. Other gods on Rügen had seven heads. *Below*: head of a deity carved in oak, from Jankowo, Poland. *Right*: a double-headed cult-figure 1.7 metres high, also of oak, found at Fischerinsel near Neubrandenburg. The lower parts joined into an irregular seven-sided pillar. (17,19)

Christianity came to the Slavs during the ninth century, but the process of conversion was slow. This silver belt-end, found at Mikulčice, may continue a pagan iconographic form with the addition of a Christian cross, or may be an adaptation of the *orans* pose. (18)

Bronze decorative plaque in the Jellinge style, found at Carwitz, near Neustrelitz, dating from the eleventh or twelfth century. (2)

THE NORTHERN SLAVS

THE FALL of the Roman Empire and the rise of the barbarian kingdoms in the fifth century AD mark the beginning of a new era in European history. It was not only the south and west of Europe that was affected; even outside the Empire, in eastern, central and northern Europe, the economic, social and cultural consequences of these events were far reaching. One of the groups to attain prominence as a result was the Slavs.

The Slavs, as a distinct linguistic and cultural division of the Indo-European family, seem to have crystallized as far back as the Neolithic, probably in the north European plain between the Vistula and the Dnjeper. In the east they were in contact with nomadic steppe tribes, who, among other things, transmitted a strong Iranian element to the Slav language. In the west, close relation with the coastal tribes of the Baltic had existed from remote times, and by the last centuries BC we find Slavs living as neighbours to Germanic peoples. The Germans called them 'Wends', a name also given to the east central European Veneto-Illyrian tribes. Tacitus, in the *Germania* (late first century), our earliest documented reference, calls them 'Venedi'.

In the first centuries AD some of the Germanic tribes moving south, for example the Goths and the Burgundians, encountered Slavs. There were skirmishes along the Vistula and occasionally in the area to

◁ **Arab coins** in staggering numbers have been found at many Slav as well as Scandinavian sites, bearing witness to the extent of the trade passing between north and south. The most outstanding of all finds was made at Ralswiek, on Rügen – a hoard of 2,270 coins (*opposite*). Most of them came from central Asia or Arabia and were probably brought by a merchant via the Volga and Staraja Ladoga. Arab traders usually came no further than Bulgar, at the confluence of the Kama and Volga rivers, and there exchanged their goods. By the same route the Viking mercenaries known as Varangians travelled south through Russia to the emperor of Byzantium. (20)

the east, between the Vistula and the Dnjeper. Some Slav tribes seem to have attached themselves to the Ostrogothic kingdom, or came under its sway. Others were in close touch with the Roman provinces on the middle and lower Danube and in Dacia. These relations were of considerable importance for economic developments in the region of the Vistula and in the eastern foothills of the Carpathian mountains. Roman industrial and craft traditions were transmitted from the provinces both indirectly, by way of the neighbouring Slav tribes who adopted Roman methods of manufacture, and directly by skilled craftsmen from the provinces who came to the Slav heartlands either as refugees or as captives. In some places formal economic centres developed. Around Crakow on the upper Vistula, for instance, a centre of industrial pottery production grew up in the second century. The iron mines at Swietekrzyskie Gory, which involved underground mining, were also worked. These mines supplied large tracts of the area in east central Europe covered by what is known as the Przeworsk culture, and there are even some indications that iron from Swietekrzyskie Gory reached the Roman Empire. An analysis of traded objects in central and eastern Europe has shown how many goods of Roman or provincial Roman origin were acquired by some of the Slav tribes. Seen in this light, the Przeworsk culture, which is at least partially Slav, belongs to the margin of the Roman world. Roman influence can be traced not only in the fairly obvious areas of metalwork, pottery and jewellery, but also in agriculture: the common introduction of rye cultivation among the Slavs and the use of iron tools, including the iron-shod plough in some areas, were decisive innovations.

These contacts with the developed Roman world were of great importance to the history of the Slavs in two respects. Social and economic advances, and consequent increased production potential within the tribes, led to a rapid growth of population in the fourth to sixth centuries. And this in turn was the main cause of

193

the Slav migrations and expansion from the fifth century onwards. The Roman provinces acted as a magnet to which new bands of warriors and tribal groups were constantly attracted. Slav incursions into the Balkan provinces began early in the sixth century. These were followed in the mid-sixth century by more substantial Slav settlement south of the Danube on the territory of the east Roman Empire. This opened a new corridor to Mediterranean culture, and in the centuries that followed cultural and economic impulses originating in this area were transmitted as far as the Slav tribes on the Baltic coast. The Mediterranean colouring thus given to Slav culture is of great importance in considering the part played by these tribes in the history of the southern Baltic.

Slav tribes reached the south coast of the Baltic at different times and under different conditions. From the fifth and sixth centuries onwards dense Slav settlement was established between the mouth of the Vistula and the Bay of Kiel, at times even stretching as far as the lower Elbe. This was the territory of the western Slavs, who can be divided into four main groups. Further west lived the Obodrites, an umbrella term for Obodrites proper, Wagrians, Polabs and Warnoi; the Poles, of the region of Gniezno and Poznan, were to play an important role in the history of the Baltic peoples, as the kingdom which emerged between the Oder and the Vistula in the tenth century was based on this tribe. The Wilti settled east of the Obodrite territory as far as the Oder; the Woliners at the mouth of the Oder, and the Pomeranians, so called because of their coastal settlements (*pomorzane* = seaside inhabitants), further east still. At times the Rugians or Rügen Slavs, the inhabitants of the island of Rügen, were a major factor in the western Baltic. The Venerable Bede in the eighth century knew of this tribe and names them alongside the Danes and the Huns. By that date the Rugians had presumably already come into contact with Willibrord's Anglo-Saxon mission.

Whereas the western Slavs occupied a long stretch of the Baltic shore as early as the sixth century, the eastern Slavs only reached the eastern side of the Gulf of Finland in the eighth and ninth centuries. During this little-known migratory and colonizing movement the Ilmen Slavs emerged as an identifiable group through a process of assimilation of tribes of Finno-Ugrian extraction. Important routes to central Asia and the Near East passed through their territory. Both the Volga and the Dnjeper routes began here, on the lower Neva, Lake Ladoga, and the Volkhov and Ilmen rivers. Staraja Ladoga, Beloezero and finally Novgorod became the dominant centres on this Continental trade and circulation route. The Krivichi created another point of access to the Baltic for the eastern Slavs by their general expansion towards Lake Peipus and by the foundation of Isborsk and Pskov.

Since time immemorial Baltic tribes, of which the Prussians, the Lithuanians and the Letts were the most important, had inhabited the area between the lower Vistula and the western Dvina. Finno-Ugrian tribes such as the Livonians, the Estonians and the Votes had settled to the north of the Dvina. These tribes would have preferred to adopt an isolationist policy, but for various poorly understood reasons they were unable to defend their territories in the south and south-east against the expanding Slavs. The Krivichi dominated such geographically crucial areas as the Smolensk region and the vicinity of Lake Peipus until the ninth and tenth centuries and at times even annexed them.

This ethnic pattern which emerged during the early Middle Ages has remained fundamentally the same until the present day.

Changing structures

These three groups – Slavs, Baltic and Finnish tribes – played various roles in the political and cultural development of northern and western Europe, depending on their social structures and the opportunities given them by their locations.

The western Slavs were undergoing important internal changes. Tribal customs were slowly lapsing from the sixth century onwards, yielding to a system that may be called 'military democracy'. Tribal chieftains and the nobility sought to establish their personal sphere of power. They created bands of armed followers, built private forts and increasingly kept more of the tribal wealth for themselves. Their power, however, was balanced by that of the free farmers on their freeholds, who accepted military obligations but had the right to speak on tribal matters at popular assemblies. Gatherings of these warrior-farmers were consequently just as much a feature of society at this time as the bands of personal followers of the tribal chieftains. A lower social stratum of slaves, villeins and serfs worked on the manors of the nobles and on the freeholdings of the warrior-farmers. The Slav languages still to some extent have words in common for these social strata. The tribal lord was known as *Knez* or *Knjas* and the later word for feudal princes developed from this root. For instance, a *Knez*, Jacza of Köpenick, as he styles himself on his coins, owned Berlin-Kopenick about 1150. The more important farmers were known as *Kmetz* or *Kmets*; smaller, more or less independent farmers were called *Smirdz*. These are the *Smerds* or *Smurds* encountered in medieval manuscripts from the Elbe-Saale region and Mecklenburg. Finally, the slave, villein or serf was known as *Cholop* (Cholp). These social groups are well known from ecclesiastical chronicles, above all those of Thietmar of Merseburg, Adam of Bremen (both of the eleventh century), Helmold of Bosau and the biographer of St Otto of Bamberg who travelled to the towns at the mouth of

Reconstruction of Slav block-houses at Meissen. These log constructions, built on wooden platforms without footings, have left few remains, but can be reconstructed from oak fragments. The carpentry was of a high order, the roof being laid directly on the topmost row of beams. Fireplaces seem to have been close to the door, and the smoke escaped through holes under the gables. (3)

the Oder. The states which emerged in the territories of the Obodrites and the Poles in the ninth century AD must be seen against this background.

It was a violent and troubled time. Neighbour fought neighbour, tribe fought tribe, kingdom fought kingdom for supremacy. From the documentary evidence we know of various Frankish incursions into Slav territory east of the Elbe from the seventh century onwards, at one point almost reaching the mouth of the Oder. Certain tribes were at times vassals, and some regions on the Elbe and Saale were even annexed to the Frankish Empire. In 929, under Henry I, the Germans began a great attempt to conquer the Slavs as far as the Oder. The archbishopric of Magdeburg was founded by Emperor Otto in 968; there were German bishops in Brandenburg and Havelberg from 948 and in Meissen and Oldenburg from 968. However, a great rebellion of Wilti tribes, who had formed a special alliance known as the Lutizen federation, put an end to German feudal rule beyond the Oder in 983. In the main the Obodrites and the Wilti managed to retain their independence until the middle of the twelfth century.

How did these events affect the social organization of the western Slavs and in what ways did they influence their relations with other tribes in the Baltic? As we have seen, their Mediterranean contacts gave them distinct advantages in technology and agriculture. The introduction of rye in the sixth century, one of the most important innovations, had an important stabilizing effect on Slav agricultural practice. Rye could be grown instead of barley and wheat every third year; we know that this happened, for instance, at the Slav fort of

Tornow, south of Berlin. In the climatic conditions which prevail in the Baltic region, rye is indeed a more reliable crop than wheat, even though the preparation of the soil before sowing requires greater care. It was presumably from here that it was introduced to Scandinavia in the ninth and tenth centuries. In other areas, Livland for example, slash-and-burn agriculture was only replaced by rye cultivation in about 1000.

The extraction of iron-ore, in the south, bog iron-ore, increased markedly in all countries around the Baltic from the mid-third century onwards. Iron sickles, scythes, axes, hoes, harness mounts and plough-shares have been found in abundance. In Norway and Sweden, as well as in the lands of the western Slavs, iron ingots commonly occur in the form of axes and other implements such as sickles and spades.

The use in some areas of the collar harness and the breast-strap harness made it possible to extend the use of horse traction considerably. The horse could now be used to pull the plough, as well as the heavy carts and sledges. The Slavs received the collar harness, originally a Chinese invention, from nomadic tribes to the south-east. The breast-strap harness occurs sporadically in late classical times. It was known in Scandinavia by the beginning of the ninth century at the latest. A form of horse collar, on the other hand, a wooden yoke which rests on the withers of the horse and takes the reins, is first attested in the tenth century. This wooden yoke is not depicted on the horse harnesses on the ninth-century Norwegian tapestry from Oseberg. The use of the horse collar alongside the breast-strap harness in Scandinavia is probably due to the influence of the collar harness used by the eastern Slavs. Numerous finds from Novgorod date the use of the latter to the tenth century. Rich Scandinavian chieftains had horse collars ornamented with elaborate incised decoration and metal plaques.

The distribution of the various new types of harness in the various Baltic countries demonstrates how they adapted the basic innovation – horse traction – to their own indigenous farming traditions.

As horses are more effective than oxen it was possible to cut down on work hours and above all to plough faster. Such an improvement was essential to increased production, especially in regions with light soils where large areas had to be tilled. The horse-drawn plough was almost twice as fast as the ox-drawn, as the chronicler Helmold among others tells us in relation to Slav agriculture in Mecklenburg. With its introduction, the iron-clad plough-share became the basic agricultural implement in the lands of the eastern Slavs, Finns and Baltic peoples.

Other important changes were taking place: goods were being produced to exchange for local raw materials; crafts and industrial activities were being concentrated in permanent centres; above all, production was being reorganized on a basis either of large manors or of the seigneurial establishments of the tribal nobility. Sources of iron ore were increasingly exploited, and salt mines began to be worked on a large scale from the seventh century onwards. One of the first areas to rise to prosperity on this industry was Kolobrzeg in lower Persenta. Other salt mines were located in Mecklenburg and in east Holstein. Quernstone quarries were opened up in suitable areas. Apart from occasional imported Rhenish quernstones and locally manufactured boulder quernstones, central German quarries apparently supplied large areas of the Elbe and Oder regions. Tar was essential to boat- and ship-building and archaeological finds demonstrate the growth of tar-burning in coastal areas later in the period. The extensive forests provided not only local requirements of honey and wax but also a surplus which was important in relation to trade with western Europe and the Arabs. The hunting of fur-bearing animals and the collection and working of amber were also of

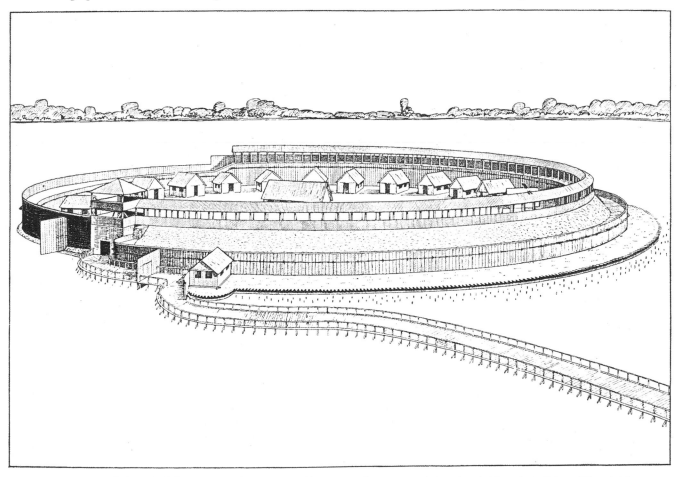

The lake settlement of Behren-Lübchin, as it may have appeared in the eleventh century. Circular in plan, like Tornow and many other forts, it was given added security by being surrounded by water.

Access was only by a long bridge; the building of these bridges, several of which have been excavated, was one of the most remarkable achievements of Slav technology. (4)

196

economic importance. The tribal nobility and the emerging ruling class of feudal lords organized the extraction, working and distribution of such raw materials and natural products, and a great part of their wealth derived from them. The building of fortifications and defended manors, the choice of collecting points, and the establishment of merchant settlements, fairs and trading towns were all part of this organization.

A land of forts

To the Scandinavians the territory of the eastern Slavs was known as the land of forts (*Gardarike*). This was an apt description of the Slav lands as a whole, particularly in the region south of the Baltic. The forts were the focal points of settlement and of economic, social, religious and cultural life. More than two thousand of them survive on the plain between the Vistula and the Elbe. The areas of settlement that grew up around these forts varied in size. Some consisted of between five and twenty villages and were known as *Opole* in Polish, *Gefilde* in German and as *civitates* in Latin. The inhabitants of such communities were bound together by common economic relations. The eastern Slavs and the Baltic tribes had a similar organizational pattern. Several of these units taken together were known as *regiones* in the Latin chronicles and often formed the territorial base of a tribe or clan. Physically they were cultivated clearings of varying extent surrounded by primeval forests.

On the map the emerging settlement pattern in central and eastern Europe can be likened to the irregular spots of a leopard. A similar pattern is found in Scandinavia but here the forts and the associated social and economic organization had little importance.

Several forts of the Slavs and the Baltic tribes have been excavated, and it has been possible to gain an understanding of their construction and function. It is clear the different forts had different functions. The earliest and most common were tribal centres or places
5 of refuge. Feldberg near Neustrelitz is an example of this type of fort, of which several have been excavated in Pomerania and Mecklenburg. Feldberg, with an enclosed area of five hectares, was at times inhabited by more than a thousand people. The houses were built in rows inside the fortified area. There was a small shrine or temple as well as a water source and a harbour. This type of fort occurred only in the period 600–800 and was then superseded by the forts of the emerging nobility.

Another type of fort combined two functions, being both the seat of the tribal leader and a refuge. At
6 Tornow in Niederlausitz both the fort and the village associated with it have been found; an eighth-century
6 fort had been replaced by a later seigneurial castle. The main house was surrounded by nineteen store-rooms as

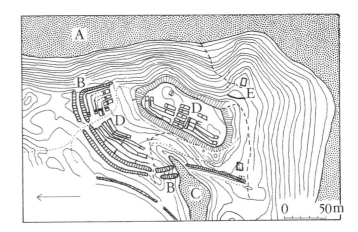

Plan of the fort of Feldberg, strategically placed on a headland partly surrounded by a lake (A). A double rampart with ditch between (B) defended the rows of houses (D), some of which were immediately behind it, some on higher ground further back. A pond (C) penetrated the defences, providing a water-supply. On the tip of the headland stood the temple (E). (5)

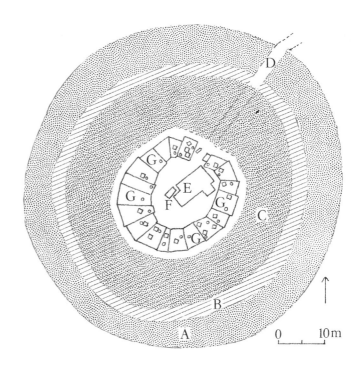

Plan of Tornow (see reconstruction on p. 187). The defensive works consisted of a ditch (A), a flat platform (B) and a rampart (C). The long entrance (D) was via a bridge and a passage. Inside the enclosure stood a house (E) probably belonging to the tribal leader, with a well (F) next to it. Occupying all the space round the wall were nineteen store-rooms (G) containing grinding stones and containers for grain. (6)

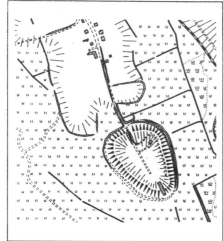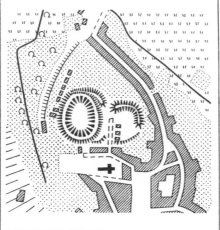

Far left: plan of the castle of Mecklenburg, near the Baltic, the seat of the rulers of the Obodrites. It was one of the largest of Slav defensive structures. The wall, timber framed and built of earth and stones, was more than ten metres high. (7)

Left: plan of the trading centre of Oldenburg, showing the ancient citadel in relation to the later Christian church and town. There was a German bishop in Oldenburg as early as 968. (8)

well as lodgings for the lord's retinue. The farmers living in front of the fort brought their grain to these store-rooms. More than seventy different parcels of grain, stored in wooden chests, clay containers, pottery vessels and sacks, were found during the excavations – obviously the last harvest before the destruction of the fort at the beginning of the ninth century. At a later date the seigneurial castle was rebuilt in front of the fort and the village. The fort itself was left in ruins.

At Gross Raden near Schwerin, the excellent preservation of parts of the wooden structures has enabled archaeologists to make a reliable reconstruction of a ninth- and tenth-century settlement and fort, including even details of the interior and of the implements used. One of the most spectacular finds was a ninth-century wooden temple situated on the periphery. The walls of the 10- by 7-metre building were constructed of vertical oak planking, the façade ends of which were carved into symbolic male and female heads. An aurochs head, the symbol of primeval force, was suspended over the door. A finely fashioned pottery drinking cup served as a chalice for ritual ceremonies. The seigneurial castles built after about 900 were of a different character and much better fortified. The castle of the rulers of the Obodrites was situated in Mecklenburg not far from the Baltic near Wismar. Mecklenburg is first mentioned as Michelinburg, in accordance with the Saxon way of speaking, in a document of 995. Latin chronicles call it Magnopolis, and an Arab traveller, Ibrahim ibn Jacub, probably recorded its Slavonic name, Wiligrad. The meaning is always the same, 'large fort'. This fort was indeed one of the largest Slav defensive structures on the whole Baltic coast; its wall, made of earth and stone and timber framed, was more than 10 metres high and 12 metres thick, and the area enclosed was about 15,000 square metres. Only the fort of the Polish rulers further south at Gniezno was of comparable size. Apart from a royal palace these forts also contained lodgings for the

rulers' retinue of warriors, farm buildings, stables and workshops, primarily for the manufacture of weapons and ornaments. Similar forts also existed in the lands of the eastern Slavs and of the Baltic tribes. Well defended and provisioned, they were virtually impregnable.

They needed to be. Inside them the whole wealth of the tribe, as well as the private treasure of the rulers, was concentrated, and they were the objects of repeated attacks by warrior bands from Scandinavia. One such attack in the 840s is described in the *Vita Anskarii*, a chronicle by Rimbert of the life and deeds of St Ansgar, a missionary to Denmark and Sweden. 'Then it happened that they [the Danes] had to go to a far distant fort in the land of the Slavs . . . There they made a surprise attack on the peaceful, unsuspecting inhabitants, captured the fort and returned to their homeland laden with stolen goods and many treasures.' In 852 a Danish fleet attacked Kurland: 'In this territory there were five regional forts. The inhabitants retreated to one of these after they had learnt of the Danish landing, in order to protect their territory by valiant defence. They were victorious and half the Danes were killed and half their ships destroyed. They won gold, silver and rich booty . . .' A renewed attack on Kurland by the Swedes under King Olaf led to the capture of the Seeburg. Another fort further inland resisted successfully and an agreement was reached during the siege. The Swedes withdrew with a ransom and a promise of tribute. These three instances could be considerably amplified. All the evidence shows that the elaborate system of forts protected the tribes on the southern coast from attacks by Franks, German feudal lords and Scandinavians. They were also refuges in times of intertribal feud and conflicts with neighbouring kingdoms.

The Slavs, however, did not merely sit behind their defences waiting to be attacked. The Obodrites for instance were within reach of such important centres as Hedeby across the narrow isthmus of Schleswig. At the end of the tenth century their army marched into

Hedeby and destroyed it. From the second half of the eleventh century the Rügen Slavs and the Pomeranians began to build fleets, beating the Danes several times and even settling on some of the Danish islands. Similar expeditions probably attacked Gotland, Öland and southern Sweden. Not only have many finds of Slav origin been made in these areas, but, from the mid-tenth century onwards, we find earlier strongholds being re-fortified, as exemplified by Eketorp on Öland. Mårten Stenberger, the excavator of Eketorp, reached the conclusion that the numerous finds of Slav origin were evidence of trade, 'but it may also mean that Öland was occupied by Slavs from the southern coast of the Baltic, as is indicated by Saxo and the Scandinavian Knýtlinga Saga'.

p.150(4)

The western part of the Baltic was at times known as the *Mare Rugianorum*, on account of the activities of the fleet of the Rügen Slavs. However, the interaction of the Slav tribes and kingdoms with the Scandinavians was more or less intermittent and sporadic. The main concern of the Slav kingdoms of the Obodrites, the Pomeranians, the Poles and above all the Kiev Rus' was with territorial questions and national administration. There were never any serious national attempts to gain a foothold in Scandinavia.

But war between the Slavs and the Scandinavians was only one side of the coin. Economic, trade and cultural relations were of far greater importance.

'The way from the Varangians to the Greeks'

The migrations and tribal movements south of the Baltic coast during the fourth to sixth centuries disrupted traditional routes between Scandinavia and central and southern Europe, or at least made them dangerous to use. The Oder and Vistula routes to the Danubian countries and to the Balkans and ultimately to Byzantium were no longer the safe highways they had been during the first century AD. In the mid-sixth century, communications between Scandinavia and Byzantium along these routes broke down or were at least greatly reduced. It was some time before the Scandinavians became aware of the new situation and could begin to make arrangements with the new Slav tribes and kingdoms, but numerous archaeological finds show that this had been accomplished by the eighth century. Trade formed the basis of these new relations. The stage was set by about 700 when the new ethnic groups had established themselves in their territories south of the Baltic. The economic boom in these areas and the emergence of a class structure within the Slave tribes were also important factors.

Markets and industrial centres would often grow up next to the forts of the tribal leaders and nobility, from the second half of the eighth century onwards. In the kingdom of the Obodrites the trading port of Reric was

of great importance. Its exact location is not entirely clear, but most of the evidence points to its being at Mecklenburg and situated in the immediate vicinity of the royal fort. Already at the beginning of the ninth century there were traders here. This settlement was attacked by the Danish king Godfred in 808 and the merchants were abducted and forced to settle in Hedeby. Soon afterwards the Obodrite king was treacherously assassinated by Godfred's men in his own trading settlement of Reric.

There is no mention in our main source, the Frankish annals, of the nationality or number of these merchants. It is not unlikely that there were Saxons, Franks and Frisians among them, as Mecklenburg and its hinterland was the Baltic town closest to the Frankish kingdom. This does not exclude the possibility of Reric having become the main Frankish access point to the Baltic after the conquest of the Saxons by Charlemagne, assisted by the Obodrites, around 800. Relations between the Frankish emperor and the Obodrite leaders were very close in the decades around 800, due to the common Saxo-Danish enemy. The numerous finds of hoards with Arab coins are evidence of the importance of the trading settlement at Mecklenburg-Reric even at this early date.

Oldenburg (known as Starigard by the Slavs, and *8* Brandehuse by the Scandinavians) was another trading centre in the territory of the Obodrites. In the eleventh century it was acknowledged as a *civitas maritima*. Excavations in Oldenburg itself and its Wagrian hinterland have brought to light a large number of goods of Scandinavian origin.

The trading centre of the Wilti was situated on the lower Peene near present-day Menzlin. Excavations here have revealed occupation levels with numerous imported artifacts as well as a cemetery containing some burials in boat-shaped stone settings. This burial type is alien to the Slav tradition and indicates the presence of Danes or Swedes who found their last resting place here. Their graves form an integral part of the cemetery, so one must assume that the Scandinavians were accepted as inhabitants of the town. But clearly they were in a minority: the predominant material remains are indigenous and Slav. Both in the settlement and in the cemetery, moreover, the evidence is purely of traders and craftsmen – there are no weapons. Weapons have, however, been found at a nearby settlement of the same date, located some 100 metres away on the river Peene. It is clear that this was the military and political centre, and that the port had grown up in its vicinity.

In recent years extensive excavations have taken place in Rügen, especially at Arkona and Ralswiek. At *1* Arkona there is already evidence of connections with Scandinavia and north-west Europe in the ninth century. Among the finds was a merchant's hoard

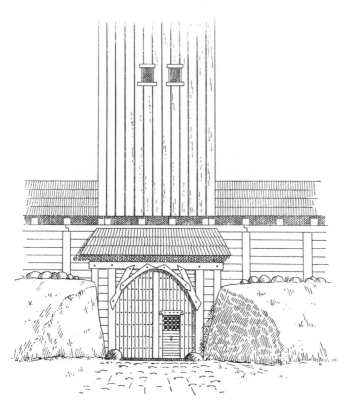

Reconstruction of the town gate of Arkona. The wooden door occupied a gap in the earth rampart. It was surmounted by a tower, making any attack on the gate itself extremely hazardous. The top of the tower, for which no evidence exists, is not reconstructed. (9)

consisting of knives, axes, arrowheads, metal orna-ments for drinking cups and a gilded bronze plaque bearing the sun motif, a symbol which probably originated in either Scandinavia or Ireland. The fort at Arkona was the Rugians' religious centre. Many trading and market activities were associated with the harvest ceremony. The Danish chronicler Saxo Grammaticus gives a lively description of this festival, albeit later than the ninth century:

Once a year, after the harvest, all the people of the island gathered in front of the temple of the idol and, having sacrificed an animal, partook of a ceremonial meal dedicated to their religion. It was the custom that the priest, distinguished by his beard and long hair, should on the previous day carefully sweep the temple, which only he may enter, with a broom. He took care not to breathe out inside the temple and each time he had to take a breath or breathe out he ran outside so as not to defile the idol with mortal breath. On the following day when the people were gathered outside he examined the cup which he had removed from the idol with care. If there was less liquid than before he took it as an omen of a bad harvest the following year, in which case he ordered that the present harvest be stored in the temple. If all the liquid was still there he would prophesy times of plenty in the fields. In accordance with the prophecy he would admonish the people to be either more careful or more

generous during the coming year. After he had emptied the old liquid on the ground in front of the idol's feet he refilled the cup. When he had honoured the idol by pretending to drink to it, he prayed in solemn language, both on behalf of himself and the country, for wealth and victory for the inhabitants. When he finished his speech he emptied the cup in great gulps and replaced it in the safe-keeping of the idol. An offering was also made of an almost man-sized round cake made of honey. The priest placed the cake between himself and the people and then asked them if they could see him. If they replied that they could, he expressed the wish that next year he would be completely hidden by it.

Every man and woman had to pay a coin to the idol every year for the maintenance of the cult. The idol was also granted a third of all captured booty, since it had been gained with its help. The god also had 300 specially selected horses and their riders in his service and any treasure they obtained, be it in war or through robbery, was placed at the disposal of the priest. He then had various cult objects and temple ornaments made from the proceeds. He kept them in locked rooms which contained not only a great deal of money but also a number of purple robes decayed by age.... (ch 825)

Apart from all this the idol also owned a white horse and it was regarded as sacrilege to pull hairs out of its mane or tail. To ensure that the sacred horse did not lose its prestige through frequent use only the priest had the right to groom and mount it. The Rugians believe that Svantevit, for this is the idol's name, wages war on the enemies of his sanctuaries on this horse. Sometimes, although it had been in its stable all night, the horse was found covered in sweat and dirt as if it had travelled a long way; this was regarded as specially significant. The horse was also used for prophecies. (ch 826)

Excavation results and the analysis of the animal bones show that feasts such as that described above were already held in Arkona at a much earlier date. There is also evidence of intermittent visits by traders from the ninth century onwards. But the settlement there seems never to have been permanently occupied.

That at Ralswiek, in the centre of the island of Rügen, however, certainly was a permanent settlement. It was founded in the eighth century, and was on the sea route to the mouth of the Oder and the countries of the eastern Baltic. At that time all navigation hugged the coast. At Ralswiek a settlement consisting of fifteen to twenty-five house-plots was established on an island-like hill between the bay of Jasmund and a lake which today has silted up. Anchorages for ships were constructed on the lakeward side by digging channels from the lake to individual house-plots and by building jetties of piles and planks, some of which supported buildings. Seventeen of these berths have been identified to date.

The farmsteads consisted of one main house and other smaller buildings, some of which served as workshops for producing antler and bone artifacts, iron, wood, amber and, in some places, glass and silver goods. In the different settlement layers were numerous imports from Scandinavia and the Baltic countries, including Norwegian soapstone, annular brooches from Gotland, and disc brooches from Sweden. But the most spectacular find was a silver hoard consisting of 2,270 Arab coins, mostly from central Asia or Arabia (the largest number of pre-850 Arab coins so far discovered in the Baltic), and a bracelet of Perm type. They were in a woven basket in a house dated to the mid-ninth century. Probably belonging to a merchant permanently resident at Ralswiek, the hoard seems to have come from Bulgar on the Volga by way of Staraja Ladoga and the southern Baltic route.

From Ralswiek, too, three sea-going ships dated to the period 900–1100 are known. The best preserved is 14m long, 3.4m wide and could carry about 9 tons of cargo – that is, roughly the same as ship no. 3 from Skuldelev in Denmark, which is dated to the early eleventh century.

So far over four hundred tumuli have been identified at Ralswiek, of which nearly two hundred have been excavated. Certain differences in grave-goods indicate that even in Ralswiek foreign merchants, probably Scandinavians, lived alongside the native Slav merchants and craftsmen. Ralswiek was in the vicinity of the old tribal centre and the fort of the ruler of the Rügen Slavs at Rugard near Bergen.

We have seen that there were also trading centres at the mouth of the Oder, at Menzlin, and (from the latter half of the ninth century) at Wolin and Szczecin. During the tenth century Wolin became pre-eminent and in the eleventh was known as a metropolis throughout northern Europe. Adam of Bremen gives the following description of it: 'It is truly the greatest of all towns in Europe; Slavs and other tribes, Greeks and Barbarians live there; even strangers from Saxony have been granted equal terms of residence . . . For the town is filled with goods from all the northern countries and nothing desirable or rare is lacking . . .' Archaeological evidence from Menzlin and Ralswiek confirms that foreign merchants were permitted to reside and trade alongside the native merchants and craftsmen. Excavations over many years have elucidated the main development of the settlement to Wolin.

Another trading settlement which had colonies of foreign merchants or craftsmen grew up at the old salt centre of Kolobrzeg. At the mouth of the Vistula, on the borderlands between the Slavs and Baltic tribes, the Prussian trading settlement of Truso – known to us from the writings of the English king Alfred the Great – flourished in the ninth century. It must have been of some considerable importance as Wulfstan, a farmer and warrior merchant from northern Norway, sailed directly there from Hedeby without calling at any Slav, Danish or Swedish ports on the way. Similar settle-

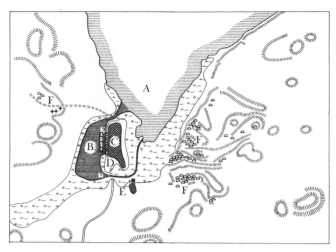

Ralswiek, on the island of Rügen. Here, at the end of the eighth century, between an inlet (A) and a now dried-up creek (B), a settlement of about twenty houses (C) was established. Each house had its own jetty (D). Three boats were found slightly to the south (E). On the higher ground nearby were over 400 burial mounds and graves (F), of which more than 150 have been excavated. (10)

ments were situated on the lower Niemen and Dvina. An important trade route to the upper Dnjeper and on to Byzantium followed the Dvina.

Important trading settlements grew up along the route from the Baltic to Byzantium and on to the land of the Bulgars and central Asia. On Lake Ladoga stood Staraja Ladoga, a joint Finno-Ugrian Slav settlement, probably visited by western Slav, Scandinavian and Frisian merchants as early as the eighth century. Soviet scholars even hold that Frisian craftsmen lived here. From Staraja Ladoga one went on to the upper Volga and central Asia. Bulgar, situated at the confluence of the Kama and Volga rivers, was the capital of the kingdom of the Volga-Bulgarians and a meeting place for merchants from the Arab and the Baltic countries. Here goods from the Baltic and the Arab world were

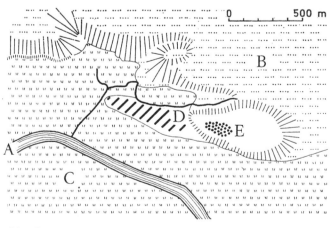

Menzlin, an important Slav trading settlement at the mouth of the Oder (A). Here the town (D) was situated where dry subsoil (B) met wet (C). The burial mounds (E) are on higher ground behind. (11)

exchanged; it was rare for either party to venture further. An Arab geographer, Mohammed Mugaddosi, writing about 985, says: 'Sable, deer skin, ermine, steppe fox, fox, beaver skins, colourful pheasants, goat skins, wax, arrows, birch bark, coins, fish bones, fish teeth, castorum, amber, shagreen, honey, hazelnuts, hawks, swords, armour, maple wood, Slav slaves, small livestock and cattle: all these things come from Bulgar.' Already sixty years earlier, about 921/922, the Arab geographer ibn Hauqal had witnessed in person the trading in Bulgar. He travelled in a caravan of 5,000 men and 3,000 horses, donkeys and camels which covered the 1,250 miles from Chorezm on the Oxus (now the Amu-Darya) to Bulgar in under two months. In Bulgar he met Rus' merchants who were selling furs 'from the Scandinavian countries of Gog and Magog'. From another of ibn Hauqal's books we know that some of the merchants from Chorezm even continued beyond Bulgar and the Volga route as far as Scandinavia.

Other Arab merchants reached central and northern Europe from Islamic Spain. One of these was Ibrahim ibn Jacub who described a journey of around 965 which touched at Hedeby, Mecklenburg, Magdeburg, Prague and other places. His account includes a description of the Polish kingdom and the land of the Obodrites:

To the west the land of Nakon [the king of the Obodrites] borders on Saxony and some of the Danes. His land has so many horses that they are exported. They [the Obodrites] have complete sets of arms, that is coats of armour, helmets and swords . . . The fort [i.e. Nakon's fort] is called Wiligrad which means the big fort . . .

As for the land of Mescheqqo [the Polish king] it is the largest of their lands and it is rich in grain, meat, honey and fish. Taxes are paid to him in coined money and this is used to keep his soldiers, each man receiving a set sum every month. He has 3,000 men-at-arms and 100 of them are the equivalent of 10,000 others. He provides the soldiers with clothes, steeds, weapons and all that they need. . . .

On the basis of these various snippets of information, Arab geographers made the first maps of eastern and northern Europe, noting down important towns and routes and above all river and sea communications. Only one collection of such maps survives, that made in the twelfth century at the court of Emperor Frederick II in Sicily by the Arab geographer Al Idrisi.

The northern trading settlements struck Arab merchants, used to the richness and variety of Arab bazaars, as poorly equipped and lacking in refinements. Ibrahim ibn Jacub wrote as follows of Hedeby: 'Schleswig is a very large town situated at the farthest limit of the ocean . . . The town has a dearth both of merchandise and the blessings of nature . . . Fish, of which there is an abundance, is the staple food of the inhabitants . . . Never have I heard less pleasing song

than that of Schleswig; it is a kind of growling emitted from the throat like the barking of a dog . . .' Yet for all their northern desolation and lack of social amenities, these south Baltic trading towns were for the Scandinavians the gateway to another world – western Europe, the Danube, Byzantium, central Asia and the Arab countries. And just as the southern merchants passed through them on the way north, so the northerners did, before setting forth on one of the great trade routes to the south and east.

Political control over these trade routes varied. Sometimes they existed in a power vacuum, and were independent communities under their own merchant warriors, who extorted tribute from the surrounding area. Some were so well established that foreign traders not only lived in them for long periods, but died and were buried. We have a very vivid and detailed description by the Arab chronicler ibn Fadlan of the funeral of a merchant of the Scandinavian Rus'. The dead man's ship is dragged ashore and propped up with stakes. Horses, a dog and a hen are sacrificed. Much of the ritual is directed by an old woman called the Angel of Death. On the ship's deck a tent is pitched. The body is laid in it and a slave-girl volunteers to die with him:

Then some men came who had shields and sticks, and they handed her a beaker of liquor; she sang over it and drank it up. The interpreter told me: 'Now with this she is bidding farewell to all her friends.' Next, another beaker was handed to her; she took it, and made her singing long drawn out; but the old woman hurried her, to make her drink it up and go into the tent where her master was. I was watching her, and she looked quite dazed; she tried to go into the tent, but stuck her head between it and the ship's side. Then the old woman took her by the hand and led her into the tent, and the old woman herself went inside with her. The men then began to beat their shields with sticks, so that no sound of her shrieking should be heard, for fear other girls should become frightened and not want to seek to die with their masters. Then six men went into the tent, and all made love with her. After this they laid her beside her dead master; two held her legs and two her hands, and the woman called the Angel of Death wound a cord with knotted ends round her neck, passing the ends out on either side and handing them to the two men to pull. Then she stepped forward with a broad-bladed dagger, and began to drive it in and pluck it out again between the girl's ribs, while the two men choked her with the cord, and so she died.

After this, whoever was the closest kinsman of the dead man came forward. He took a wooden stick and set light to it; then he walked backwards, with his back to the ship and his face to the people, holding the stick in one hand and with the other hand laid on his backside; he was naked. By this means, the wood they had put just under the ship was set on fire, immediately after they had laid the slave-girl they had killed beside her master. Then the people came forward with

Schleswig
Plön
Bosau
Oldenburg
Rerik
Rostok
Mecklenburg
Schwerin
Bremen
Arkona
RÜGEN I.
Ralswiek
Bergen
Bornholm
Kolobrzeg
Truso
Wolin
Neubrandenburg
Szczecin
Neustrelitz
Feldberg
Tornow
Havelberg
Spandau
Berlin
Köpenick
Brandenburg
Magdeburg
Gniezno
Poznan
Peene
Elbe
Weser
Oder
Vistula
NIEDERLAUSITZ
Merseburg
Leipzig
OBERLAUSITZ
Meissen
Dresden
Saale
SWIĘTOKRZYSKIE MTS
200 Kms
120 Mls
Bamberg
Prague
MORAVIA
Crakow

L. LADOGA
Neva
L. BELOE
Staraja Ladoga
G. OF FINLAND
Volkho...
Novgorod
Bulgar
BALTIC SEA
Gotland
L. PEIPUS
L. ILMEN
Pskov
SKÅNE
KURLAND
Dvina
Smolensk
Niemen
Vistula
Oder
Bamberg
Regensburg
CARPATHIAN MTS
Dnjester
Kiev
Dnjeper
Don
Volga
Beloezero
DACIA
CAUCASUS MTS
Danube
BLACK SEA
Byzantium

wood and timber; each brought a stick with its tip on fire and threw it on the wood lying under the ship, so that the flames took hold, first on the wood, and then on the ship, and then on the tent and the man and the woman and everything inside the ship. Thereupon a strong, fierce wind arose, so that the flames grew stronger and the fire blazed even more . . . not much time passed before the ship and the timber and the slave-girl and her master had all turned into ashes and so into dust.

After this, on the spot where the ship had first lain when they dragged it up from the river, they built something that looked like a round mound. In the middle of it they set up a big post of birch wood, on which they wrote the name of this man and the name of the king of the Rus'; then they went on their way.

Similar scenes were no doubt enacted in Gnezdowo-Smolensk, Staraja Ladoga, Beloezero, Novgorod, Truso, Swielubie, Menzlin and Birka, where Frisians, Finns and Slavs lived and were buried among the Swedes.

The trading settlements on the coast and along the Continental trade routes were intertribal centres. It was here that people of different tribal and ethnic origin met and that cultural traits were exchanged. But within the tribal areas, where a strong political and social structure already existed, the development of these centres depended upon stable conditions in the host country. Here the trading settlements were in the first instance dependencies of their respective hinterlands. Hedeby remained a Danish town despite its multinational population; in the same way Reric-Mecklenburg was Obodrite, Wolin a town of the Wolin Slavs; Truso, Prussian; Staraja Ladoga, Slav and Finno-Ugrian; and Novgorod an international mercantile centre of the Ilmen Slavs.

Trade and culture

The cultural importance of the trading settlements has already been suggested. For Slavs and Scandinavians alike, they were the points of contact with the outside world, the places through which travellers and goods had to pass even if their final destinations were far away. Archaeology amply supports written history, and the tens of thousands of Arab coins that have been found in the vicinity of such settlements are alone sufficient to prove their commercial vitality. They would obviously have handled both utility and luxury goods, weapons and ornaments, raw materials and foodstuffs, but since not all these survive equally well, we shall confine ourselves to those goods that are most easily traced in the archaeological record.

Some trade and trade routes can be deduced from pottery. Frisian jugs from the lower Rhine, for instance, probably contained wine. Others, probably made to hold honey, wax, fats or other foodstuffs, are evidence

for the movement of these commodities. Much of the Slav pottery found in Scandinavian trading ports no doubt often arrived there as containers, but it may also have been in demand as tableware, for it was greatly superior, both in form and decoration, to the crude Scandinavian pottery. It appears to have been copied in south Scandinavia, possibly by Slav potters imported for the purpose. The distribution of Slav pottery in the earlier period therefore reflects the intensity of Scandinavian-Slav relations, even though it is not necessarily the result of direct trading. The so-called Feldberg and Fresendorf pottery of the seventh to tenth centuries produced by the Wilti copying classical pottery types was itself an object of trade. Carl Schuchhardt, one of the first scholars to identify it, called this pottery the 'Meissen of the Middle Ages' on account of its fine finish and high technical standard. Long-distance trade ensured its wide distribution in the countries around the Baltic.

In the eighth and ninth centuries silversmiths in the forts and trading settlements of Poland and Pomerania were greatly influenced by styles and fashions from the lands along the Danube and from Moravia. The Tempelhof type of earring, for example, can ultimately be traced back to Byzantian prototypes. They were most widely distributed in the tenth century, when they occurred in great numbers on Bornholm and Gotland, odd ones even reaching Sjoelland and Skåne. Silver basket earrings and silver belt and cloak clasps have the same pattern of distribution. Other metal artifacts such as crescent-shaped pendants, ornaments and female fertility symbols also reached the Baltic, generally by way of the territory of the eastern Slavs. Arab prototypes have even been found in the Slav heartland, where they were copied and elaborated further. Among these there were filigree-decorated crescent pendants, earrings with basket-shaped beads or beads ornamented with filigree.

The kaftan worn in Persia and the Arab world was very much in vogue in the Swedish town of Birka in the period from the late eighth to the tenth century. Here, as in Poland and even Pomerania, the native tunic was adapted, possibly due to the influence of the kaftan or of the Byzantine riding coat. Patterned linen shirts found in the earliest graves at Birka dating to the ninth century were foreign to Scandinavia and had obviously reached these parts from the lands of the eastern Slavs.

One specific problem has been much discussed, namely the trade in weapons, above all the supply of good quality swords. In the past, more on *a priori* than empirical grounds, it used to be maintained that only the Vikings supplied swords to eastern and central Europe. Such a theory ignores unequivocal statements in the Frankish sources. In 805, Charlemagne, in order to preserve the monopoly of the Frankish counts, issued a proclamation prohibiting certain towns from selling weapons to the Slavs; the towns are listed by name, as are the places where merchants crossed the frontier. The fact that the prohibition had to be repeated on several subsequent occasions only proves how well established the trade had become. It is clear that not only weapons, but also a great many other goods reached Slav territory through trading centres located on important routes of circulation. Names such as Ulfberht, Ingelreht and Hilpreht are inscribed on their blades. The high quality of Frankish swords made them objects of great demand even in the Arab world. Slav, Baltic and probably even Scandinavian smiths attempted to produce swords of the same quality. Swordsmiths sometimes even copied the names of the Rhenish masters, apparently taking them to be ornamental but inscribing their own names as well. One sword recently found in Foscevataja in the Ukraine bears an inscription in Cyrillic script: 'Ljudota the smith made this.'

A developed iron technology, the prerequisite for producing similar weapons, was known to the south of the Baltic; for example in Greater Moravia, Bohemia, Poland, in the Baltic countries and of course in the important early towns of the Kiev Rus'. The manufacture of steel, the welding together both of different types of steel and of soft forged iron with steel were known to Slav smiths as early as the seventh and eighth centuries, as they were in parts of Scandinavia.

A similar story is told by the leaf-shaped spear-head; originally of Rhenish manufacture, this weapon was later produced at many Scandinavian, Slav and Baltic centres, as was the battle-axe which was copied from late classical and Persian prototypes. It is at present almost impossible to gauge the volume of the trade in weapons on the basis of the available archaeological evidence, especially as no weapon workshop has yet been excavated.

It is easier to trace the origin and distribution of other items of trade, Norwegian soapstone, for example, amber, ornaments of the types mentioned above, certain pottery and mould types and coins. Some items can by their nature be known only from documentary sources, slaves for example. Slav, Baltic and Finno-Ugrian slaves were sold in large numbers at Bulgar, Magdeburg, Regensburg and other border towns, mainly to Arab countries.

The trade in furs was both widespread and extremely lucrative. It flourished particularly between Frisia and the Baltic countries. In the eleventh century Adam of Bremen raged against the trade in furs from Lapland 'which has brought the death-bringing poison of ostentation into our world . . . For we thirst for a marten fur coat at any cost as if it were eternal salvation. They therefore offer us marten furs in exchange for our woollen cloth which we call *falsones*.' As a consequence of the importance of the fur trade a few Old Russian

words crept into some Low German patois. In Old Russian the word *kuna* meant marten, marten-skin, money. In Old Frisian the word recurs as *cona* meaning coin. The Russian *sobol* found its way into Middle High German as *sabel* and *zobel*. In English it occurs as *sable*, meaning both the animal and its fur. The Old Slavonic word for fur, *kozych*, is probably the origin of the medieval Latin *crusna*, *crusina* and the Old High German and Old Saxon *kursinna* and the Old Frisian *kersua*.

The slave trade and the fur trade were by far the most profitable in north-south and east-west trade. On the Volga, for instance, a marten skin cost about one dirhem, i.e. 3 grams of silver at the most, the value of one green glass bead. One could therefore buy a fortune in skins and furs for a handful of beads. In Arab markets this wealth could be realized at a profit of 1,000 per cent or more. This single example, which is one of many, shows how the mutually exclusive ranges of goods and price differentials between northern and eastern Europe and the developed world provided the incentive for a trade which was often hazardous. Some 150,000 Arab coins, most of which occur in more than 1,500 silver hoards found in the various Baltic countries, clearly show the extent of this trade in the ninth to eleventh centuries. Slav traders and Slav markets played an important part in this Baltic trade, merchants acting both as principals and as middlemen.

Only towards the end of the tenth century did trade with central and western Europe increase in importance; this is indicated by the eleventh-century concentration of coins, mainly of German origin, in the Baltic region.

Some trading settlements, as well as some trade and craft centres located outside forts which had emerged in the interior in the ninth to tenth centuries, formed the nuclei of medieval towns. Between 50 and 80 per cent of medieval towns on Slav territory and about 50 per cent of the German towns east of the Elbe can be traced back to these ninth- and tenth-century foundations.

Religion and temple cults

The territory of the north-western Slavs was one of the few areas in medieval Europe which retained pagan beliefs and cults well into the twelfth century – a stumbling block for the ecclesiastical hierarchy of the neighbouring feudal states, and to some extent a thorn in the side of Christian Europe. From about 700 onwards Christian missions, therefore, attempted to convert these areas and to integrate them under Christian control. The tribes of the north-western Slavs, however, were equally steadfast in warding off these attempts, the more so as they were more or less veiled pretexts for conquest and suppression by either the Frankish or the German kingdom. In such circumstances the pagan religion of the north-western Slavs also became the focal point of resistance to foreign conquest. The display of religious and cult practices was therefore of great importance and was stressed by Christian apologists.

According to the chronicler Thietmar (*c.* 1015), each tribe had its own god: 'There are', he said, 'as many temples as there are tribes.' Some of the names of the gods can be traced back to old Indo-European roots. The Wagrians around Oldenburg worshipped a god called Prove; those at Plön the god Podaga; the Polabs had a god Siwa and the Obodrites at Mecklenburg the god Radigost. Swarozyc was the principal god of the Wilti. He was worshipped at a ceremonial fort at Rethra (Riedegost) in the vicinity of the modern town of Neubrandenburg in Mecklenburg. The temple is described as follows: 'The outer walls, as far as one can discern, are decorated with various splendidly carved images of gods and goddesses. Inside are statues of gods each inscribed with a name; they are awe-inspiring and clad in helmets and armour; the highest of the gods is called Swarozyc and he is specially revered and worshipped by all heathens. The standards may only be removed in times of war and then only by warriors on foot.'

One of the characteristics of the Slav gods was that they had many heads. In Arkona the Rugian god Svantevit is supposed to have been depicted with four heads. Other gods in Rügen are described as having had seven heads. Triglaw, a three-headed god, stood in Brandenburg, and the town of Szczecin also had a Triglaw as its special communal god. A few years ago a two-headed wooden statue was excavated on the island of Tollensesee near Neubrandenburg. At Wolin a miniature wood carving with four faces interpreted as Svantevit was associated with strata datable to the end of the ninth century.

Slav places of worship brought to light in excavations in Poland and the USSR show that in some regions the modes of worshipping gods in temples and by means of statues differed. The earlier places of worship of both the Slavs and the Baltic tribes usually consisted of a circular setting enclosing either symbolic posts or wooden figures. The best known of these sites is devoted to Perun at Novgorod. Archaeology shows that this type of site also occurred in Poland and east of the Oder. It is possible that the particular north-west Slav tradition of idols and temples may be due to Celtic influences from southern Poland and Bohemia.

From both documentary and archaeological sources we know of fertility and cattle gods such as Volos; gods of war and primeval power such as Svantevit; sky gods such as Perun; sun and fire gods such as Svarog and Svarozyc and war gods such as Gerovit. There were also numerous other divinities and demons. Rethra is an example of a place where a complete pantheon was created and priests or groups of priests established to serve it. Such priests were the religious leaders of the community and influenced social and politico-military life.

The north-western Slavs and the Germans

The north-western tribes played a special role in the evolution of the German nation. Large parts of the medieval German territories east of Hanover and Bamberg were originally settled by Slav-speaking peoples; in some places this remained the case up to the sixteenth century. After the confusion of the Migration Period they had helped to bring the land into cultivation, and the Frankish and Saxon feudal lords welcomed their contribution. They suffered the same oppression as Frankish, Saxon and Thuringian farmers and enjoyed the same limited rights. Hence they became amalgamated with the German nation at an early stage.

East of the Elbe-Saale, however, things were different. The tribes that were settled here fiercely resisted the attempts of the German lords to subdue them. Developments here were consequently marked by serious strife and unrest which lasted almost 400 years. It was only in the middle of the twelfth century that Slav power really collapsed between the Oder and the Elbe, and the Slav tribal rulers paid allegiance to either German or Danish lords and became their vassals and intermarried with them. The ruling family in Mecklenburg until 1918 could trace its origins back to the Slavic Obodrites. Their arms bore a bull's head, the symbol of primeval force and fertility.

The ordinary people, who had to bear the burden of these wars, had developed the land, in some areas to a high degree of efficiency. From the twelfth century, however, farmers from Flanders, Saxony, Frankonia and Thuringia settled in and around their villages. Although often under great stress, the two elements gradually merged, and new German tribes such as Mecklenburgers, Pomeranians, Brandenburgers and 'new' Saxons emerged from this process of assimilation.

This historic Slav settlement is reflected even today by the many Slav place-names both in the land of the Wends around Hanover but above all to the east of the Elbe-Saale line. About half the villages in the German Democratic Republic trace their origin back to the period of Slav settlement and bear Slav names. The same is true of the towns – Schwerin, Rostock, Leipzig, Dresden, Brandenburg and Berlin-Spandau all originated in the Slav period and formed the nucleus of later medieval towns. The ethnic minority known as the Sorbs, distant descendants of the tribe of the Sorbs mentioned as living in the Elbe-Saale region by a Frankish chronicle in 630, still live in the Ober- and Niederlausitz area in the midst of a German-speaking neighbourhood.

8
ROMANTICISM
AND
REVIVAL

JÖRAN MJÖBERG

> '*The White God is coming northwards;*
> *I will not stay to meet him. The old gods are not as mighty*
> *as they were; they are asleep, or sit like shadows*
> *of themselves.*'

Henrik Ibsen
Hjördis, in *The Warriors at Helgeland*

1857

The heroic age of the sagas made a sudden and very dramatic impact upon the imagination of the late eighteenth century. In part this was due to a new sense of national identity, so that Englishmen, Scotsmen, Irishmen, Germans, Norwegians, Swedes, Danes were no longer content to look for their origins in the classical-Christian culture that they all shared, but to demand something more tangible and particularized. This went hand in hand with an intellectual movement away from the qualities valued by the Age of Reason – urbanity, sophistication, taste – and towards the primitive and the barbaric. Both currents – nationalism and Romanticism – had one consequence in common: a revival of interest in the Northern World and a revaluation of its achievements.

While poets and artists allowed their fantasy to roam among bards, heroes and gods, the scholars were patiently piecing together the evidence. The old texts (the Eddas, the sagas, *Beowulf*, the *Nibelungenlied*) were carefully edited and published. Old Norse, Anglo-Saxon and Old High German were revived as university subjects on an equality with the classical languages. Folklorists collected stories that were still being told round country firesides. Antiquarians recovered carved stones, jewellery, ships and the foundations of buildings. Gradually fiction was brought into broad conformity with fact. In a few cases poet and scholar were the same man. William Morris, the author of long romances in verse and prose based on Norse and Germanic legends, also studied and translated the sagas, and in 1871 and 1873 actually went to Iceland to pursue his researches on the spot. On one of these journeys he was accompanied by the artist W. G. Collingwood. From drawings made on the site of the old Icelandic parliament, Thingvellir, Collingwood painted this picture (*opposite*) which is still considered to be generally accurate. The Great Assembly ('Althingi') of the Norsemen is constantly mentioned in the sagas. Here the independent farmers set up their booths, paid visits and debated public affairs; legal decisions and sentences, such as outlawry, etc., would be reached and promulgated by democratic consensus. The painting is very typical of its age in utilizing all available knowledge to produce a vivid reconstruction of the past. (1)

On previous page: an engraving of one of the most famous Danish rune-stones, the Tullstorp stone, from Ole Worm's 'Monumenta Danica', of 1643. Scholarly research into Norse antiquities goes back to the Renaissance, but scientific recording was in its infancy. Here the runic inscription (which is what interested Worm) is accurately copied, but the animal – the wolf Fenrir – is hopelessly wrong. (1)

The Ossianic mirage

Ossian was a genuine bard of the third century, but the works purporting to be translations and published in the 1760s were in fact fabricated by James Macpherson. Ossian was nevertheless hailed as a northern Homer and translated into nearly every European language. *Left: Ossian's Last Song* by N. A. Abildgaard, 1781. *Below*: engraved title-page of the 1761 edition of *Fingal*. (2,3)

The craze for Ossian spread to France, Germany, even America, but illustrations to *Fingal* by both the American artist John Trumbull (*above*) and the German Otto Runge (*right*) show how hard it was for artists to free themselves from classical conventions. Runge's work seems intended to rival Flaxman's illustrations to the *Iliad*, but he crowns his 'acropolis' with a sort of Stonehenge. (4,5)

Romantic nationalism reaches a climax in Girodet's painting *Ossian receiving the warriors of the Revolution into Paradise*, 1803. Ossian was one of Napoleon's favourite poets, which may account for the widespread attempts to create an Ossianic iconography. Jacques-Louis David wrote: 'It is in Homer and Ossian, and in the primitive peoples among whom their works were written, that we shall find the means to regenerate our soul and our spirit.' (6)

A vision of history

'**Viking**' originally meant a man who took part in sea raids. In the later Middle Ages it came to mean simply a pirate, but by the eighteenth century it was beginning to acquire the romantic overtones that it still has today. What it meant to the seventeenth century may be judged from an illustrated copy of *Grettirs saga* in Copenhagen (*right*). Grettir's great-grandfather is described as 'a great viking, who used to harry away in the West over the sea'. (7)

The long ships, so central to the modern image of the Vikings, were only partially understood for most of the nineteenth century. The Gokstad ship was discovered in 1880, the Oseberg not until 1904. In 1889, Hans Gude painted this view (*below*) of *Viking ships under sail in Sognefjord*, and on the whole achieved a remarkably convincing result. Such paintings were officially encouraged, and scenes from national history adorned town halls, universities and houses of parliament in every country of northern Europe. The same period saw the rise of the historical novel, its details becoming more and more accurate as research deepened. (8)

Where history melted into legend, the patriotic imagination had its freest scope. Ragnar Lodbroke was a Scandinavian ruler who perhaps lived in the eighth or ninth century and who was said to have invaded France and England. He was captured by Ælla, king of Northumberland, and thrown into a snake-pit. His sons revenged him by killing King Ælla. Above: *Ælla's messengers before Ragnar Lodbroke's sons*, by J. A. Malmström. (9)

The discovery of America by Leif Eiriksson was another favourite episode on the borderline between legend and history. In Christian Krohg's painting of 1893, the Viking explorer grasps the tiller and points excitedly to the land. (10)

The world of the sagas

Nostalgia for the past produced paintings which at the time seemed authentically barbaric, but which with the passage of time now seem to us to bear the unmistakable stamp of the nineteenth century. *Left*: Johannes Flintoe's *Duel at Skiringsal*, of the mid-1830s. (11)

Winged helmets became indissolubly associated with the Viking Age, though in fact no such Viking helmets have ever been found. *Above*: *The Viking's Farewell*, by Herbert Gandy. In Nils Bergslien's *King Harald Finehair at the Battle of Hafrsfjord* (*left*), the king wears a plumed helmet and carries an Arabian sword. (12,13)

A vein of sentiment often betrays nineteenth-century sensibility in spite of painstaking detail. F. N. Jensen's *Viking abducting a southern woman* (*below*) is given a classical setting, and Malmström's *Ingeborg* (*right*) sits in a chair with a convincingly Viking arm-rest as she hears the news of Hjalmar's death. Malmström in fact experimented with 'Nordic' furniture and ceramics. (14,15)

Balder's funeral inspired Sir Frank Dicksee's *Funeral of a Viking* (*below*), of 1893. Snorri Sturluson and other sources relate how Balder's body was placed on a ship which was set on fire and launched into the lonely sea. Such funerals no doubt actually took place, but could leave no material record. (16)

Mythological painting drew its inspiration purely from literary sources; it was a deliberate attempt to challenge classical art on its own ground. Two examples from the first half of the nineteenth century are by Constantine Hansen (*above*) and C. W. Eckersberg (*below*). In the first, Loki, having managed to get himself invited to a banquet given by the giant Ægir, systematically insults all the guests, exposing their private lives and holding even the gods up to mockery; he was finally driven from the hall by Thor. In the second, the blind god Hod has accidentally killed Balder by throwing a branch of mistletoe at him. Every object in nature had sworn not to harm Balder, except the mistletoe, which was too young to take the oath. The gods amused themselves by throwing things at the invulnerable Balder, and Loki cunningly put a branch of mistletoe into Hod's hand. (17,18)

The gods reborn

'The wild hunt of Odin' by the Norwegian artist Peter Nicolai Arbo comes close to Wagner in its evocation of barbaric power. Odin was perhaps originally a sky-god and the noise of storms is explained in the folklore of many Germanic countries by a horde of wild horsemen galloping above the clouds. The riders were the ghosts of dead warriors collected by the Valkyries (literally 'choosers of the slain') from battlefields. This scene was painted in 1872, within a few years of the composition of *Die Walküre*. (19)

Drama and romance

To explore the past was for many novelists and playwrights a means of asking profound questions about the present. The hero of Oelenschläger's play, *Earl Håkon the Mighty* (1808), represents the doomed tradition of the old religion succumbing to Christianity. *Left*: Adolph Tidemand's illustration of Håkon's death; having taken refuge in a pig-sty he was killed by his own slave. *Below left*: *Thora at Håkon's bier*, by C. W. Eckersberg. Thora was Håkon's mistress. (20,21)

The theatre boldly invented what eluded the historians. *Below*: two representations of pre-Christian temples, by Johannes Flintoe (Temple of Thor) and Thomas Bruun (Temple of the goddess Hertha). Neither has the slightest archaeological foundation. (22,23)

Frithiof's Saga by Esaias Tegnér
(1825) was the first serious attempt to
revive the saga form. It tells the story
of Frithiof, the son of a Viking, who
falls in love with the king's daughter
Ingeborg and after many setbacks and
adventures marries her. *Below*:
Ingeborg's Lament by J. A. Malmström.
(24)

The end of the story: Frithiof and
Ingeborg are united in Balder's temple,
another illustration by Malmström,
whose work is distinguished by its
concern for archaeological accuracy.
By 1888 this was perfectly possible.
Earlier versions of *Ingeborg's Lament*,
such as those by Boehmer, 1846 (*left*),
and Jensen, 1830 (*right*), use a strange
mixture of historical features.
(25,26,27)

219

Odin or Christ?

The confrontation between paganism and Christianity appealed strongly to nineteenth-century artists for its stark juxtaposition of light and darkness. In the twentieth century, interest shifted to paganism itself. The painter Carl Larsson was a keen antiquarian, and between 1911 and 1915 he produced a large mural (*above*) depicting the midwinter ritual sacrifice of a king at Gamla Uppsala. Costumes, armour, musical instruments and architecture are drawn from a variety of sources, but the result is a powerful impression of an ancient rite. (28)

St Columba came from Christian Ireland to pagan Iona probably in the year 563. From there he journeyed to the mainland preaching to the heathen Picts. In William Hole's fresco in the National Portrait Gallery in Edinburgh (*left*) he has assumed something of the character of a Victorian evangelical. (29)

St Sigfrid, traditionally a priest from York, preached the Gospel in Sweden, dying at Växjö about 1045. F. L. Blackstadius's painting of 1866 (*right*) has all the ingredients of popular iconography – the holy bishop baptizing; the children, symbols of innocence; a black-robed priest of the old order; warriors with winged helmets; a disconsolate bard, his occupation gone; even a rune-stone copied from a real example. (30)

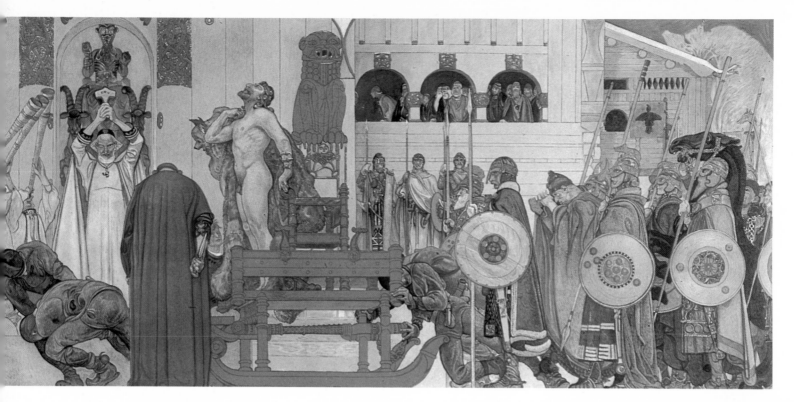

The Valkyries

Warrior maidens, daughters of Odin, the Valkyries carried the bodies of the slain to Valhalla and there waited upon them at an eternal banquet. Stories about individual Valkyries abound in the Eddas and in Saxo Grammaticus's *Gesta Danorum*; the most famous was Brynhild, who became the beloved of Sigurd. *Opposite*: a spirited rendering of the Valkyries' ride by Arbo. (34)

Shield maidens resembled Valkyries and were often confused with them, but they lacked the Valkyries' supernatural status. *Left*: the tragic end of the story of Stikla and Rusla, an illustration to Saxo by Louis Moe. *Below*: *The Valkyrie's Death*, again by Arbo. (31,32)

Wagner's Valkyries play their traditional role of bearing heroes to Valhalla. Brünnhilde's story is also very close to that related in the Edda: having forfeited Wotan's favour by disobedience she is laid asleep, surrounded by a wall of fire that only Siegfried will dare to penetrate. *Right*: four of the nine Valkyries from the English National Opera production of 1970. (33)

'Corn-field summer': one of the woodcuts made by the Danish artist Sigurd Vasegaard for a new edition of Saxo Grammaticus in the 1960s – an indication of this century's interest in phallic ritual. (2)

ROMANTICISM AND REVIVAL

DURING THE LAST three centuries the ancient past of Scandinavia has been enriched with a great wealth of imaginative writing produced in Scandinavia, England, Germany, France and America: writing ultimately based on ancient sources, particularly the Icelandic sagas, the Eddic and scaldic poetry and Saxo Grammaticus' Danish chronicle, *Gesta Danorum*.

The saga literature may be divided into three categories. The first is the great work by Snorri Sturluson, *Heimskringla*, the tales of the kings of Norway, a broadly based realistic and picaresque account of Norway's history from heathen times to the end of the twelfth century. This great classic (written by Snorri in Iceland between 1225 and 1240) is said to have lain next to the Bible in almost every farmhouse in Norway in the nineteenth century when that country was reaching towards independence. The second category is made up of the Icelandic sagas, for example *Njals saga*, *Laxdæla saga*, *Egils saga*, *Grettirs saga*, *Gunnlaugs saga* and *Eyrbyggja saga*, written down in the second half of the thirteenth century. The third category comprises the *Fornaldar sögur* (heroic sagas) which were written later, but which, treating of earlier periods, are of a more romantic and popular character.

The manuscript of the Poetic Edda was discovered in Iceland in the 1640s by Bishop Brynjulfur Sveinsson. Some of the individual poems in this Edda are of a mythological, that is a religious, character, while others are written in a heroic vein. They are thought to have been written down in the same period as the sagas.

The so-called *Edda of Snorri*, written by Snorri Sturluson, outlines important rules for constructing poetry and includes some mythological writings in both verse and prose. Scaldic poems, by named writers, are also included in individual sagas, particularly in *Heimskringla*.

The Latin chronicle of Denmark's history, *Gesta Danorum*, was written by a Danish monk, Saxo Grammaticus, presumably in the last decade of the twelfth century, and the first two decades of the thirteenth. Here are described events up to the end of the twelfth century, but the earlier portion of the chronicle contains a highly apocryphal list of Danish kings, which purports to go back to the time of the birth of Christ. In the famous thirteenth-century German epic *Nibelungenlied* the same material is found as in *Volsunga saga* and some Eddic poems.

In the seventeenth and eighteenth centuries, scholars in Scandinavia, England and Germany began to issue translations of this Icelandic literature. Among the works published in this fashion were both Eddic and scaldic poems, Saxo's chronicle and Snorri's history and some sagas. From this period to the present day, literary scholars have continued to publish translations of these works in Swedish, Danish, Norwegian, English and German.

◁ **English history** received much the same sort of patriotic treatment as did Scandinavian, though there was nothing corresponding to the Eddas and the sagas to make a wholly original national mythology. But the novels of Walter Scott and Bulwer Lytton invested the past with heroic glamour, and Daniel Maclise was among the numerous artists who pursued a similar course in painting. His *Alfred disguised as a minstrel in the tent of Guthrun the Dane*, of 1852, may be dubious history but it was first-class romance. If episodes like this did not happen, said Winston Churchill, they *ought* to have happened. (35)

Sagas reborn

This nostalgia for an era of past glory on the part of Scandinavian writers was fed by the almost mystical aura assumed by places of historical or national significance, when seen in a romantic perspective. In Denmark these included the supposed residence of the ancient kings at Lejre on Sjælland; nearby Roskilde, the p.134(17) site of the well of the pagan saga king Hroar; and Jelling in Jutland, sanctified by its remarkable rune-stones and the tenth-century burial mounds of King p.136(21) Gorm and Queen Thyre.

The Temple at Old Uppsala, as imagined by Erik Dahlbergh in 1720. Each tower is sacred to a different deity. In the foreground various priestly activities are taking place; the two birds just below the tree are Odin's ravens. (3)

In Sweden the most important national sites of pre-Christian origin are two towns in the Uppland region: p.134(16) Gamla Uppsala, with its great royal burial mounds, 3 which is also presumed to be the site of the temple of the Æsir, and Sigtuna; and in Norway the towns of Oslo, Bergen and Nidaros (Trondheim), semi-mystical sites in an ancient kingdom which existed before and around the time of the introduction of Christianity. In Iceland the fount of historic tradition is the ancient place of 1 assembly, Thingvellir, but other important sites from the Icelandic sagas reappear in modern literature. One might compare such places with English sites like Stonehenge, Runnymede and Hastings.

Certain common archaeological features and objects became archetypal and symbolic in Romantic literature. Of these, the most important are rune-stones and burial mounds; swords, spears, helmets and drinking horns; temples and ships.

On occasions of great public ceremony such archaeological stereotypes were used as stage settings. Thus after the assassination of King Gustaf III in 1792 at a masked ball at the opera, the choir of Riddarholm church in Stockholm was decorated for the funeral with a specially constructed burial mound flanked by standing stones. In the performance of contemporary plays with ancient Nordic themes the stage-designers would employ burial mounds and rune-stones to create the right atmosphere. In Denmark in 1801, for example, V. T. Galeotti produced the Norwegian Christopher Pram's ballet *Lagertha* with music by Schall. The Danish writer Oehlenschläger and the Norwegian

Henrik Ibsen both wrote plays about burial mounds – respectively *Fostbrødrene* (the foster-brothers) and *The Warrior's Barrow*.

Rune-stones and burial mounds are of varied ideological significance. They may become a vehicle of an elegiac longing for a morally superior past age, as for instance in the case of the leading Swedish Romantic writer Atterbom. They may also, more resolutely, inspire high-flown appeals for national unity and cooperation, as in the poem *Mindesang paa Fædres Gravhøj* (a song of remembrance on the burial mound of our fathers), written by N. F. S. Grundtvig in 1813 (founder of the Danish People's High School Movement and instigator of a religious and patriotic revival in the period 1840–1880). In Norway such symbols were used by writers to appeal for the better care of ancient monuments. In a poem by the Norwegian Henrik Wergeland, about the burial mound of Frithiof in Sogn, these features are used in a polemic against the more timid interpretation of the Scandinavian character found in Esaias Tegnér's great poem about the same ancient hero, *Frithiof's Saga* 24–27 (1825). Tegnér's poem is in parts a rather sentimental pastiche of an Icelandic saga: it tells how Frithiof, the son of a Viking, grows up to love Ingeborg, the king's daughter. He sees with bitterness how her brothers marry her off to a neighbouring king, an older man. Frithiof then accidentally burns down the temple of the god Balder. To forget his love and guilt he departs on Viking raids, but when Ingeborg's husband dies he rebuilds the temple to placate the god, and wins the hand of his beloved. During the minority of her son he becomes regent of the country.

Swords, spears, axes and helmets are important possessions of the ancient warriors. In the sagas swords are named and invested with supernatural properties. In the Old English poem, *Beowulf*, the hero has a sword called Hrunting; Hrolf Kraki's sword is called Skofnung, and in battle it sings when it touches the head of an enemy. In *Njals saga* Skarphedinn has an axe called Rimgyge, which gives off a ringing sound before it kills. In the Norwegian, J. S. Welhaven wrote an epic poem *Koll med Øxen* (Koll of the axe), the axe of the title singing when Koll sees his mortal enemy, intent on revenge, enter the room. Nineteenth-century authors like Ling and Carsten Hauch, and in the 1920s the Nobel laureate Sigrid Undset, wrote of swords with such names as Mimring (taken from a ballad) and Grimsbane, and axes called Jarnglumra and Ættarfylgja. In English literature a sword is a sign of premonition in Rudyard Kipling's *Puck of Pook's Hill*, which contains a considerable amount of old popular superstition.

Several different kinds of helmet are described in literature and art: Roman helmets, plumed helmets, 12,13 winged helmets and horned helmets. Frithiof in Tegnér's poem wears a helmet with eagles' wings, while in the early productions of Wagner's *Ring* the characters also wear winged helmets. Such helmets do not occur in the Viking Age, although a few isolated archaeological finds from Denmark suggest that horned helmets did exist in a much earlier period; but helmets were highly romanticized by later authors and artists.

Towards the end of the nineteenth century, however, Scandinavian artists and writers became more concerned with archaeological accuracy. Thus, when Snorri Sturluson's tales of the Norwegian kings were to be published in a popular Norwegian edition in 1899, Erik Werenskiold, the art editor and main illustrator, 4 chose to depict a helmet without wings or horns, but with a nose guard, of a type which had appeared in Hefner-Alteneck's survey of dress and household goods of the period 1060–1220.

In 1831 Nicolai Wergeland, a Norwegian priest and literary critic (the father of the writer Henrik Wergeland), observed in a review that no Nordic drama was complete without its drinking horns. He was clearly commenting on an expressed custom: in Sweden, for example, when the poet Erik Gustaf Geijer took up his appointment as Professor of History in Uppsala in 1817, a group of students presented him with a drinking horn. Silver-mounted horns like this have been presented to the restaurant at the royal burial mounds at Gamla Uppsala since those days and from them the privileged can still drink mulled beer.

The harp is the most popular musical instrument in Romantic literature. It is frequently mentioned in the sagas. The god Bragi, for example, played the harp and *Ynglinga saga* tells of King Hugleik's harp-players. As well as the more familiar larger harps, there was also a smaller instrument, which was used in more aristocratic circles and is documented in medieval ballads; one is reminded of the oval lyre from the seventh-century

Historical research led to greater accuracy in the illustration of such details as armour. In his plates for an edition of Snorri Sturluson in 1899, Erik Werenskiold discarded romantic notions of winged and horned helmets and showed one with a realistic nose guard. (4)

Anglo-Saxon burial at Sutton Hoo. On the portals of some early twelfth-century Norwegian stave churches, Gunnar, one of the heroes of *Volsunga saga*, is depicted p.33(2) playing the harp with his toes. Romantic writers and artists envisaged the scald declaiming his poetry to his own harp accompaniment: one of the best examples of this is Geijer's poem *Den siste skalden* (the last scald). The frequency with which harps are mentioned in Romantic writing may be due to the influence of the Celtic revival, for in the songs of Ossian the bards are 2 described as playing harps and singing.

Few motifs from Scandinavian antiquity have inspired writers and artists to such heights of Romantic extravagance as the temples of the gods (*hoven*). Factual information about the temples dedicated to the Æsir is lacking; the Romantic writers had therefore to rely on written sources. Adam of Bremen, the German historian who visited Scandinavia in the eleventh century, described the temple at Uppsala; *Eyrbyggja saga* includes a description of a *hov* in western Iceland, and Saxo Grammaticus tells of the temple of the god Svantevit on the island of Rügen, which was burnt down by the Danes. But no building has been conclusively identified archaeologically as a temple.

The most curious representations of pre-Christian temples occur in the art and literature of the end of the eighteenth and the beginning of the nineteenth century. In 1785 an 'heroic drama' by Brigitte Catherine Boye was produced in Copenhagen. The artist Thomas Bruun designed a set depicting a temple to the godess 23 Hertha which consisted of a cave in a mound, flanked by rune-stones, in which was a draped idol and an altar shaped like a dolmen. A temple of Thor painted in 1818 22 by the Norwegian artist Johannes Flintoe depicts a building in the style of a Gothic church; in the foreground are a sacrificial table and bowl, while in the

Pictures of Viking ships became much more accurate after the discovery of the Oseberg and Gokstad ships. An engraving of Frithiof's ship Ellida (top) for Esaias Tegnér's 'Frithiof's Saga' of 1825 represents the extreme of Romanticism. By contrast, Eric Palmqvist's ship for Jan Fridegård's Trägudars Land (1961) is archaeologically respectable. (5,6)

background an image of the god Thor stands, Christ-like, in the apse behind a choir screen.

In *Frithiof's Saga* Esaias Tegnér provides a strange and eccentric design for the temple which Frithiof builds to appease Balder, the god of goodness. The round temple stands behind a forged-iron fence and has two rows of pillars, a dome and a door made of copper. One scholar has interpreted Tegnér's temple as symbolic of a union between the Nordic and classical worlds, while another believes that Tegnér intended to create the impression that Stonehenge had been rebuilt in Norway.

Thomas Bruun's dolmen-like altar is paralleled in the writing of the Danish theologian and hymn-writer Grundtvig: in 1808 he wrote a poem about a megalithic tomb in Gunderslev Skov on Sjælland. The tomb is seen as an altar to which he runs weeping, to kneel before it in honour of the gods.

In nineteenth-century Romantic literature, an image often associated with the Vikings was the ship or 'dragon'. For the greater part of the century little was known of the appearance of their Nordic forebears' ships. The two ships from Gokstad and Oseberg, which are now a symbol of the Vikings, were not excavated until 1880 and 1904 respectively. In *Frithiof's Saga* the stern of Frithiof's ship is embellished with the curly tail of a fabulous dragon. In 1879, the year before the Gokstad ship was found, the Norwegian artist Nils Bergslien painted King Harald Finehair at the battle of Hafrsfjord, standing at the stern of his ship, wearing a plumed helmet and carrying a curved Arabic sword. The ship itself is both fanciful and unseaworthy, reminiscent perhaps of a Renaissance carvel. The demand for greater archaeological accuracy is exemplified in recent years by Eric Palmqvist's illustrations to Jan Fridegård's novel of ninth-century Scandinavia, *Trägudars Land* (land of the carved idols) published in 1944 (illustrated edition 1961), in which a shaven monk is seen boarding a vessel which is an accurate representation of the Gokstad ship.

Gods and men
The Poetic Edda describes both gods and heroes. At the end of the eighteenth century and in the first half of the nineteenth, representations of gods seem to be more common in the visual arts, and in particular in sculpture, than in literature. Among those who wrote of these gods was the great Danish Romantic writer Oehlenschläger, who produced numerous novels, dramas and lyric poems on mythological subjects, as did his younger contemporary Grundtvig. The gods who occur most frequently are Odin, Thor, Frey, Balder, Bragi, Heimdall, Frigg, Freyja, and the demon and trouble-maker Loki. In such literature they are at times portrayed as pale, stilted figures in the neo-classical mode, and at others as archaic personages, evoking the world of bloody sacrificial rituals.

The nineteenth century also saw numerous competitions for essays and paintings on old Nordic themes. The Swedish Academy of Art organized a number of such competitions between 1840 and 1880. The subjects were either mythological or heroic: the first mythological subject was 'Heimdall gives the jewel Bryting to Freyja', and in 1873 it was 'Thor unwittingly injures his son'. In Moscow the Imperial Academy of Art celebrated its centenary in 1864 with a competition on the subject of 'A Feast in Valhalla': it was stipulated that Odin should be portrayed surrounded by Æsir and heroes, with the ravens Hugin and Munin perched on his shoulders.

In literature the gods are depicted in a rather archetypal manner, and this trend is even more pronounced with regard to certain human types, as for instance the Viking, the farmer, the scald, saga-woman and Valkyrie (a figure that has been much associated with folklore).

The word 'viking' has been the subject of much controversy; it was early used in the phrase *ligga i viking*, meaning to engage in war-like raids at sea, and it is known in this sense even before the beginning of the Viking Age proper. As early as the seventh century the word occurs in the English poem *Widsith* in the sense of a sea-based warrior, but after the Viking period its meaning seems to have become debased, so that in the later Middle Ages, and until the eighteenth century, it came to mean 'pirate'. In the Romantic literature of the nineteenth century the word 'viking' is used along with *kämpe* (a land warrior) and *søkonge, sjökonung* (a warrior at sea). The Swedish writers Tegnér and Geijer were probably responsible for the continuing idealization of the name and concept of 'viking'.

The moral calibre of the different Viking characters varies considerably from author to author. Some of them – Oehlenschläger, Tegnér and Runeberg for example – manifestly civilize their Vikings. In the personalities of Oehlenschläger's King Helge, Tegnér's Frithiof and Runeberg's King Fjalar, there is a noticeably conciliatory, almost Christian aspect. But other writers have fewer reservations about accepting all sides of the Viking temperament: in Geijer's famous poem *Vikingen* (the Viking) there is no criticism of the principal character as he sets out on a gory rampage, raiding foreign lands, engaging in violent combat and raping women. When the newly elected Swedish Crown Prince – Karl August of Holstein – arrived in his new country in May 1810, Pehr Henrik Ling (the originator of Swedish gymnastics) wrote a poem describing feasts in ancient times at which the Swedish warriors would drink both mead and blood with the same composure and fortitude.

In complete contrast to the Viking is the farmer, who is also eulogized in the Romantic literature. As well as *Vikingen*, Geijer wrote a poem called *Odalbonden* (the farmer). The farmer's tranquil existence symbolized historical continuity. A number of Romantic writers consciously juxtaposed and contrasted the adventurous Viking and the constructive pacific farmer: these include Geijer, Tegnér, Oehlenschläger, the Norwegian Bjørnstjerne Bjørnson, the Swede Verner von Heidenstam, and finally the Icelandic novelist Gunnar Gunnarsson.

In Romantic Celtic literature, as for example in the poems of Ossian, the poet is typically called a 'bard', and is depicted striking a statuesque pose at the summit of a cliff. This conception of the poet is also found in Scandinavian literature from about 1800, but is much less common than the type of poet known from the Icelandic sagas. The Romantic writers would sometimes make use of the scalds named in the better-known sagas, but they also created their own scalds,

based on these models. Such characters either manifest a harsh severity or a gentle tenderness. The same contrast is found in descriptions of the women of the saga period. Cruel saga-women are based on Brynhild in *Volsunga saga*, Hallgerd in *Njals saga* and Gudrun in *Laxdæla saga*: they are all proud women who incite men to revenge. Such women are found in the works of Grundtvig, Oehlenschläger, Ibsen and Bjørnson; while women of the gentle, tender and loyal type occur, for example – often alongside their harsher sisters – in literary works by Oehlenschläger and Tegnér. The mural dated 1849 by the painter Hans Gude in Oscarshall's Castle, Oslo, is a fantasy on the gentle and tender love life of the Viking woman Ingeborg.

The last of these archetypes, the Valkyrie, is a 31–34 supernatural figure who arrives at the battlefield when the fighting is done and leads the dead warriors to Valhalla, the house of the gods. Literary descriptions of the Valkyries became more common after the appearance of Wagner's operas, set in the ancient Nordic mode, in the middle of the nineteenth century.

The roots of Romanticism

Eighteenth-century literature from Scandinavia and other European countries already shows a marked interest in ancient Nordic motifs. A number of writers, for instance the Swiss Paul-Henri Mallet, translated old Nordic literature and used related motifs as a basis for their creative writing. Klopstock, who like Mallet visited Copenhagen in the third quarter of the eighteenth century, includes the names of some Nordic gods and a hymn to Woden (Odin) in his drama *Hermanns Schlacht* (Hermann's battle), but the world is basically that of Ossianic poetry; while the poem *Skulda* tells of the eponymous Norn who decides the fates of all poets.

Ossian was a legendary Celtic bard who probably lived in the third century AD, but none of whose works in fact survive. In 1761, however, James Macpherson published *Fingal, an Ancient Epic Poem in Six Books, composed by Ossian the Son of Fingal, translated from the Gaelic language*. Other epics followed, and in 1765 he brought out *The Works of Ossian*. Although Macpherson claimed to have translated all these from original texts, he was never able to produce them, and it is now clear that he was actually weaving together fragments of genuine oral poetry into long romances that were essentially his own invention. At the time, however, the poems were regarded as authentic productions of Nordic genius, worthy to stand beside the *Iliad* and the *Odyssey*. They influenced practically all the writers who 2–6 adopted Nordic themes at the end of the eighteenth century and the beginning of the nineteenth, and even accompanied Napoleon on his campaigns. Sentimental and elegiac rather than heroic, they yet contain many purely Nordic elements. In *Fingal*, for instance, the Irish prince Cuthullin is attacked by a fleet commanded by the Norwegian Viking king, Swaran, who is described by Cuthullin's scout Moran in a manner more poetic than realistic:

I beheld their chief, tall as a glittering rock. His spear is a blasted pine. His shield the rising moon! He sat on the shore, like a cloud of mist on the silent hill! Many, chief of heroes!, I said, many are our hands of war. Well are thou named, the mighty man; but many mighty men are seen from Tura's windy walls.

In England, translations were produced by Thomas Percy, the collector of folk songs (*Five Pieces of Runic Poetry*, 1763), by Amos Cottle, in 1797, and by the great pre-Romantic poet Thomas Gray, who also wrote *The Bard*, which is an example of the sentimental fusion of Nordic and Celtic elements:

> *On a rock whose haughty brow*
> *Frowns o'er old Conway's foaming flood*
> *Rob'd in the sable garb of woe*
> *With haggard eyes the Poet stood*
> *(Loose his beard and hoary hair*
> *Streamed, like a meteor, to the troubled air)*
> *And with a master's hand, and prophet's fire*
> *Struck the deep sorrows of his lyre* . . . .

Gray's 'pindaric ode' ends with the bard throwing himself from the summit of the cliff into the abyss below.

One of the great Romantic poets, Robert Southey, planned an epic poem based on the story of Harald Finehair in *Heimskringla*, and (in an amicable tribute to the translator Amos Cottle) he characterizes the Nordic spirit as one of wildness:

> *Wild the Runic faith*
> *And wild the realms where Scandinavian Chiefs*
> *And Scalds arose, and hence the Scald's strong verse*
> *Partook the savage wildness* . . . .

Inspired by Mallet, French writers also took up the old Nordic themes. Bernardin de Saint-Pierre used Scandinavian mythology, drawn from his impressions of a journey to Finland, in his didactic novel *L'Arcadie*, and the composer Lesueur wrote an opera called *Ossian, ou les bardes*; this even attracted the attention of Napoleon himself, who showed his appreciation in the form of a snuffbox. It is doubtful, however, if the French painter Anne Louis Girodet received even so small a reward for the 'Ossianic' design he painted in 1803 at Bonaparte's Malmaison: French warriors marching into Valhalla are greeted by bards (shades from Ossian's world of romance), surrounded by Valkyries and harp-playing mermaids. In Finland, the poet J. L. Runeberg in the 1840s wrote his tragic story *King Fjalar* as a hybrid of romantic poem and Greek drama, with many Ossianic place-names and characters.

Of the Danish writers, Johannes Ewald is a typical representative of the sentimental pre-Romantic move-ment. His tragedy, based on the life of the saga king Hrolf Kraki, is inspired by Klopstock's *Hermanns Schlacht*, the poems of Ossian and Saxo's chronicle, as well as by Shakespeare and Voltaire. His aim was to create a tragedy in the classical mode, which he attempted again in a drama about the death of Balder a few years later. Ewald's knowledge of old Nordic mythology and culture was scanty. He was greatly interested in the poems of Ossian, and attempted to contact Macpherson by letter, with a view to finding melodies for the Ossianic songs. He even conceived a plan to travel through northern Scotland to Orkney and Iceland, to look for any songs which might have escaped Macpherson's notice.

Two Danish authors, P. F. Suhm and O. J. Samsøe, produced short stories about the distant past of Scandinavia. Suhm (who also wrote a history of Denmark in fourteen volumes) used Saxo's chronicle as his source, and employed a long-winded, sentimental and tendentious style. In places he created some highly improbable situations; in *De Tre Venner* (the three friends) a group of fishermen sing the Eddic poem *Voluspa* as a sea shanty!

In the 1770s a number of Norwegian writers active in Copenhagen formed Det Norske Selskab (The Norwegian Society), which exhibited pronounced nationalistic tendencies. Among them was Johan Nordahl Brun, later Bishop of Bergen. He wrote a tragedy about Olaf Tryggvason's famous archer Einer Tambeskielver. The tragedy conforms to French taste, but in one scene, in which Einer's wife Bergljot dreams of revenging the murder of her husband, Brun creates an authentic old Nordic atmosphere.

In Sweden several eighteenth-century authors used old Nordic motifs in their writings. As early as the 1730s, Olof von Dalin, who was for a while the tutor of the future King Gustaf III, wrote a tragedy in the French style about Brynhild, the uncompromising heroine of *Volsunga saga*, which was later to attract the attention of Richard Wagner. Rather later Jacob Mörk, a clergyman, wrote novels based on ancient Nordic themes, inspired by the Swedish conquests of the previous century, while Thomas Thorild, a writer of the *Sturm und Drang* school, who ended his days as professor at the then Swedish university of Greifswald, wrote a poem *Harmen* (anger) about the god Thor. The author expresses his own revolutionary fervour and his indignation at the wretchedness of the world in his portrayal of the god of strength flourishing thunder-bolts across the sky.

Images of Nordic antiquity

The architecture of Balder's temple as described by Tegnér in *Frithiof's Saga* was, as we have seen, of classical inspiration. Artists and writers alike were totally ignorant about period and location. In 1836, the

Norwegian Adolph Tidemand illustrated Tegnér's work portraying a tender scene between Frithiof and Ingeborg, the former wearing helmet, skirt and breastplate of Roman type, while Ingeborg is dressed in classical, or rather neo-classical, costume. Another Norwegian artist, P. N. Arbo, portrays two Scandinavian warriors in Roman helmets riding full tilt in a Roman chariot drawn by two horses. The Swedish artist J. A. Malmström, who illustrated *Frithiof's Saga* in 1868, included many details of Bronze Age date; while the German illustrators of the later nineteenth century, such as Boehmer, Huhn, Naue, Hoffman and Klein, display a motley variety of styles. The High Middle Ages provided the background for Schnorr von Carolsfeld's illustrations to the Siegfried saga, which in their turn helped to inspire Wagner. The style of Oehlenschläger's great cycle *The Gods of the North*, on the other hand, appears to be in deliberate imitation of the Italian Renaissance.

In literature, a considerable number of Scandinavian writers were inspired by the English Renaissance. Translations of Shakespeare began to appear at the beginning of the nineteenth century, shortly after the German translations. Scenes like that of the witches in Macbeth stimulated numerous imitators, but were transposed into the context of Scandinavian antiquity. Other works have a gruesome quality that seems to derive from the Gothic novel. In Grundtvig's tragedy *Vagn Aagesen*, Håkon Jarl wishes to sacrifice his slave Karker on a mound of his enemies' skulls – a scene inspired by the saga of Ragnar Lodbroke. In the tragedy *Sigurd ring*, by the Swedish writer Erik Johan Stagnelius, the daughter of the Danish king turns in disgust from King Sigurd and describes him as a barbarian who has eaten wolves' entrails and drunk blood from skulls. Leconte de Lisle's *Poèmes barbares* (1862) include seven or eight poems with old Nordic motifs. *L'épée d'Angantyr* is based on the *Hervarar saga*. The Valkyrie Hervor begs her dead father in his burial mound to give her his sword – if he does not grant her request she will call on the wild wolf to drag his bones from the grave and crush them. In *Le Coeur d'Hialmar*, the dying saga hero Hjalmar asks the raven to cut the heart from his breast and carry it to his beloved.

So we can trace influences from the Middle Ages, from the Renaissance, and from neo-classicism. There is even a trace of the Rococo. In Denmark, Adam Oehlenschläger revels in his description of the seductive Queen Oluf in her bath, her round hips, full thighs and fine silken drapery reminiscent of a nymph painted by Pater or Boucher. In Sweden, Tegnér speaks with pleasure of Ingeborg's beautiful bosom, while Pehr Henrik Ling casts a lascivious eye at the bare knee of Lofn, goddess of love! In the late nineteenth century, Scandinavian artists developed a kind of Wagnerian style, typified by representations of beautiful Valkyries, usually sporting winged helmets. A painting of Odin's hunt by the Norwegian Arbo (1872) may be compared to the final scene of a Wagner opera; and in the 1880s and 1890s Stephen Sinding's Valhalla frieze and Hans Heyerdahl's *Helheim and Brynhild* are both reminiscent of Wagner.

The rise of realism and naturalism (Dickens, Flaubert, Tolstoy, Zola) led to the desire for greater historical verisimilitude in the representation of antiquity by artists and writers. Well-documented background descriptions were expected. It is striking, for instance, that the Swedish graphic artist J. A. Malmström, who had illustrated *Frithiof's Saga* in the 1860s using artifacts from the Bronze Age, produced an edition of the same work twenty years later in which the objects are much more authentic.

The end of the eighteenth and the beginning of the nineteenth century was a time of exhaustive discussion about the relative merits of old Nordic and classical motifs in works of art. Herder published a dialogue on this theme between Frey, who champions classical culture and finds the Nordic gods exaggerated and brutal, and Alfred, who represents Herder's own view and argues for the nobility of Nordic mythology. Schiller took up the question a year later, but his attitude was more negative: he considered the Nordic gods bore too close a resemblance to himself and his fellow countrymen and that poetry should stand apart from daily life. Goethe saw the Nordic saga heritage as amusing and stimulating to the imagination, but at the same time shrouded in Ossianic mists, and not graphic enough to inspire the poet.

In 1799 the University of Copenhagen offered a prize for an essay based on the question whether it would be an advantage to literature if Greek mythology were replaced by that of ancient Scandinavia. All the entrants answered the question in the affirmative. Adam Oehlenschläger was one of these: he found Nordic mythology fresher and less hackneyed than classical. Other Scandinavian writers took different sides in the debate which followed. Grundtvig, in 1808, found the Greek gods superior in outward appearance but the Scandinavian surpassing them in personality and strength. Wilhelm Grimm, in 1820, held Greek mythology to be richer than Nordic in spiritual symbolism. A more satirical attitude was adopted in 1820 by the Swede J. M. Stiernstolpe in a poem entitled *Mythologierne eller Gudatvisten* (the mythologies, or the quarrel of the gods), in which Thor gets drunk and approaches goddesses in an unseemly manner. Zeus, the foremost of the Greek gods, also appears and pokes fun at the Nordic gods, asking if it is right to praise barbarians who have shed blood on their altars. Among the Vikings, says Stiernstolpe, it is those with a gift for fighting and heavy drinking, who will be happiest in the warriors' paradise in Valhalla.

Odin or Christ?

In the first half of the nineteenth century the confrontation between paganism and Christianity became one of the most popular motifs both in writing and in the visual arts. Three basic attitudes may be distinguished: the main emphasis is placed on the pre-Christian religion itself; or paganism is represented as anticipating Christianity; or the introduction of the new religion is seen with hindsight as the ultimately desirable objective.

Among writers who placed their main emphasis on the old religion were Grundtvig in Denmark (in his earlier years), Erik Gustaf Geijer in Sweden, and (to some extent) the leading Norwegian Romantics Henrik Wergeland and J. S. Welhaven. Grundtvig declared in 1808 that his most painful childhood experience was learning from Huitfeldt's Danish chronicle that no facts were known about the old gods. At about this time he wrote the poem *Gunderslev Skov* (Gunderslev woods), in which he wishes to throw himself on his knees before the altar of the Æsir, and asks rhetorically, 'How can anyone experience the great struggle between darkness and light without worshipping the Æsir?' In plays written in 1808 and 1810 he expresses heartfelt sympathy for the saga warrior Palna-Toki, who becomes a symbol of the dying Scandinavian paganism.

In the poetry of his contemporary Erik Gustaf Geijer we find two figures who similarly symbolize the old religion: *Den siste kämpen* (the last warrior) and *Den siste skalden* (the last scald). The former, he explains, is baptised not in water, but in blood; he rejects the Christian paradise and longs for Valhalla. His faith in the glory and strength of the Æsir is unshakeable, and like Gray's bard he throws himself into the sea from a cliff-top. Similarly, the last scald hears a voice calling him to Valhalla: both warrior and scald are doomed and fated figures, who perish in a new era; but in their Promethean defiance they express a romantic rebellion against the effeminacy and decadence of contemporary society.

In Norway Henrik Wergeland wrote *A Viking's Hall*, about 1830. This poem presents everyday details of the old pagan world in a manner which, although at times stereotyped, is nonetheless evocative:

> Pent in a western valley's fold,
> Like a berserk hemmed by foes,
> A timbered hall did, in days of old,
> Its sombre length expose . . .
>
> A sail in the corner moulders grey;
> Keen bills in the beams bite fast:
> The flickering flame in a fitful ray
> From shields in the loft is cast .
>
> And bows from hooks in the wainscot hung
> Their writhen arms spread wide;
> With bundles of arrows, and cordage strung
> From bear-gut and sinew dried.

> Forth two gods, at the table's end,
> Flash out as the pine-logs flare :
> Thor and Odin their presence lend
> To hallow the master's chair . . . .

His contemporary J. S. Welhaven produced pious romances about the saintly King Olaf, but also wrote some poems in the 1840s which emphasize the pagan side of the human soul. In the romance *I Kivledal* the Christian message, represented by the preaching of the priest *herr* Peder, is set against the savage power of nature and the giantesses outside the church, who exercise a strong attraction on the congregation. The second poem, *Asgaardsreien*, tells of Odin's wild hunt, a motif we have already encountered in the visual arts. Welhaven's powerful and dramatic poem concerns two berserks, with the pagan sounding names of Grim and Ulv, who break into a wedding feast to kill the bridegroom. While the fight is raging Odin's hunt rushes through the air above the farm. Grim is killed, and the bridegroom taken into the house severely wounded. Christian culture and the forces of order have managed only with great difficulty to repel this attack from the pagan world of primitive instincts.

Schelling's theological view of history is echoed in Oehlenschläger's play *Earl Håkon the Mighty* (1808), in which the main character embodies the last glimmering of the old Nordic power. This also reflects A. W. Schlegel's opinion that the fight between old and new gods is a suitable theme for dramatic writing. In a much later play, *Olaf den hellige* (Saint Olaf) of 1838, Oehlenschläger focuses on another of the great missionary kings of Norway, Olaf Haraldsson. One of the king's followers, the highly educated Kalf Arnason, asks himself these questions: did not love, justice and compassion exist in the Æsir cult, just as in Christianity; were not the fairies of light comparable to angels; and was it not true that the god Balder was known as 'Balder the Good'? The idea that Balder's goodness lived on in the Christian faith was also suggested at this time by the Swedish sculptor Bengt Erland Fogelberg: his Balder is strongly reminiscent of Christ, and in particular of the famous portrayal by Thorvaldsen, which Fogelberg had seen in Rome.

Certain Scandinavian Romantic writers who dealt with Viking subjects would include a conversion to Christianity, normally towards the end of the story. Grundtvig, for instance, did so in *Atle og Gjukongerne* (Atle and the Gjukungs) in 1811 after his religious crisis. In this play the priest Thorkild discerns a Christian spirit in the dying Odrun and initiates her into the new faith with the sign of the cross. In Ibsen's first play *The Warrior's Barrow* (first performed in 1850), the Scandinavian poet becomes so impressed by the Christian message that he remains in the south rather than returning to his pagan homeland in the north. Hebbel's drama *Die Nibelungen* also concludes with a

Christian message. Strindberg's early play *The Outlaw*, 1870, follows the example of Oehlenschläger and Ibsen; the stern Earl Thorfinn turns Christian in the closing words of the play. In the same year Bjørnstjerne Bjørnson wrote the epic poem *Arnljot Gelline*: in a manner reminiscent of Oehlenschläger's *Earl Håkon the Mighty*, he describes the confrontation between the two religions, setting cross against hammer, faith against defiance, and self-sacrifice against mercenary might.

Political idealism in old Nordic disguise

Nostalgic Romanticism can be a purely literary or intellectual fashion, but it can also take on political overtones. In 1801 the Danish navy successfully defended Copenhagen against an attack by the English fleet, and Oehlenschläger praised this great national achievement in a poem, speaking of the revival of 'the spirit and glory of the ancient past'. In another of his poems the ancient kings step out of their burial mounds along with the god Thor, to inspire the Danish soldiers by their valour. And a few years later (in 1808) we find Grundtvig employing similar imagery in his *Drapa om Villemoes* (Ode to Villemoes) in which the halls of Valhalla open to receive the dead hero Villemoes, a Danish officer killed in a naval battle against the English. P. H. Ling, in the same year, was expressing the grief of the Swedes at losing Finland in an allegorical poem of the saga king Gylfe sitting on a burial mound and mourning the loss of his beloved Aura. Another reaction to the same event comes in Tegnér's patriotic poem *Svea*, in which the poet has a vision of his forefathers rising from their burial mounds and, with hands as shadowy as Ossian's poetry, applauding the Swedish soldiers who have recaptured Finland.

Another manifestation of the same cast of thought is the foundation of patriotic societies inspired by the past. The first was Götiska Förbundet (the Gothic Alliance), started by the author Jacob Adlerbeth in Stockholm with the aim, on the one hand, of reviving the ancient spirit of freedom, fostering courage and preserving national independence, and on the other of promoting research into the sagas and traditional history. The members of Götiska Förbundet took the names of ancient heroes, and their journal, *Iduna*, published Geijer's poems *The Viking*, *The Farmer*, *The Last Warrior* and *The Last Scald*.

A comparable society, Manhemsförbundet (The Manhem society), was founded in Stockholm in 1815 by the author C. J. L. Almqvist. Like the Freemasons, its members were divided into orders, nine in number, with names based on such different concepts of life as that of the warrior in Valhalla, of the patriot, of *Ragnarok* (the End of the world), of chivalry and of religion: the ninth order was – in the spirit of Rousseau – based on the farmer's life. Elsewhere dreams of the

ancient past reflected political events. Nordahl Brun's song *To Norway*, written in Copenhagen in 1772, which supposedly expressed separatist sentiments, was prohibited by the Danish police. Brun, indeed, did not dare to acknowledge its authorship; but in later years it became a Norwegian national song. Throughout the nineteenth century, indeed, it was commonplace to arouse patriotic sentiments by appealing to the heroic past.

Some writers and artists went further and used the past to convey not merely general patriotic values but a specific ideological programme. When Richard Wagner completed the first prose version of his music drama *The Ring of the Nibelung* in the autumn of 1848, Siegfried had become the personification of his own revolutionary ideals: Siegfried represents the liberated p.27(27) man of the future in an egalitarian society. The composer was indeed an ardent supporter of the Revolution of 1848, and was even sought by the police in Dresden as an enemy of society; Wagner believed that immediate change was essential to German society, and demanded 'the total destruction of aristocratic prejudices'. The fundamentally anti-capitalist aspect of this work was reinforced in the final version of 1852. It is curious that a feudal ruler such as Ludwig II of Bavaria should have been Wagner's patron, not least in the construction of the magnificent theatre at Bayreuth, which was specifically designed for the performance of Wagner's operas.

Wagner's interest in the story of Siegfried had been stimulated by reading not only *Nibelungenlied*, but also such Icelandic literature as the *Volsunga saga* and the Edda. He had also been deeply moved by Friedrich de la Motte Fouqué's dramatic poem *Der Held des Nordens* (the hero of the north). Although unsatisfactory in terms of psychology, the poem is interesting in form, with blank verse alternating with scaldic and alliterative songs in the old Nordic style. The first volume was published in 1808 and the third in 1810, the year of Grundtvig's dramatic work *Norners og Asers Kamp* (the battle of the Norns and Æsir), which also treats of the Siegfried theme.

At the same time as Wagner, Friedrich Engels was preparing a dramatic sketch entitled *Der gehörnte Siegfried*, which is philosophically related to Wagner's work. Hebbel's *Die Nibelungen* (mentioned above) was written ten years later, and operates on different levels of mythology, heroism and Christianity and in this regard it is reminiscent of Grundtvig. Hebbel's drama is approximately contemporary with Ibsen's tragedy *The Warriors at Helgeland* (1858): the hero, Sigurd, is drawn from *Nibelungen saga*. Ibsen's work resembles that of Hebbel in the tension among the mythological, heroic and Christian elements, and also in its Christian bias.

In England about this time William Morris was

8 working on a great poem, *The Story of Sigurd the Volsung and the Fall of the Niblungs* (1862). Morris's work is expansive and detailed in its presentation, and is sustained by dramatic and psychological intensity as well as artistic purity, but this splendid poem does not have a truly Nordic atmosphere. In the same year, Leconte de Lisle wrote his *Poèmes barbares* (see above). In *La mort de Sigurd* a mood of savage despair surrounds the dead hero: the poem ends with a description of Brynhild's arrival at Sigurd's bier, where she expresses her sorrow at the death of her lover, and her hatred of Gudrun, before drawing her dagger and taking her own life.

A few more instances in which Nordic imagery was used to embody a political statement may briefly be noted. The 'Viking Movement' in Finland, which arose in the last three decades of the nineteenth century, was dedicated to retaining the use of Swedish (spoken by twenty per cent of the inhabitants) instead of Finnish. A journal, *Vikingen*, published around 1870, ran for four issues, but the only great writer to emerge from the Movement was Arvid Mörne (1876–1946), who combined fervour for the Swedish language with an active belief in Socialism. The Norwegian lyric poet Per Sivle used his poems about the saga kings and heroes in a similar way, to express his own liberal, socialist and patriotic beliefs. With their forceful articulation of liberal idealism, these poems from the period 1880–1900 are still frequently read and quoted in Norway today.

Finally, as late as 1942 and 1943, the German occupation of Denmark provoked two newspaper articles in which a contemporary message was expressed under the guise of history. Their author was Martin A. Hansen. The first was about the tale of Uffe, as told by Saxo; Uffe is a dullard, the despair of his

The sacrifice of King Domalde, an episode from the 'Ynglinga saga' by Snorri Sturluson: an illustration from the Norwegian edition of 1899. (7)

father, until he is transformed into the saviour of his people in their battle against invaders from Saxony. The second analyzes Saxo's poem *Hrolf Kraki*, in which the hero, a Christ-like but manly figure, is surprised and murdered in his castle by brutal invaders. Both these articles, with their richly symbolic allusions to the invasion of Denmark by modern intruders, must have seemed political dynamite to Danish citizens reading their morning papers during the troubled years of the occupation.

At a more personal level, Nordic themes are given new social and psychological significance by such writers as Strindberg, Rydberg and Fridegård. Strindberg's anarchist poem *Lokes smädelser* (Loki's abuses), written in 1884 is a variation on the theme of the Eddic poem *Lokasenna*. Through the person of Loki, an evil, demonic figure among the Æsir, Strindberg gloats over the recent political assassinations in Europe, and hurls threats at the powerful figures of society. Some years later, in the early 1890s, Victor Rydberg, an older Swedish writer, wrote a version of the Eddic poem *Grotta Songr*, using the myth of the thralls who drive the mill Grotte for King Frodi. In Rydberg's poem the mill which grinds gold becomes a symbol of industrialism, the thralls represent the industrial proletariat, and the King Frodi of the Eddic poem becomes a representative of the employers' class. The poem gives vent to a social indignation comparable to *Oliver Twist* or *Uncle Tom's Cabin*. Rydberg's artistic register is rich and varied, ranging from irony and sarcasm, through stark realism and biblical pathos, to emotional commitment and deepest despair. Perhaps foremost of those interested in the lowest class of Viking Age society is the Swedish writer Jan Fridegård, who wrote three simple and sensitive novels about ninth-century Sweden, choosing to see Viking society entirely from the thralls' point of view. The first novel of the trilogy was published in 1944 with the evocative title *Trägudars land* (land of the carved idols).

Strindberg's anarchistic tendencies were at one time shared by the Swedish painter Carl Larsson (1853–1919); but at the beginning of the twentieth century Larsson's political sympathies developed in a reactionary and chauvinistic direction. In 1908 he published an article recommending the construction of a Swedish pantheon on the Uppsala burial mounds, for the safekeeping of such national treasures as the Vendel helmets (excavated a few years previously) and the heart of Gustavus Adolphus. He also spoke enthusiastically of the old pagan temple which was supposed to lie hidden beneath the church at Gamla Uppsala. Between 1911 and 1915 Larsson worked on a large painting representing the midwinter ritual sacrifice at Gamla Uppsala. The painting, *Midvinterblot* (*Midwinter* *28* *Sacrifice*), is magnificently colourful, but from an archaeological point of view it presents a bewildering

The Pre-Raphaelites absorbed an interest in Germanic legends from William Morris, but transposed them into a mood of dreamy romanticism that is far from the heroic originals. Right: Burne-Jones's 'Sigurd', a wood engraving of 1862. (8)

mixture of styles: a pair of figures dressed in costumes of Oriental type are seen blowing into Bronze Age trumpets; fabulous beasts carved in wood, resembling Chinese sculptures, stand in the corner of the temple; and women dressed in Lapp-Finnish costumes are performing a folk-dance.

The central motif in Larsson's painting, based on 7 *Ynglinga saga*, is the king who sacrifices himself for his country. It is significant that Valdemar Rørdam, a profoundly nationalistic Danish writer (who was to manifest pro-Nazi sympathies in the 1930s and 40s), wrote a play on a similar theme a decade after Larsson painted *Midvinterblot*. *Kongeofret* (the sacrifice of a king), is based on Saxo Grammaticus's tale of Hrolf Kraki and also on *Beowulf*: it has a profoundly conceived archaeological and religious atmosphere.

Icelandic literature of the 1930s also manifests a strong chauvinistic element, most pronounced in the works of Gudmundur Kamban, a writer who lived in Denmark during the occupation. He sympathized with Nazism, and was accidentally shot in May 1945 by Danish freedom-fighters who came to interrogate him. His novel of 1936, *I See a Wondrous Land*, is an inspired description of how the men of the north conquered Vinland. It is based on the sagas, but uses archaeological material to provide rich local colour. Kamban's impression of the Vikings is, however, extremely idealized, and seems almost to echo the sentiments of the Nazi writer Alfred Rosenberg, whose *Der Mythus des 20. Jahrhunderts* (1930) had proclaimed the superiority of the Nordic race. Kamban describes the Vikings as 'the ultimate product of the free Nordic

235

countries, their bodies perfected by the practice of sport, courageous in the face of the unknown, unsubmissive against the evil powers of fate and of nature, contemptuous of danger and of death, but with a true spirit underlying their courage, and a true virtue underlying their strength.'

This quotation makes clear the radical transformations that the whole concept of the Nordic world has undergone during the last two hundred years. Nostalgic and romantic in the first half of the nineteenth century, liberal and Utopian in the second, it became populist and even racist by the twentieth. It seems to have been about the middle of the nineteenth century that preoccupation with the past became a matter of general cultural and educational interest. Chairs in Scandinavian languages, including Icelandic, were created at the universities of Copenhagen, Uppsala and Oslo between 1840 and 1870. The teaching of Icelandic in schools was discussed in the press, and was finally attempted in Sweden and successfully introduced in Norway, where it has continued ever since. At the age of twenty-two, Strindberg suggested in a newspaper article that Icelandic should replace Latin in the schools; in the People's High Schools the old Nordic literature was studied for its moral teachings. Some passages taken from the Eddic poetry and the sagas are still part of the curriculum of Scandinavian grammar schools and universities, although few have any illusions about their moral content. In the late nineteenth century and throughout the twentieth, new translations of the Poetic Edda and the sagas have appeared, just as in England the pre-Raphaelite period saw a similar renaissance in the translation of Old English literature. Archaeologists and historians have contributed to this renewed interest, deepening and enriching our thinking in historical, national and political matters.

What of the other arts? In Sweden and Norway particularly, considerable interest was shown in supposedly old Nordic architecture and design. Lofts with exposed roof timbers, first floor verandas and small Romanesque windows were often incorporated in new buildings, typical examples being Biologiska Museet in Stockholm and Frognersæteren, the restaurant just outside Oslo. In the 1860s and 70s, the painter J. A. Malmström experimented with designs for furniture and ceramics in the old Nordic style. The drawing rooms of many wealthy homes were heated by porcelain stoves decorated with motifs of this kind, and such designs were very common in textile art. At a military masque in Stockholm in 1869, Malmström and the ballet-master S. H. Lund even created an old Nordic quadrille.

The world of music was also smitten with a fascination for this period. The twenty-four songs of *Frithiof's Saga* were set to music by the Swedish composer Crusell, and were sung throughout Scandinavia. Many of Oehlenschläger's works were set to music by the Dane J. P. E. Hartmann in the period 1830–85, as were the Eddic poems *Thrymskvida* and *Voluspa*. Niels W. Gade (1818–90) worked on a composition called *Baldurs Drøm* (Balder's dream) during the 1850s, and produced the outline of an opera *Siegfried og Brynhilde*, but he made his name as a young man with the concert overture *Echoes from Ossian*. In Norway, Edvard Grieg wrote music to Bjørnson's drama *Sigurd Jorsalfar* (about the Viking king who goes on a pilgrimage to Jerusalem) and also worked on an opera about Olaf Tryggvason. In England, Edward Elgar used Longfellow's *Saga of King Olaf* (based on *Heimskringla*) as the basis of his melodramatic cantata *King Olaf* (1896), which was the first of his works to win public acclaim. Other motifs from the sagas inspired Johan Svendsen and Richard Nordraak, while Carl Nielsen used similar ideas as the basis for his symphonic work *Sagadrøm* (a saga dream) from 1890. Recent films have sound-track music which aims to recreate the atmosphere of the Viking period; and in Fritz Lang's film version of the Siegfried story, the visual images are p.27(28) embued with a distinctive brand of Nordic pathos.

But there is one area in which the Scandinavian countries show a probably unique degree of attachment to the old Nordic traditions – the choice of names. Steam-boats were given names from Nordic mythology even before the middle of the nineteenth century, and these names were later conferred on numerous naval vessels. The first Danish locomotive was named *Odin* in 1846. In many Scandinavian towns and cities, streets are named after gods or characters and localities from the sagas. At the end of the nineteenth century, insurance companies took their names from the Nordic gods: Balder, Odin, Thor. Children were often given Nordic Christian names around the turn of the century, and in Norway and Iceland they are still very popular. Sports clubs often have names with old Nordic associations; there is a Norwegian chocolate factory called 'Freia', while a Swedish shoe-polish manufacturer and a Norwegian hotel are called 'Viking'.

A few writers have been critical of the idealization of the ancient past and its people. The earliest was A. O. Vinje (1818–70), a luckless genius and contemporary of Ibsen and Bjørnson. Employing vituperative sarcasm, he attacks the Northmen's brutality on the battlefield and their treatment of women and children, and comments ironically on such barbaric behaviour at feast-times as throwing gnawed bones at each others' heads. He even goes so far as to describe the whole Viking Age as a 'cellar full of corpses', remarkably strong criticism for the mid-nineteenth century.

Ibsen and Bjørnson both criticized the reckless and assertive nature of the Vikings, their plays developing into works of self-examination. In his several plays about the saga kings, Bjørnson condemns the lust for power, the inability to compromise and the desperate tendency to throw common-sense to the winds. A true leader must consider his actions in a balanced and logical fashion; and must be able to tolerate injustice and personal misfortune.

Here again we meet Strindberg. In a short story, written in the beginning of the twentieth century, Strindberg describes the priestess Hildur Horgabrud, whose sacrifices and cruel ritual murders at Uppsala epitomize the powerlessness of the individual in a world full of hatred. In another story, *Vikingaliv* (Viking life), he directly attacks the lovelessness, egotism and violence of the Viking world, and approaches the views held by Bjørnson when he censures the ruthless treatment of women, who were always subjected to great suffering.

The Icelandic Nobel Prize winner Halldor Laxness published *The Happy Warriors* (under the title of *Gerpla*) in 1951. Laxness used the *Fostbroedra saga* (the saga of the sworn brothers) and other sagas, along with the Eddic poetry, as basic sources in his description of the life and times of two foster-brothers, Thormod and Thorgeir. But the work also satirizes the heroic ideal, the author's attitude being coloured by his uncompromising socialist ideals. In *The Happy Warriors* the Vikings are stripped of all their idealized qualities. They are small, ugly, bow-legged and grotesque, and behave in the most cruel fashion: they burn the farms of their enemies, maim the aged and the very young, and hang the severed heads of recently raped women from their belts. King Olaf (later Saint Olaf) plays an important role in the novel, and is depicted as an expert torturer, who delights in putting out the eyes of captured and dethroned kings. Laxness skilfully piles on irony and sarcasm: the Norsemen lose no opportunity, he says, to kick their enemies when they are down and to stab them in the back.

Today's perspectives

In the last decades of the nineteenth century and the first half of the twentieth, a completely new view of the old Nordic culture and life-style has emerged. Exacting demands for naturalistic detail, combined with increased historical knowledge, have made the achievement of archaeological truth something of an obsession. The fantastic shadowy visions of the ancient past seen by the Romantics have been repudiated. Writers have also tried to see the whole history of Scandinavian culture as a continuity. Works in this genre include a novel in six volumes by the Dane Johannes V. Jensen, *The Long Journey*, 1924, and *The Tree of the Folkungs*, by Verner von Heidenstam, which follows the Swedish royal family, the Folkungs, from the eleventh century to the thirteenth when they became the rulers of Sweden. The novels of the Icelander Gunnar Gunnarsson also belong here, as they trace the history of Iceland of the sagas from its colonization through the centuries' struggle for peace, freedom, justice, spirituality and culture. The first, *Edbrødre* (*Brothers*, 1918), is set in the ninth century, while the subsequent novels are set in the eleventh and twelfth. The publication of his second novel, *Jord*, coincided with the primitivist movement in Western Europe and the popularity of the novels of D. H. Lawrence and Sherwood Anderson, as well as of the *Blut und Boden* (blood and earth) concept of Nazi Germany; but his novels had only superficial ties with primitivism. This was not the case with some later artists and writers. Jan Fridegård's three novels, *Trägudars land* (land of the carved idols), *Gryningsfolket* (people of the dawn) and *Offerrök* (sacrificial smoke), 1944–49, describe Holme, chief of the thralls, and his struggle for freedom. This work is clearly primitivist, including, for example, a description of sexual excesses at the midwinter sacrifices at Gamla Uppsala. Vilhelm Moberg (best known for his later novels on Swedish emigration to America) completed in 1946 *Brudarnas källa* (the brides' spring), which he called 'a legend'. The action takes place at four different periods at a pagan cult-place in the Swedish province of Småland. In the earliest, Moberg gives a very spicy account of ancient phallic rituals and the sacrifice of virgins. *2*

Phallic ritual is also depicted on Bror Marklund's richly sculptured doors, known as 'The Doors of History' (1939–52), which form the entrance to the *p.19(7)* Statens historiska museum in Stockholm. One of the door handles is actually a phallus, and the sketches for the doors include the scene of a dance around a fertility symbol which is a phallic stone from the Östergötland region.

A group of writers who rose to prominence after the Second World War – including Martin A. Hansen, Ole Wivel and Thorkild Bjørnvig – offer further modern perspectives on the Nordic world. Hansen's *Orm og Tyr* (the serpent and the bull), 1952, is a bold and sweeping historical meditation on pre-Christian and medieval Scandinavia. Bjørnvig's view, on the other hand, is fundamentally atheistic, and is exemplified in his great poem of 1955, *Sejdmændene paa Skratteskær* (the wizards of Skratteskær), in which King Olaf Tryggvason uses the tide to drown some wizards in west Norway. The poem is an allegory of modern man's desire to establish his own rule over a godless universe, and of his failure to achieve this, due to his own inadequacy.

Pastiches and parodies of the old Nordic literature appeared as early as the nineteenth century. *Frithiof's Saga* itself is a pastiche in which the author sometimes, but not always, succeeds in recreating the spirit of ancient Scandinavia. The New England poet J. G. Whittier was the author of a romantic poem called *The Norseman*. In the 1860s Longfellow wrote a series of pastiches in the heroic manner based on Snorri's saga of Olaf Tryggvason. The construction of his verse is highly skilful, and is at times reminiscent of Tegnér and Runeberg, both authors whom he knew well, but the characterization is very superficial. William Morris's great poems, *The Lovers of Gudrun* and *Siegfried*, are in reality pastiches, the former written in blank verse and the latter in the authentic *Nibelungen* measure. In a more contemporary style, one of Jack London's stories, published around 1900, 'An Odyssey of the North', deals with a Viking who comes to an Indian village in North America.

Eric Linklater's novel *The Men of Ness* (1932) recreated with no little success the astringent style of the sagas, departing rarely from the saga of Olaf Tryggvason (in its longer form in *Flateyjarbók*) and *Orkneyinga saga*. He describes the execution of the captured Jomsvikings after the victory of the Norwegian Earl Erik at Hjorungavag, and also the death of the Earl Sigurd: the latter carries the severed head of his enemy, Earl Melbricta, on the pommel of his saddle, but contracts blood-poisoning when the head bites a deep wound in his thigh.

J. R. R. Tolkien is another British writer who has written pastiches based on the literature of ancient Scandinavia, although his work also contains elements from early English literature such as *Beowulf* and the Arthurian legends. A linguist and literary historian, Tolkien early showed an interest in the ancient history of Scandinavia, and learnt the Scandinavian languages, including Icelandic. The several parts of *The Lord of the Rings* cycle all contain elements from the Icelandic sagas and the Eddic poems. Names borrowed from the dwarfs in *Voluspa*, caps to make a man invisible, racy songs and magical devices, riddles, transformations into animals, riding on wolfback, the ship as a funeral pyre – all combine to show the enormous influence of the Nordic sagas on Tolkien's mind.

The mixture of parody and heroic form also occurs elsewhere. In 1941 and 1945 the Swedish essayist Frans G. Bengtsson published the two volumes of his novel *The Long Ships* (published in Swedish under the title *Röde Orm*). The work is permeated with a dry sense of humour, which combines well with the author's unfeigned admiration for the courage and resourcefulness of the Vikings he described. Bengtsson indeed recreated some important features of the ancient Nordic literary style, such as a laconic harshness and macabre humour. He avoided archaic expressions and refrained from psychological speculation: as in the sagas the characters are presented directly through their actions. This, however, also gives to his portrayal of the period, their people and their philosophy a more

superficial character than that of, say, Eric Linklater and of contemporary Norwegian writers like Vera Henriksen. Bengtsson's curt pronouncements are indeed often of a frivolous nature. During the later years of his life, Hemingway, whose style was influenced by the Icelandic sagas, is said to have read Bengtsson with great interest.

In the search for a valid modern interpretation of the ancient past of Scandinavia and its people we need not confine ourselves to Europe. In South America we encounter writers whose interpretation of the ancient Nordic world seems to be close to the spirit of the Icelanders. The Brazilian João Guimarães Rosa, who died in 1967, wrote a thrilling short story about blood-feuds, *Vendetta* (1947). The title of the collection of short stories in which this appeared, *Sagarana* (saga-like), expresses the author's affinity with old Nordic literature. In Argentina, Julio Cortázar writes of Snorri Sturluson in his best-known novel *Rayuela*; and one of the greatest of Latin American authors, Jorge Luis Borges, often alludes to the ancient literature of Scandinavia and England. He has written some acerbic poems about a Viking chief Hengist, and in another poem gives vent to his yearning for Iceland, its mythology and ancient culture.

Our knowledge of the northern world and its peoples has grown immeasurably during the last hundred years, as the other chapters in this book have abundantly shown. We might expect such an increase of knowledge to have had an inhibiting effect on what may be called the 'myth' of the north, the north as a symbol; but curiously that seems not to be the case. It was perhaps Goethe who first formulated the contrast between north and south in psychological terms: the classical south standing for warmth, clarity, intellect and art, the romantic north for harshness, storm and heroic struggle. Whenever life seems *too* sophisticated, *too* civilized, it is to our Teutonic ancestors that we instinctively turn. Like all myths that reach down into the subconscious, it has its dangers. To one society it means self-assertion and healthy independence, to another primitivism and brutality. The appeal of Nordic imagery to the Nazis has already been noted, and we remember Dr Goebbels' boast: 'They call us barbarians. We *are* barbarians. We glory in the name of barbarian.' But, for better or worse, 'the Northern World' is now part of the mental furniture of Western man, and the wealth of literature and art that it continues to produce is a witness to its potency. What is peculiarly fascinating is to trace the links between the reality and the myth, and to see, through the swirling mists of the imagination, the dim forms of those living men and women whose children we are.

Select Bibliography

The sources listed here are intended as a means of access to further reading. They are not intended to be exhaustive in scope.

1. Gods and Heroes of the Northern World

Bellows, H. A. *The Poetic Edda*, 1923, reprinted 1957
Fell, C. E. *Egils Saga*, 1975
Hatto, A. T. *The Nibelungenlied*, 1965
Hallberg, P. *The Icelandic Saga*, 1962
Page, R. I. *Life in Anglo-Saxon England*, 1970
Shippey, T. A. *Old English Verse*, 1972
Turville-Petre, E. O. G. *Myth and religion of the north*, 1964
Young, J. *The Prose Edda*, 1954, reprinted 1963

2. The Germanic Tribes in Europe

Dixon, P. W. *Barbarian Europe*, 1976
Hermann, J. (ed.). *Die Germanen*, i, 1976
Holmqvist, W. *Germanic Art during the First Millennium AD*, 1955
Lasko, P. *The Kingdom of the Franks, North-West Europe before Charlemagne*, 1971
Musset, L. *The Germanic Invasions*, 1975
Thompson, E. A. *The Early Germans*, 1965
Wallace-Hadrill, J. M. *The Barbarian West 400–1100*, 3rd ed. 1967

3. The Anglo-Saxon Settlement of England

Alcock, L. *Arthur's Britain*, 1971
Gelling, M. *Signposts to the past. Place Names in the History of England*, 1978
Hills, C. M. *The Anglo-Saxon cemetery at Spong Hill*, i, (East Anglian Archaeology, Norfolk Archaeological Unit, 1977)
Hunter-Blair, P. *An Introduction to Anglo-Saxon England*, 1956, 2nd ed. 1977
Leeds, E. T. *Early Anglo-Saxon Art and Archaeology*, 1936
Page, R. I. *Life in Anglo-Saxon England*, 1970
Wilson, D. M. *The Anglo-Saxons*, 1st ed. 1960, revised 1971
Wilson, D.M. *The Archaeology of Anglo-Saxon England*, 1976
Whitelock, D. (ed.) *English Historical Documents c.500–1042*, 1955

4. The Celtic Contribution: Picts, Scots, Irish and Welsh

Alcock, L. *Arthur's Britain*, 1971
Ashe, G. (ed) *The Quest for Arthur's Britain*, 1968
de Paor, M. and L. *Early Christian Ireland*, 1958
Henderson, I. *The Picts*, 1967
Henry, F. *Irish Art in the Early Christian Period to AD 800*, 1965
Laing, L. *The Archaeology of Late Celtic Britain and Ireland, c. AD 400–1200*, 1975
Thomas, C. *Britain and Ireland in Early Christian Times, AD 400–800*, 1971
Ordnance Survey *Map of Britain in the Dark Ages*, 1966

5. The Scandinavians at Home

Arbman, H. *Svear i Österviking*, 1955
Jones, G. *A History of the Vikings*, 1968
Krogh, K. J. *Viking Greenland*, 1967
Loyn, H. R. *The Vikings in Britain*, 1977
Sawyer, P. H. *The Age of the Vikings*, 2nd ed. 1971

6. The Viking Adventure

Brønsted, J. *Danmarks Oldtid*, iii, 2nd ed. 1960
Bass, G. (ed.) *A History of Seafaring, based on underwater archaeology*, 1972
Foote, P. G. and Wilson, D. M. *The Viking Achievement*, 3rd impression 1978
Magnus, B. and Myhre B. *Norges Historie*, i, 1976
Stenberger, M. *Det forntida Sverige*, 1964
Wilson, D. M. *The Vikings and their origins*, new ed. 1980

7. The Northern Slavs

Bosau, Helmold von *Slawenchronik (Ausgewählte Quellen zur deutschen Geschichte des Mittelalters xix)*, 1963
Cross, S. and Sherbowitz-Wetzor (ed.) *The Russian Primary Chronicle*, 2nd ed. 1953
Gimbutas, M. B. *The Slavs*, 1971
Hensel, W. *Die Slawen im frühen Mittelalter. Ihre materielle Kultur*, 1965
Herrmann, J. *Zwischen Hradschin und Vineta. Frühe Kulturen der Westslawen*, 1971
— *Die Slawen in Deutschland*, 1970
Merseberg, Thietmar von *Chronik* (ed. V. W. Trillmich). (Ausgewählte Quellen zur deutschen Geschichte des Mittelalters ix), 1958

8. Romanticism and Revival

Most of the literature on this subject is published in Scandinavian languages. For further references see J. Mjöberg, *Drömmen om sagatiden*, I-II, Lund 1967–8; and E. Simon, *Réveil national et populaire en Scandinavie*, Uppsala 1960.

Sources of Illustrations

The page in which an illustration appears is shown by the first set of numbers in bold type, its plate or figure number by the second. Photographic sources are italicized. Where no other source is given, photographs were supplied by the museum or gallery. The following abbreviations have been used:
AIC Arnamagnaean Institute, Copenhagen
ATA Antikvarisk Topografisk Arkiv, Stockholm
Bibl. Nat. Bibliothèque National
BL British Library
BM British Museum
DOE Department of the Environment
IMK Ian Mackenzie-Kerr
NMAS National Museum of Antiquities of Scotland, Edinburgh
NMC Nationalmuseet, Copenhagen
NMI National Museum of Ireland
NMR National Monuments Record
NO Nasjonalgalleriet, Oslo
NS Nationalmuseum, Stockholm
Rh. Bild. Rheinisches Bildarchiv
Riksant. Riksantikvarieämbetet, Stockholm
SDO Scottish Development Office
SHM Statens Historiska Museum, Stockholm
SMK Statens Museum for Kunst, Copenhagen
St Joseph J.K.S. St Joseph, University of Cambridge, Committee for Aerial Photography
UOS Universitetets Oldsaksamling, Oslo
VSH Vikingskipethuset, Oslo
WF Werner Forman Archive
ZIAGA Akademie der Wissenschaften der DDR, Zentralinstitut für Alte Geschichte und Archäologie

Introduction

10 *1.* Ogham alphabet
2. Pictish stone with ogham inscription
3. Runic alphabet. Eva Wilson
4. Rune-stone from Ed, near Stockholm. IMK
11 *5.* Detail from the *Cathach* of St Columba; 7th c. Royal Irish Academy, Dublin
6. Northumbria: page from a Bible; early 8th c. BL
12 *7.* Oath imposed on the Saxons; c.820. From the library of Fulda Abbey, Germany. Domstiftsbibliothek, Mersenburg
8. Page from the Anglo-Saxon Chronicle; late 11th c. BL
13 *9.* Page from the Greenlanders' Saga; 1387–94. From the *Flateyjarbók*

1. Gods and Heroes of the Northern World

16 *1.* Gosforth, Northumberland: detail of sculpture. IMK
17 *1.* Woden: from illuminated ms.; 13th c. By courtesy of the Master and Fellows of Corpus Christi College, Cambridge
18 *2.* Odin on Sleipnir: detail of picture stone from Alskog, Tjangvide, Gotland; 10th c. SHM. *WF*
3. Odin being eaten by Fenrir: detail of the Thorwald Cross, Andreas, Isle of Man; 10th c. Manx Museum, Douglas, Isle of Man. *WF*
4. Pehr Hörberg (1746–1816): 'Odin builds his capital Sigtuna', tinted drawing; 1812. Nordiska Museet, Stockholm
19 *5.* Odin: coloured drawing from an Icelandic ms. of the Prose Edda; c.1680. AIC
6. Dagfin Werenskiold (b.1892): 'Odin on Sleipnir', painted wood relief in courtyard of Oslo State House; 1945–50. *Otto Vaering*
7. Bror Marklund (b.1907): 'Odin', detail from 'The Porches of History'; c.1950. SHM
20 *8.* Henry Fuseli (1741–1825): 'Thor, in the boat of Hymir, battering the Midgard Serpent'; 1790. Royal Academy, London
9. Olafur Brynjólfsson (c.1713–65): 'Asa-Thor catches the Midgard Serpent', illustration to the Prose Edda; c.1760. Royal Library, Copenhagen
10. Smith's mould for making Christian crosses and Thor's hammers; 10th c. *WF*
21 *11.* Mårten Eskil Winge (1825–96): 'Thor's fight with the Giants'; 1872. NS
22 *12.* Nils Jakob Olsson Blommér (1816–53): 'Freyja searching for her husband'; 1852. NS
13. Odin, Thor and Frey, with Freyja in background: tapestry from Skog church, Hälsingland; 12th c. SHM. *WF*
14. Bengt Erland Fogelberg (1786–1854): statue of Balder; c.1844. NS
23 *15.* Mårten Eskil Winge (1825–96): 'Loki and Sigyn'. NS
16. Arthur Rackham (1867–1939): 'Freyja'; from Richard Wagner, *Ring of the Nibelung*, tr. Margaret Armour, London; 1911
17. Hermann Ernst Freund (1786–1840): statuette of Loki; 1822. Ny Carlsberg Glypothek, Copenhagen
24 *18.* Nicolai Abraham Abilgaard (1743–1809): 'The Giant Ymir and the cow Audumbla'. SMK
25 *19.* 'Yggdrasil'; coloured drawing from a ms. of the Prose Edda; c.1680. AIC
20. Axel Revold (1887–1962): 'Yggdrasil', fresco in the vestibule of the University Library, Oslo; 1933. *Otto Vaering*
21. Vinje Gunnerud: 'Fenrir wants to get loose', sculpture at Asköy, Bergen, Norway. *Vinje Gunnerud*

241

Museum dür Ur und Frühgeschichte Frühgeschichte
191 17. Jankowo, Poland: wooden cult figure; 11th/12th c. Archaeological Museum, Poznan
18. Mikulčice, Moravia: buckle *in situ*; 9th c. *Brno Museum*
19. Fischerinsel, Neubrandenburg: wooden cult figure. *K. Hamann, ZIAGA*
192 20. Ralswiek, Rügen, E. Germany: silver coin hoard. *K. Hamann, ZIAGA*
193–201 All drawings adapted from illustrations in J. Herrmann, *Die Slawen in Deutschland*, Berlin, 1970

8. Romanticism and Revival

207 *1*. Tullstorp, Denmark: carved stone, from Ole Worm, *Monumenta Danica*; 1643
209 1. W. G. Collingwood: 'Thingvellir, meeting of the Althing'. BM. *John Webb*
210 2. Nicolai Abraham Abilgaard (1743–1809): 'Ossian's Last Song'; 1787. SMK
3. Title-page: engraved by Samuel Wale for 1762 edition of Ossian's 'Fingal' (by James Macpherson). University College, London, Scandinavian Library. *Eileen Tweedy*
4. John Trumbull (1756–1843): 'Lamderg and Gelchossa: scene from Ossian's "Fingal"'; 1792. Toledo Museum of Art (Gift of Florence Scott Libbey)
5. Otto Runge (1777–1810): 'Comhall's Death and Fingal's Birth', from a series of illustrations to Ossian. Hamburg Kunsthalle. *Ralph Kleinhempel*
211 6. Anne-Louis Girodet de Roucy-Trioson (1767–1824): 'Ossian receiving the Warriors of the Revolution in Paradise'; 1801. Château de Malmaison
212 7. 'Grettir': illustration from a ms. of Icelandic family sagas; late 17th century. AIC
8. Hans Gude (1825–1903): 'Viking ships under sail in Sognefjord'; 1889. NO. *Otto Vaering*
213 9. August Malmström (1829–1901): 'King Ælla's messengers before Ragnar Lodbroke's sons'; 1857. Norrköping Museum
10. Christian Krogh (1852–1925): 'The Discovery of America by Leif Eiriksson'; 1893. NO. *Otto Vaering*
214 11. Johan Flintoe (1786–1870): 'Duel at Skiringsal harbour from the time of the Sagas'; mid-1830s. NO. *Otto Vaering*
12. Nils Bergslien (b.1853): 'King Harald Finehair at the Battle of Hafrsfjord', illustration to 'History of Norway'; 1879. *Otto Vaering*
13. Herbert Gandy (fl. late 19th c.): 'The Viking's Farewell'. *Mansell Collection*
215 14. Fredrik Nicolai Jensen (1818–70): 'Viking abducting a southern woman'; 1845. Bergen Art Gallery
15. August Malmström (1829–1901): 'Ingeborg hears of the death of Hjalmar from Orvar Odd'; 1859. NS
16. Sir Frank Dicksee

(1853–1928): 'Funeral of a Viking'; 1893. Manchester City Art Gallery
216 17. Constantin Hansen (1804–80): 'Aegir gives a banquet for the gods'; 1861. SMK
18. Christoffer Wilhelm Eckersberg (1783–1853): 'Death of Baldur'. SMK
217 19. Peter Nicolai Arbo (1831–92): 'The Wild hunt of Odin' (Åsgårdsreier); 1872. NO. *Otto Vaering*
218 20. Adolph Tidemand (1814–76): 'Håkon Jarl's Death'. *Otto Vaering*
21. Christoffer Wilhelm Eckersberg (1783–1853): 'Thora by Håkon's bier'; c.1810–16. SMK. *Hans Petersen*
22. Johan Flintoe (1786–1870): 'Temple to Thor'; 1818. *Jöran Mjöberg*
23. Thomas Brunn (1742–1800): stage set for the play 'Gorm den Gamle' – temple to the goddess Hertha; c.1790. *Jöran Mjöberg*
219 24. August Malmström (1829–1901): 'Ingeborg's Lament', illustration to Esias Tegnér's 'Frithiof's Saga'; 1888 edition. University College London, Scandinavian Library. *Eileen Tweedy*
25. 'Ingeborg's Lament': from German translation of 'Frithiof's Saga'; 1846. Illustrated by Boehmer. Credits as 24
26. August Malmström (1829–1901): 'Ingeborg with her son and Frithiof in Baldur's temple'. See No. 24
27. Fredrik Nicolai Jensen (1818–70): 'Ingeborg's Lament'; c.1830. Bergen Art Gallery
220 28. Carl Larsson (1853–1919): 'Midvinterblot'; 1915. Archiv för Dekorativ Konst, Lund. *Press Association*
29. William Hole (1846–1917): 'St Columba preaching to the Picts', fresco in the National Portrait Gallery of Scotland. *Tom Scott*
221 30. Johan Zacharias Blackstadius (1816–98): 'St Sigfrid'; 1866. Nordiska Museet, Stockholm (Inv. no. NM84.565)
222 31. Louis Moe (b.1859): 'The shieldmaidens Stikla and Rusla', illustration from Horn's translation of Saxo Grammaticus, 'Gesta Danorum', Copenhagen; 1898. *Jöran Mjöberg*
32. Peter Nicolai Arbo (1831–92): 'The Valkyrie's Death'. NO. *Otto Vaering*
33. Valkyries: from the 1970 production by the English National Opera of Wagner's 'Valkyries'. *John Garner*
223 34. Peter Nicolai Arbo (1831–92): 'Valkyries'; 1869. NO. *Otto Vaering*
224 35. Daniel Maclise (1806–70): detail from 'Alfred disguised as a minstrel in the tent of Guthrum the Dane'; 1852. Tyne and Wear County Museums Service, Laing Art Gallery
225 2. Sigurd Vasegaard: *Kornmark Sommer*, from an illustrated edition of Saxo Grammaticus, *Gesta Danorum*; 1960
226 *3*. Gamla Uppsala: temple, from Erik Dahlbergh, *Suecia Antiqua et*

Hodierna, Stockholm; 1720
227 *4*. Erik Werenskiold: illustration to an edition of Snorri Sturluson; 1899
228 *5*. Illustration to Esaias Tegnér, *Frithiof's Saga*; 1825
6. Eric Palmqvist: illustration to Jan Fridegård, *Trägudars Land*; 1961
234 *7*. Illustration to a Norwegian translation of Snorri Sturluson's *Ynglinga Saga*; 1899
235 *8*. Edward Burne-Jones: *Sigurd*, from *Good Words*; 1862

Sources of Quotations

The translation of the *Poetic Edda* (p. 16) is by A. G. Brodeur; of the *Nibelungenlied* (p. 28) by Margaret Armour; of Gregory of Tours (p. 48) and Gerald of Wales (p. 96) by Lewis Thorpe; of *Beowulf* (p. 93 and p. 146) by Kevin Crossley-Holland; of 'The Ruin' (p. 87) and 'The Dream of the Rood' (p. 94) by R. K. Gordon; of Snorri Sturluson (p. 128) by Samuel Laing; of the *Greenlanders' Saga* (p. 160) by Magnus Magnusson and Hermann Pálsson; of Saxo Grammaticus (p. 184) by O. Elton; of Ibn Fadlun's account of the Viking burial (p. 202) by Jacqueline Simpson; and of Ibsen (p. 208) by R. Farquharson Sharp.

Index

Page numbers in *italic* refer to the illustrations and their captions.